Terrorism and the Politics of Response

This inter-disciplinary edited volume critically examines the dynamics of the War on Terror, focusing on the theme of the politics of response.

The book explores both how responses to terrorism – by politicians, authorities and the media – legitimise particular forms of sovereign politics, and how terrorism can be understood as a response to global inequalities, colonial and imperial legacies, and the dominant idioms of modern politics.

The investigation is made against the backdrop of the 7 July 2005 bombings in London and their aftermath, which have gone largely unexamined in the academic literature to date. The case offers a provocative site for analysing the diverse logics implicated in the broader context of the War on Terror, for examining how terrorist events are framed, and how such framings serve to legitimise particular policies and political practices.

The book will be of much interest to students and researchers of critical security studies, political geography, political theory, terrorism studies and IR in general.

Angharad Closs Stephens is Lecturer in Human Geography at the University of Durham, UK, and Co-Convenor of the British International Studies Association (BISA) Post-Structural Politics Working Group. **Nick Vaughan-Williams** is Lecturer in International Relations at the University of Exeter, UK, and Co-Convenor of the British International Studies Association (BISA) Post-Structural Politics Working Group.

Routledge Critical Terrorism Studies

Series Editors: Richard Jackson, Marie Breen Smyth and Jeroen Gunning
University of Wales, Aberystwyth, UK

This book series will publish rigorous and innovative studies on all aspects of terrorism, counter-terrorism and state terror. It seeks to advance a new generation of thinking on traditional subjects, investigate topics frequently overlooked in orthodox accounts of terrorism. Books in this series will typically adopt approaches informed by critical-normative theory, post-positivist methodologies and non-Western perspectives, as well as rigorous and reflective orthodox terrorism studies.

Terrorism and the Politics of Response
Edited by Angharad Closs Stephens and Nick Vaughan-Williams

Terrorism and the Politics of Response

Edited by Angharad Closs Stephens and Nick Vaughan-Williams

LONDON AND NEW YORK

First published 2009
by Routledge
2 Park Square, Milton Park, Abingdon, Oxon OX14 4RN

Simultaneously published in the USA and Canada
by Routledge
270 Madison Ave, New York, NY 10016

First issued in paperback 2010

Routledge is an imprint of the Taylor & Francis Group, an informa business

© 2009 Selection and editorial matter Angharad Closs Stephens and Nick Vaughan-Williams; individual chapters, the contributors

Typeset in Times by Wearset Ltd, Boldon, Tyne and Wear

All rights reserved. No part of this book may be reprinted or reproduced or utilised in any form or by any electronic, mechanical, or other means, now known or hereafter invented, including photocopying and recording, or in any information storage or retrieval system, without permission in writing from the publishers.

British Library Cataloguing in Publication Data
A catalogue record for this book is available from the British Library

Library of Congress Cataloging in Publication Data
A catalog record for this book has been requested

ISBN13: 978-0-415-45506-0 (hbk)
ISBN13: 978-0-415-60951-7 (pbk)
ISBN13: 978-0-203-88933-6 (ebk)

Contents

Notes on contributors   vii

Foreword   x
MARIE FATAYI-WILLIAMS

Acknowledgements   xiii

Introduction: London, time, terror   1
ANGHARAD CLOSS STEPHENS AND NICK VAUGHAN-WILLIAMS

PART I
Cartographies of response   17

1 Biopolitics, communication and global governance:
London, July 2005   19
JENNY EDKINS

2 Security, multiculturalism and the cosmopolis   44
VIVIENNE JABRI

3 Seven million Londoners, one London: national and urban
ideas of community   60
ANGHARAD CLOSS STEPHENS

PART II
War on terror/war on response   79

4 'Foreign' terror? Resisting/responding to the London bombings   81
DAN BULLEY

5 The shooting of Jean Charles de Menezes: new border politics?   96
NICK VAUGHAN-WILLIAMS

6 Terror time in Toronto: a response to the response to the arrests
   of the Toronto 17   112
   PATRICIA MOLLOY

7 Response before the event: on forgetting the war on terror   130
   LOUISE AMOORE

PART III
Possibilities of response?   145

8 Cosmopolitanism vs terrorism? Discourses of ethical possibility
   before and after 7/7   147
   JAMES BRASSETT

9 Finding meaning in meaningless times: emotional responses to
   terror threats in London   164
   CHRIS RUMFORD

10 The ontopolitics of response: difference, alterity and the face   178
   MADELEINE FAGAN

11 2 July, 7 July and metaphysics   190
   COSTAS DOUZINAS

   Index   211

Contributors

Louise Amoore is Reader in the Geography Department, University of Durham. Her research focuses on three key areas: global geopolitics and the governance of worker and migrant bodies; the politics and practices of risk management (with specific reference to the rise of risk consulting as a technology of governing); and political and social theories of resistance and dissent. Her books include *Globalisation Contested: An International Political Economy of Work* (2002) and *The Global Resistance Reader* (2005). She has published in several leading journals including *Political Geography, Security Dialogue, Review of International Studies* and *International Studies Perspectives*.

James Brassett is RCUK Fellow and Assistant Professor of International Political Economy in the Centre for the Study of Globalisation and Regionalisation (CSGR), University of Warwick. His research concerns the politics of global ethics and how moral arguments are increasingly sought and deployed in domains such as global economic governance, global civil society and global migration. His work has been published in leading international journals including *Ethics and International Affairs*, *European Journal of International Relations*, *International Studies Quarterly*, *Millennium: Journal of International Studies* and *Review of International Studies*.

Dan Bulley is Lecturer in International Relations in the School of Politics, International Studies and Philosophy, at Queen's University, Belfast. His research focuses on the ethics and politics of foreign policy, and the thought of Jacques Derrida. He has published in the *Review of International Studies*, the *British Journal of Politics and International Relations*, and is currently preparing a manuscript for publication entitled *Ethics and Foreign Policy: Negotiating Undecidability*.

Angharad Closs Stephens is Lecturer in Human Geography at the University of Durham and studied for her PhD in International Relations at Keele University. Her research work focuses on contemporary attempts to imagine political community without unity and investigations into the relationship between time and politics, inspired by postcolonial and feminist theories in particular. She has recently published in *Alternatives: Global, Local,*

Political and she is working on a monograph entitled *Oppressed by Our Utopias: The Politics of Communities, Origins and Temporality*. She is co-convenor of the BISA Poststructural Politics Working Group.

Costas Douzinas is Professor of Law, Pro-Vice Master for International Relations and Director of the Birkbeck Institute for the Humanities. He joined Birkbeck College in 1992 to establish the Birkbeck School of Law. He was Head of the School from 1996 to 2001 and Dean of the Faculty from 2002 to 2006, when he founded the Institute for the Humanities. Costas is a founding member of the Critical Legal Conference and the managing editor of *Law and Critique: The International Journal of Critical Legal Thought* and the Birkbeck Law Press. Costas specialises in political philosophy, jurisprudence human rights, aesthetics and critical theory. His many books include *Postmodern Jurisprudence, Justice Miscarried, The Logos of the Nomos* (with Ronnie Warrington), *The End of Human Rights, Law and the Image* (with Lynne Nead), *Nomos and Aesthetics, Critical Jurisprudence* (with Adam Gearey), *Adieu Derrida* (Palgrave Macmillan) and *Human Rights and Empire* (Routledge). His work has been translated into eight languages.

Jenny Edkins is Professor of International Politics at Aberystwyth University. Her books include *Trauma and the Memory of Politics* (2003), *Whose Hunger? Concepts of Famine, Practices of Aid* (2000, 2008), *Sovereign Lives: Power in Global Politics* (with Véronique Pin-Fat and Michael J. Shapiro, 2004), *Critical Theorists and International Relations* (with Nick Vaughan-Williams, 2008), and *Global Politics: A New Introduction* (with Maja Zehfuss, 2008).

Madeleine Fagan is a Doctoral Candidate in the Department of International Politics, Aberystwyth University. Her research is on the intersection of ethics and politics, particularly the themes of response and responsibility as found in the work of Jacques Derrida and Emmanuel Lévinas. Recent publications include *Derrida: Negotiating the Legacy* (Edinburgh University Press, 2007) and 'The Inseparability of Ethics and Politics: Rethinking the Third in Emmanuel Levinas', in *Contemporary Political Theory* (forthcoming 2008). She is convenor of the Aberystwyth Post International Group (APIG).

Marie Fatayi-Williams is author of *For the Love of Anthony* (2007) and initiator of the Anthony Fatayi-Williams Foundation to encourage multicultural debate, education and international peace.

Vivienne Jabri is Professor of International Politics in the Department of War Studies, King's College London. Her most recent publications include *War and the Transformation of Global Politics* (Palgrave Macmillan, 2007), and articles in *Review of International Studies, International Political Sociology, Security Dialogue, Millennium: Journal of International Studies* and *Alternatives*. Jabri's current research and writing focus on the implications of late modern warfare and the politics of security for understandings of the international, the cosmopolitan and postcolonial.

Patricia Molloy has a PhD in Education from the University of Toronto and has published extensively on narratives of sovereign violence, nation, and identity in media and popular culture. She is currently finishing a manuscript entitled 'Til Death Do Us Part: Canada/US and Other Unfriendly Relations' and is about to begin work on a co-authored book on death, loss and trauma in American television since 9/11. She teaches in the Department of Communication Studies at Wilfrid Laurier University in Waterloo, Ontario and is a longtime peace activist in Toronto.

Chris Rumford is Reader in Political Sociology at Royal Holloway, University of London where he is also co-director of the Centre for Global and Transnational Politics. Recent and forthcoming publications include *Cosmopolitan Spaces: Europe, Globalization, Theory* (Routledge, 2008), *Rethinking Europe* (with Gerard Delanty, Routledge, 2005), and the edited collections *Borderwork: Citizen Empowerment through Bordering* (Routledge, 2008) and the *Handbook of European Studies* (Sage, 2008).

Nick Vaughan-Williams is Lecturer in International Relations at the University of Exeter. His research analyses borders and bordering practices and their implications for International Theory and Security. Recent work has been published in journals such as *Alternatives: Global, Local, Political*, *Millennium: Journal of International Studies*, and *Review of International Studies*. Two other books are currently in preparation: a single-authored monograph entitled *Border Politics: the Limits of Sovereign Power* and a co-edited volume (with Jenny Edkins), *Critical Theorists and International Relations*. He is co-convenor of the BISA Poststructural Politics Working Group.

Foreword

Marie Fatayi-Williams

The terrorist attacks in London on 7 July 2005 claimed 52 lives, one of whom was my first and only 26-year-old son, Anthony. Three years on, I find myself responding to academics' responses to that traumatic event.

The London bombings, following the events in New York on 11 September 2001 and in Madrid on 11 March 2004, were attacks waiting to happen. Former Prime Minister Tony Blair had decided to stand 'shoulder to shoulder' with President George W. Bush. Together, as two of the major global actors representing two major powers, they took their 'war on terror' to Iraq apparently on the grounds of 'sexed-up' intelligence. On 19 March 2003, while watching the late night news at home, I saw President Bush declare the commencement of what he termed 'Operation Shock and Awe'. The first pictures of the live bombings at Dora Farms were then beamed around the world.

'Operation Shock and Awe' was meant to leave no one in doubt as to who was in charge. It was said that the war would be swift, sharp and short with no negative or unintended consequences. The war, legitimised as it was by the coalesced decision makers, was intended to 'mop up' terrorism. This was the statesmen's attempt at governing terror. I remember thinking from the privacy of my home: 'Could this be for real?' What role had the United Nations played in this onslaught? Had I missed a declaration by the Security Council or were we about to step into a new world order whose waters were yet to be charted? I sat and wondered where all this would lead or end. My late son Anthony discussed the possibility of attending an anti-war rally in London as he believed that the 'givens' did not add up to a justified war. Suddenly, from ordinary citizens, we had both become actors in world politics. Alas! Anthony tragically became part of the 'collateral damage' of that war. He and 51 others became unintended fallen soldiers in the war on terror.

On 22 July 2005, just three weeks on from the bombings, I watched in complete amazement at the explanations put forward by those in authority to the brutal shooting of Jean Charles de Menezes at Stockwell Station. This young man was also tragically killed, unsung and betrayed in death in yet another blind shot at governing terror. Thinking about this incident now, I cast my mind back to my travails in the aftermath of the London bombings and my search for Anthony. The first set of information released claimed that the underground explosions had been caused by a power surge. I wondered at such a distortion or manipulation of information when reality seemed to be staring us all in the face. I remember the blanks we drew at every turn trying to find Anthony and what had happened to him. We, the loved ones and his friends, just like the other families, became victims ourselves, trapped in a one-way system of information gathering and control. Those that lost their lives in London that day became bare statistics and were treated as objects that were researched to assist the authorities in their search for the perpetrators of the act. Their bodies were taken, belatedly, to a resilience mortuary that had not been properly set up for the purpose, compounding their brutal treatment as a form of life devoid of human dignity. The political leaders and the state failed both the dead and the living loved ones on that day.

The events of 7 July were swept swiftly under the carpet. Tony Blair kept well away from the 'victims' of the disaster. By framing the act as something committed by those who did not share the same values of 'freedom' and the same 'way of life' as the British people, he brazenly avoided any criticism of the government's foreign policy or 'war on terror'. Meanwhile, a massive poster publicity campaign was launched, and in reference to the dead, a memorial was established on London's Victoria Embankment Gardens. Yet another wild shot at governing the effects of terror.

Some weeks after the London bombings, at our bereaved families' group meeting, it became clear that there was not going to be a forum to discuss and debate the issue of compensation. Rather, the government's Criminal Injuries Compensation Act (CICA) was to be the blueprint for a generalised form of compensation. The calculation arrived at for an unmarried young man such as Anthony was a flat-rate pay-out of £11,000: a figure deemed by the Chief Executive of the CICA as 'efficient, fair and compassionate'. To make matters worse, the paperwork and supporting documents needed for the claim ran into volumes and was cumbersome. I did not think I was ready to subject Anthony to further injustice and indignity. I certainly was in no frame of mind to go through the ordeal of filling countless claim forms. And yet, even to this day, no one in authority has shown any concern about the absence of my application for this compensation. Shockingly, one of the bereaved family members, who had filled the claim forms for his late wife, was still on the 'waiting list' almost a year later. The authorities carried out security checks on him, in his 'country of origin', while he waited for the £11,000 pay-out. The story is no different for wounded survivors. It borders on the ridiculous that injuries are classified in order of severity and costed as such. The victim with multiple injuries will have them analysed and a price tab will be put on the most severe, while the rest will be compensated on a discounted rate.

If the UK government had been aware of the £2 million awards made to the families of those people who died in the attacks of 11 September 2001 then they certainly made no reference to it. This was not an issue on which the British government wanted to stand 'shoulder to shoulder' with their American counterparts. The ethics of compensation was subsumed under this seemingly monolithic form of reasoning, devoid of all morality, that offered no opportunity for discussion and debate and yet expected the conditions to be binding on us all.

As I have sat back and reflected on the death of my son, and especially as I wrote my book, *For the Love of Anthony*, I paused to consider: How have academics situated themselves in relation to these events? Did the events of the London bombings have any resonance with the academic community? These kinds of actions are the raw materials for scholars regardless of what level of analysis they choose to work from. As a former postgraduate student of International Relations myself, I have felt rather forlorn about the loud silence of the academic community's response to the events of 7 July 2005. Even if the events in themselves did not elicit writings that fall under academic protocols, perhaps research into their aftermath would strike the right chord for linking theory with reality. I am not in a position to make judgements about the protocols of academic writing or the cold war of theories. However, I do believe that academics can and ought to problematise these actions or inactions, the monolithic reasoning of key decision makers that led to systems of inclusion and exclusion, and the violations of the fundamental human rights and dignity of those persons caught in the events of 7 July 2005. It took Tony Blair three months to write a two-paragraph letter to the bereaved families. Even then, the letter was to invite us to the government's official show of concern by way of a service at St Paul's Cathedral.

At the conference titled 'London in a Time of Terror: the Politics of Response', held at Birkbeck College in 2006, I asked: Why had the voice of academics not been heard? Have useful lessons really been learnt? Should the victims of the London bombings, dead and alive, have been treated in the way they did? Ought the Prime Minister to have ruled against a public or judicial inquiry? To what extent can we accept the official narrative of the events of 7 July released by the government, acting as judge and jury? How can academics intervene in contemporary political life, especially in the realm of foreign policy, so that the bodies do not keep piling up? These are simple but nevertheless hard questions that demand urgent attention.

July 2008

Acknowledgements

There are many institutions and individuals that we would like to thank for making this book possible. The project grew out of a conference we co-organised called 'London in a Time of Terror: the Politics of Response', which was held at Birkbeck College, London, on 8 December 2006. We acknowledge the financial assistance given to us for this conference by the Aberystwyth Post-International Group, the BISA Poststructural Politics Working Group and the BISA CRIPT Working Group. We would also like to thank all the participants at that conference, particularly Louise Amoore, Costas Douzinas, Jenny Edkins, Marie Fatayi-Williams, Steve Graham, Vivienne Jabri, Debbie Lisle, Andrew Neal, Mustapha Pasha, R. B. J. Walker and Gillian Youngs, for their generous intellectual involvement and encouragement. Many of these speakers have contributed to this volume and we also extend our gratitude to them for that. Our appreciation goes to the other authors of chapters in the book who have been excellent colleagues and friends throughout. Special thanks to Madeleine Fagan who copy-edited the entire manuscript and to Andrew Neal and John Heathershaw for their comments on the Introduction. Finally, we thank Madeleine and Rhodri for their unstinting love and support.

Angharad Closs Stephens
Nick Vaughan-Williams
March 2008

Earlier versions of some of the chapters included in this volume have appeared elsewhere and we thank Blackwell, Cambridge University Press, Sage and Lynne Rienner for granting us permission to reprint them. Chapter 1 has been published as 'Biopolitics, Communication and Global Governance', in *Review of International Studies* (2008), 34(2): 211–32. Chapters 3 and 5 were published in *Alternatives: Global, Local, Political* (2007), 32(2): 155–76 and 177–95. Chapter 4 has been published as '"Foreign" Terror? London Bombings, Resistance and the Failing State', in *British Journal of Politics and International Relations* (forthcoming 2008). Finally, Chapter 8 also appears as 'Cosmopolitanism vs Terrorism? Discourses of Ethical Possibility Before, and After 7/7' in *Millennium: Journal of International Studies* (forthcoming 2008).

Introduction
London, time, terror

Angharad Closs Stephens and Nick Vaughan-Williams

On 2 July 2005 Pink Floyd reunited to perform together on stage for the first time in 24 years. They played at the 'Live 8' concert in Hyde Park, London, which was organized by Bob Geldof and Midge Ure to raise awareness of the Make Poverty History campaign. This campaign, a coalition of more than 400 charities, unions and faith groups, formed to put pressure on world leaders' commitment to halve global poverty by 2015. It was organized in anticipation of the G8 summit of world leaders (the leaders of the world's eight richest countries) who met at the Gleneagles Hotel, near Edinburgh in Scotland, from 6 to 8 July. Top of the agenda were issues of trade, debt and aid and global climate change. The summit coincided with the meeting of the International Olympic Committee in Singapore on 6 July 2005, at which it was announced that London would host the 2012 Olympic Games, beating rival bids from Paris, Moscow, New York and Madrid. Tony Blair, then Prime Minister of the UK, and president of the G8 for that year, left the summit briefly to congratulate the city of London on its successful bid. As Blair exclaimed: 'Many reckon [London] is the greatest capital city in the world and the Olympics will keep it that way' (*BBC News Online* 2005a). The next day, 7 July, four suicide bombers targeted the London transport network killing themselves and 52 other people and injuring over 700. In the midst of such high profile and widespread discussions of global politics, justice and inequality, London experienced the worst single instance of loss of life in its recent history.

What is distinctive about the London bombings on 7 July 2005, in contrast to the events in New York, Washington and Pennsylvania on 11 September 2001, is that, despite the initial shock, many people claimed to be able to recognize instantly what kind of an event this was: the terrorist attack on London that the UK government had said that would almost inevitably happen.[1] As the Report into the bombings conducted by the London Assembly puts it: 'London had been warned repeatedly that an attack was inevitable: it was a question of when, not if' (London Assembly 2006: 6). In contrast to US President George W. Bush, who, famously, was nowhere to be seen in the immediate aftermath of the atrocities on 11 September 2001, Tony Blair interrupted the meeting of the G8 at Gleneagles at midday (three hours following the first bombings) and proclaimed that there had been 'a series of terrorist attacks in London' (*BBC News Online*

2005b). Against the backdrop of confusion on the streets and in the tube carriageways in London, as phone servers collapsed with people attempting to get in touch with loved ones, as people and bodies were being transported to and between different hospitals, and as emergency phone-lines were still being set up, Tony Blair attempted to provide clarity and meaning in confused times.

This book attempts to make the familiar events of the London bombings unfamiliar once more.[2] In contrast to proclamations by governmental leaders and politicians that frame '7/7' as self-evident and understood, we want to question the assumption that it is easy to know exactly what is going on in global politics. Rather than assume that there is general agreement over what a terrorist event looks like, what it means, and what policing, surveillance and security measures it necessitates, the collection of essays presented in this volume treat these issues as problems that require close readings and detailed engagements. The aim is to explore some of the key dynamics of the current War on Terror by focusing on the theme of what we propose to call the 'politics of response'. While many of the essays contained in this volume engage directly with the case of the bombings in London on the 7 July 2005, they also raise broader questions about the politics of identity, security, community, power, authority and sovereignty. Our rationale for focusing on this particular case is twofold. First, the London bombings, together with the so-called 'failed attacks' two weeks later and the shooting of Jean Charles de Menezes, have all gone largely unexamined in the academic literature in Politics, Political Geography and International Relations to date.[3] Second, we believe that the London case offers a provocative site for analyzing the diverse logics and idioms deployed as part of the global War on Terror. We do not seek to ask what *exactly* happened on 7 July 2005, but rather to examine in some depth how the bombings have been framed in a broader context and how such framings have served to legitimize and/or obscure certain policies and political activity. The theme of the 'politics of response' enables a double reading of how responses to terrorism, by politicians, authorities and the media, legitimize certain forms of sovereign politics, and how terrorism can also be understood as a response to global inequalities and colonial and imperial legacies. In this way the concept of response offers a particular angle which might be helpful in thinking about an array of practices that have come to be associated with global terrorism. Furthermore, as we hope will become clear throughout, the concept of response raises difficult political, methodological and ethical questions about our own abilities and *response*-abilities as academics trying to figure out ways of engaging critically and emotionally with the effects of terrorism.

The rest of this Introduction is divided into three sections. The first considers what it means to think about an act of terrorism such as the London bombings as an 'event' in global politics. We seek to raise questions about how events come to be defined as such and what is at stake, politically, in the construction of particular narratives that join lots of different events together as if they were part of a causal sequence (e.g. 9/11, 11/3, 7/7). It is suggested that this critical interrogation – or 'problematization' – of the concept of the event is a useful starting point when thinking about how the complexities of 7 July might be unpacked.

The second section then pushes this analysis of the 'event' a little further by exploring the relationship between terrorism, politics and time. Here we express a concern about the way in which events constructed simply as '9/11' or '7/7' end up legitimizing certain decisions, practices and rulings that come to dominate – or dictate even – the political possibilities of the present and future. We suggest that a focus on the relationship between terror, time and the political offers a useful avenue of thought for a critical analysis of contemporary geopolitics. Finally, in the third section, we build further on these issues by turning to the politics of response, and sketching out how this overarching theme acts as a unifying problematic throughout each of the chapters.

'7/7': London, 7 July 2005

In the absence of an official public inquiry into the bombings of 7 July 2005, the London Assembly review represents one of the only opportunities that survivors and eyewitnesses have had to put their experiences on record.[4] One of the survivors gives the following account:

> We just started leaving Tavistock Square when there was a very strange noise. It wasn't like a bang; it was like a muffled whooshing sound almost, but then the bus was very packed, and I was on the one in front. Being sort of ensconced, I didn't hear – I saw, but I didn't really hear it very loudly. There was a mass exodus off of our bus, as things were still coming to the ground and bits were flying everywhere. The only thing I do remember is the carnage and everything as it hit the floor. I remember looking at the bus, and I remember initially thinking, 'What is a sightseeing bus doing there?' because that is actually what it looked like. From the front, that is what it looked like; it didn't look like a London bus. Now I know why, but it didn't look that way to me. It looked like one of those that has the roof off. It wasn't until I actually saw the blood, and the smells, that I thought something is really wrong here and not right. It sounds almost ridiculous to say it, but it was just such a surreal thing; I still have trouble explaining it. I can see things in my head, but I just can't find the words to describe it.
>
> (London Assembly 2006: 36)

The personal stories of those caught up in the traumatic incidences of 7 July 2005 reveal the difficulty of explaining and depicting the 'event' of the London bombings. Many of the survivors speak of colours and lights, and describe the world changing 'from bright orange to nothing' or that 'Everything turned a horrible, urine-coloured yellow' (London Assembly 2006: 31, 15). It is possible to read about what people smelt, felt and touched, and of the smoke, the shock and the incomprehension. Yet, despite the sense in which this was clearly a major event, survivors' stories demonstrate that we still do not fully know what it is that we are describing when we refer to 'the London bombings' or, even more crudely, '7/7'.

In his response to the attacks on the World Trade Center and Pentagon on 11 September 2001, Jacques Derrida highlights the process through which 'brute facts' come to be recognized as 'major events' in global politics (Derrida 2003: 89). He argues that the seemingly endless and unreflective use of the slogan '9/11' ultimately suggests that 'we do not know what we are talking about': the signifier, repeated time and time again, becomes a substitute for that which we cannot describe (ibid.: 89). Derrida's response usefully informs an analysis of what is at stake in the repeated reference to what happened in London on 7 July 2005 as '7/7'. The use of this slogan to describe and package what went on that day quickly established a sense of familiarity with the radically unfamiliar: the effects of suicide bombings in the capital of the UK. One of the implications of this act of naming was to render multiple occurrences – the explosion of different devices at different sites across London, and the deaths and injuries of lots of people at staggered intervals over many hours (and in subsequent days) – as a single 'event'.[5] This way of referring to and thinking about these various happenings allows us to capture them as a coherent entity that can then form the basis for explanation within broader narratives. This is, to some extent, a necessary device. But it is also one that functions to obscure the more detailed intricacies and, perhaps more importantly, the competing understandings of what happened. Another function of the slogan '7/7' is that it ties what happened on 7 July 2005 into a number of other 'events': '9/11'; '11/3'; 'Bali'; 'Istanbul'; '21/7'. In this way, '7/7' has been emplaced within and contributes to the (re)production of a seemingly continuous sequence that has come to appear self-evident, straightforward and uncomplicated. Yet in stringing these dates and place names together, we conjure a particular view of global politics, and often forget the broader geographies and histories involved in different events at various sites.

Following Derrida, we might want to remember that moments in global politics, and the different meanings that such moments acquire, are not somehow pre-given, settled and stable but rather performatively produced, sorted and categorized. After all, it takes force to establish, uphold and maintain a continuous sequence such as this: one that organizes complex events from across a diverse geographical landscape into a singular continuum. In this example, '9/11' acts as an origin or point of departure, which, designated and media-theatricalized as a major rupture, comes to mark a series of supposed beginnings and endings: a marker that divides all that has gone before from a new world with a new politics and new necessities (Walker 1995; Derrida 2003). Consequently, in the case of an analysis of '7/7' (or indeed any of the other 'events' comprising the series) this framing obscures the way in which we might be witnessing a combination of *both* new forms of sovereign politics *and* the continuation of political techniques, discourses and laws that have a much older history. Moreover, such a framing, in its insistence upon a linearity that starts at point x and moves inexorably to point y, brings multiple and complex tragedies together in such a way that obscures the range of variegated responses occasioned by grief, anger and loss. On this basis, instead of accepting an uncritical usage of the slogan '7/7' –

thereby legitimizing a whole range of sovereign practices that follow in its name – this book insists upon a disruption of such a way of thinking. Crucially, as the next section of this chapter will outline and explore in greater detail, we suggest that critical resources for mobilizing a disruption of this sort can be found through an investigation of the relationship between time and politics. This focus offers a different framing for the way we think about global terrorism and its implications.

Terror, time and the political

What was somehow unique about the London bombings was that they were quickly described as events that we knew would take place. But what does it mean to describe the London bombings as an event that was always expected to happen? How does this influence our understanding of what happened on 7 July 2007? What range of responses does this legitimize and/or obscure? Some routes into addressing these questions are offered by John Tulloch, Professor of Media and Communication Studies at Brunel University, who was injured by the blasts at Edgware Road. In a personal and close reading of how the London bombings were framed in the media and news reports across Britain, North America and Australia, Tulloch recalls lying in hospital shortly after the bombings and studying former Prime Minister Tony Blair's response:

> One photograph I saw on 9 July from the previous day's newspaper made me very angry. It was a shot of Prime Minister Tony Blair taken at Gleneagles just after he had been told about the terrorist attacks. He is standing alone, head bowed, and body stiff as though in genuine shock – or perhaps wired, like his US presidential friend, directly to God. My immediate thought was that it was a performance, a photo opportunity to gain empathy by a politician who, because of his illegal, media-spun military entry into Iraq, was deeply unpopular. For me, lying there that day, it was a posture well-practised, an attitude thought about and rehearsed long before.
> (Tulloch 2006: 48)

At one level, we expect politicians to rehearse their lines, postures and emotions in anticipation of the need to respond to major events. However, echoing an earlier point about the way in which events on 7 July were seen as both shocking and yet somehow familiar and pre-empted, Tulloch raises a deeper and more political issue about the timing of this response, and ease with which Blair seemed to have decided what had happened and why.

Similar questions about the politics of time and timing have been raised in many critical responses to the events of 11 September 2001 and their aftermath. For example, much of this literature has concentrated on the way in which the positing of a key moment, '9/11', as exceptional, and as a fundamental rupture between a world that went before and a new world that must now follow, must be interrogated. The trick of positing such a radical break is of course typical to modern politics: it is encountered in declarations of a shift from a state of nature to a state of society to legitimize a form of sovereign politics that we must now accept. Talk of a radical break should not therefore be taken at face value but analysed for the assumptions, arguments and claims it enables. The idea of a radical break should also be interrogated for the way in which it enables a story of progress. Many people have noted the way in which the War on Terror has been framed as a war between 'us', progressive civilized people, and 'them', the backward barbarians. Derek Gregory has shown the way in which these 'imaginative geographies' are produced by 'fold[ing] distance into difference', presenting a reformulation of a familiar story of development. (Gregory 2004: 17). They rely on a particular temporal narrative: one that orders differences along a hierarchical scale ranging from the pre-modern to the modern, the underdeveloped to the developed, or from the uncivilized to the civilized (Massey 2005). This is a framing that relies on a particular and culturally specific way of seeing the world: one that can only acknowledge differences in so far as they measure up to the criteria *it* sets for what counts as a proper subjectivity or political community.

The task of resisting the particular forms and demands of sovereign politics might therefore begin by taking time to think critically about how different understandings of time both enable and constrain ways of responding to global terrorism. Judith Butler and, separately, Jenny Edkins have both engaged with questions of time and politics by pointing to the swiftness with which we were quickly invited to agree on what had happened on 11 September 2001 and on how we should respond (Butler 2004; Edkins 2003). They both refer to George W. Bush's announcement on 21 September 2001 that 'the time for mourning is over and that the time for action has begun' (Butler 2004: 29; Edkins 2003: 19). Butler and Edkins show us how these multiple events were rapidly written into a single 'event' and then co-opted into a familiar narrative of us and them, good guys and bad, war and revenge. Butler and Edkins suggest that the rhetorical rush to declarations of supremacy and self-certainty in this immediate aftermath played an important role in legitimizing ensuing US military adventurism in Afghanistan and later Iraq. However, they also argue that this direction was not necessarily pre-given or determined at that time: by reflecting on what had happened, resisting the urge to respond to violence with further violence and instead embracing an awareness of vulnerability or trauma time, Butler and Edkins emphasize that different kinds of responses could have been identified, discussed and pursued. For Butler, this might have included accepting a new understanding of the United States' position in international politics and in considering a common vulnerability, dependency and relationality (Butler 2004).

While Butler and Edkins concentrate on resisting George W. Bush's rapid and simple affirmations, Brian Massumi has argued that we should pay close attention to how Bush talks about the past, the present, and the future (Massumi 2005). For example, Massumi seizes on Bush's seemingly paradoxical statement at the time of the decision to go to war in Iraq in 2003: 'I have made judgements in the past. I have made judgements in the future' (ibid.: 5–7). Instead of casting this aside as merely another unfortunate 'Bushism', Massumi argues that it is characteristic of a significant temporal logic at the heart of the Bush administration: one that privileges a 'lightning strike' approach to decision-making (ibid.: 4–5). According to Massumi, the 'lightning strike' approach assumes the form of a foregone conclusion because it puts the present to one side in order to be seen to act without delay (ibid.: 5). Any equivocation is considered to be a sign of weakness and so this is an approach that literally seeks to 'waste no time' and act on the future before it is yet here. This, Massumi claims, can be understood in terms of a new politics of pre-emption in the context of the War on Terror whereby conventional legal and political mechanisms are by-passed as part of a shift from the present tense to the future perfect tense: from the 'will be' to the 'always will have been already' (ibid.: 6).

The common task implied by Butler, Edkins and Massumi is not only for analysts of global politics to be sensitive to questions of time and the political but also to work within and/or seek ways of developing alternative temporal registers to those of Bush, Blair and other politicians. In particular, Butler and Edkins stress that, in the face of disastrous circumstances such as those on 11 September 2001, we need not or indeed perhaps should not rush to respond by attempting to prematurely capture or make sense of these events. This point is reiterated by David Campbell, who, in his response to the events of 11 September 2001, echoes Butler and Edkins by arguing that the task of ordering things into a sequence is not only difficult but 'something we cannot and perhaps should not easily or quickly resolve' (Campbell 2002).

Inevitably, as the earlier discussion inspired by Derrida demonstrates, the activity of 'making sense' of complex and traumatic events often distorts what happens in overly simplified, crude and unhelpful ways. If these critical insights about the relationship between time and the political are applied against the backdrop of the bombings in London on 7 July 2005 then a number of salient issues arise that disrupt conventional and totalizing responses. First, such an approach encourages a critical questioning of the ways in which an initial confusion surrounding 'events' quickly becomes coded, settled and commodified. Various governmental reports into the London bombings, such as the *Report of the Official Account of the Bombings in London on 7th July 2005* offer a very coherent, straightforward and unambiguous account of what happened on 7 July 2005 but in doing so, close down multiple and contested accounts. Second, we might want to pay closer attention to the way in which events such as the London bombings quickly converge into a 'fictitious unity' that serves to affirm a united and homogenous political community (Butler 1999). Third, the focus on the relationship between terror, time and the political opens up provocative questions about the role of academics in responding to events such as the London bombings. As the next section will discuss, these and other key questions are addressed by the chapters collectively through an engagement with the overarching theme of the politics of response.

The politics of response

This book emphasizes the difficulty of understanding exactly what took place in the multiple events that have been crudely packaged as '7/7'. In concentrating on the theme of 'response' we want to question the ease with which 'terrorist events' such as the London bombings are all too often easily packaged and comprehended without due recognition of the way in which our framings affect the way we see, analyse and prescribe. The main problem with an approach to global terrorism that fails to recognize the implications of its own framings is that it tends to avoid broader discussions of the way in which such events might themselves be understood as responses to complex histories of power relations and global inequalities. Our focus on the theme of response also raises the question of how we might respond, as academics, to devastating and emotionally fraught moments in global politics such as the London bombings. Marie Fatayi-Williams, who lost her son Anthony in the bombings on 7 July, raises precisely this question in her challenging and provocative Foreword to this volume. Therefore, while the theme of response highlights a number of problems about the relationship between terrorism, time and the political, it also raises the possibility of *re*thinking the relationship between these categories and disrupting or at least de-familiarizing some of the more familiar accounts of the War on Terror. The discourse of the War on Terror places great emphasis on key dates and events and the constant positing of those dates, times and places serves to legitimize certain understandings of the present and excluding others. In beginning to think about how we might engage critically with the War on Terror we have to think about other ways of discussing and approaching these 'events' critically.

In the inaugural issue of the journal *Theory & Event*, Wendy Brown suggests that all political writings could in some way be described as responding to events, be it Locke or Hobbes on the English Revolution, or Marx, de Tocqueville or Burke on the French Revolution (Brown 1997). However, Brown goes on to distinguish between two different approaches available to academics when thinking about how to respond to 'events'. The first is to provide a close reading of the unfolding of an event, such as, we might suggest, Hannah Arendt did in her close study of the trial of the Nazi and SS member Adolf Eichmann. The second approach is one that seeks to inquire into *the conditions of possibility* of particular events. While both approaches have a valuable role to play, Brown argues that the latter might require a de-familiarizing of the event itself in order to open up a 'flourishing' of responses:

> [T]here is a world of difference between reading events and theorizing the conditions and possibilities of political life in a particular time. Indeed, understanding what the conditions of certain events means for political possibilities may entail precisely de-centring the event, *working around it*, treating it as contingency or symptom.
>
> (Brown 1997; emphasis added)

In this vein, the collection of papers presented here represents an effort to 'work around' the London bombings: to analyse how they were explained in ways that establish particular practices and forms of sovereign politics that exceed the timings and locations of the events themselves. To ask different questions about 'what happened' in London in July 2005 it is necessary to decentre the narrative that makes these events seem self-evident and which also makes those *responses* to them (such as the shooting of Jean Charles de Menezes in the feverish manhunt for the suspected bombers of the 'failed' attacks on 21 July 2005) appear as if they were the only ones available.

This de-centring is enabled by a focus on response because it takes seriously the idea that much of what we refer to as global politics can only be understood as responses and responses to those responses. Indeed, there is a sense in which all we ever encounter are responses and that any analysis of politics is always already a politics of response. Once this alternative perspective is adopted then the causal linear sequence 'event' → 'response', one which, as we have already seen, conventional discourses of the War on Terror rely upon, is rendered highly problematic. According to this sequence, 'event' is set up as being temporally prior to 'response' and therefore privileged in a given discourse: for example in the claim that the shooting of Menezes was a justified response to the event of the 'failed' attacks on 21 July. In this way 'event' is seen as a ground, source or origin and 'response' is considered to be a less important secondary by-product. However, if the 'event' itself is reconfigured as a response (for example the 'failed attacks' as a response to British foreign policy) then the simplicity and coherence of the narrative breaks down or becomes de-centred. The effect of this is to re-politicize the way that the causal linear sequence was framed to begin with: not as an obvious or somehow natural version of the way things are but as a particular rhetorical construction. We suggest that the de-centring of the event via an analysis of the politics of response offers useful critical purchase on an array of contemporary phenomena framed in the context of the ongoing War on Terror. While the London bombings offer a particular site for exploration in this volume it is hoped that our adoption of the 'politics of response' as an angle will be useful for deepening ongoing discussions about global politics more generally.

To close, we return to the question of the *response*-abilities of academics, and to Sheldon Wolin's comments on this question in the same inaugural issue of *Theory & Event* (1997). In it, Wolin argues that political theory operates according to a 'political time' that is different to the temporalities, rhythms and pace governing economy and culture. While the latter is driven and determined by the desire for change and newness, the former works according to an alternative pace, the time of deliberation. 'Political time' is that which is 'conditioned by the presence of differences and the attempt to negotiate them'. Wolin points to the 'instability' of political time, and that this is precisely what makes it difficult for political theorists to respond to events such as 1989 – and we might add, the London bombings, or the events of 11 September 2001. He argues that while traditional conceptions of the political might have assumed a common time, a common authority, and common identity, the 'instability' of contemporary politics suggests that there is no common idea of political life. In the same way that people live according to different rhythms and tempos, people also have different ideas of the political, and this makes the task of analysis more difficult. Wolin's point represents more than an acknowledgement of plurality – it is not that some people are against terrorism while others are sympathetic to terrorism, as some would have it. Rather, different people have different ideas of what politics involves, and these might not be reducible to any shared basis. We need to find a way of disrupting the familiar temporal logics within which terrorist events are framed, and the binary choices that are presented as the only ways of responding, to find a language that can recognize this complexity, and uncover some of the alternative ways in which people have woven relations, communities and solidarities in response to terrorist events. We present this collection of chapters as attempts to capture the spirit of such an approach.

The book

The book is divided into three interconnected parts designed to explore the core thematic of terrorism and the politics of response: 'Cartographies of response'; 'War on terror/war on response'; and 'Possibilities of response?' The first part maps some of the different governmental, political and analytical responses to the bombings in London on the 7 July 2005 and the various 'imagined communities' that were constructed in their immediate aftermath.

Chapter 1, written by Jenny Edkins, engages with the personal experiences of those friends and relatives that were searching for missing loved ones in the aftermath of the bombings and their encounters with different governmental authorities. Edkins critically interrogates some of the procedures that were put in place as part of the established protocols of disaster planning, and the ways in which these involved the objectification and instrumentalization of persons. Offering an analysis of biopolitical forms of global governance, Edkins draws on Giorgio Agamben's work to reveal the way in which the missing persons were produced as 'bare life', devoid of agency and humanity. In her discussion, Edkins addresses some of Marie Fatayi-Williams' concerns raised in the Foreword, by offering a response to her protests at the way in which many of the relatives of the missing were handled in the aftermath of the bombings.

Vivienne Jabri's chapter engages with the theme of political community and with the contradictions of liberalism. Jabri explores how practices of security centre on the government of social relations. More specifically, she traces the shift from discourses of multiculturalism to discourses of social cohesion in the British political context, and analyses how cultural differences came to be securitized in the governmental responses to the bombings in London on 7 July 2005. Jabri points to a paradox in the UK government's commitment to the elimination of racism and xenophobia on the one hand, and yet, on the other hand, the targeting of the Muslim subject constructed as the potentially 'radicalized' Other that is implicit in emerging security practices. The generalization of

Introduction   11

singular acts so that particular transgressions of law come to be culturally defined as common to the community as a whole ends up (re)producing the very forms of subjectivities deemed to be dangerous. Against the backdrop of London in the aftermath of the bombings, Jabri expands the analysis to explore what it means to live in the global city with its fusion of fixities and mobilities, combining the local and global, and posits this 'cosmopolis' as potentially, an alternative form of political space and political community.

This part closes with Angharad Closs Stephens' chapter, which offers a close reading of some of the governmental responses to the bombings, by concentrating on a series of poster campaigns that were disseminated by the London Assembly. Closs Stephens looks at the ways in which different ideas of community circulated in the aftermath of the events of 7 July and in particular how national ideas of belonging interweaved and contrasted with more urban multicultural narratives. Although the national and the multicultural messages offered by the British government on the one hand and the London Assembly on the other seem to offer different accounts of community, Closs Stephens argues that both worked to strikingly similar effect, by insisting on the importance of commonality and unity. She explores the politics and risks of this insistence on unity and asks how we might imagine alternative forms of community.

The second part of the book, 'War on terror/war on response', moves away from a close reading of the particular cartographies of response in the aftermath of the bombings to offer broader reflections on the politics of response in the context of the war on terror.

Dan Bulley's chapter opens with a study of how the four suicide bombers were constructed as 'outsiders' or 'others' despite the fact that these attacks were carried out by Britons. All of the bombers were raised in Britain and schooled in Britain and yet the government worked hard to make these largely typical young British men seem untypical, exceptional and 'foreign'. Bulley explores the process by which attempts were made to escape the threat of domestic chaos and insecurity through the exteriorization of the threat of terror in the aftermath of the bombings. Moreover, he locates this analysis in a broader critique of British foreign policy as it relates to the discourse of the 'failing state'. Ultimately, Bulley claims that the bombings disturb simplistic categories of inside/outside, self/other and domestic/foreign, and points to the way that the UK reveals itself as a 'failing state' according to its own designation of that term.

Chapter 5, written by Nick Vaughan-Williams, critiques the dominant framing of the shooting of Jean Charles de Menezes as a 'mistake' and seeks to re-frame this as a symptom of broader systemic features of Western politics. Vaughan-Williams argues that the discourse of the mistake stymies critical questioning about what happened and colludes in the reproduction of a particular framework of understanding within which sovereign power has retrospectively valorized Menezes' death. By contrast, he argues, the shooting can be read as one of multiple responses of the British state to the London bombings and seeks to locate it within the broader context of the global War on Terror. Rather than a simple mistake it is suggested that the shooting was symptomatic of innovations in the ways sovereign power attempts to secure the spatial and temporal borders of sovereign political community.

In her chapter, Patricia Molloy considers the relationship between time, terror and the political through an analysis of the 'Toronto arrests' of 2 June 2006 and various responses to these counter-terrorist initiatives in both policy-making and academic contexts. Molloy begins with a close reading of the ways in which, despite the absence of an act of terrorism in the Canadian context, the speaking and writing of the arrests simulated a terrorist event and mobilized fear and uncertainty among the population at a vulnerable time for the minority government. She explores the work that the myth of Canadian benevolence and tolerance to 'our multicultural others' does in reaffirming nationalist tropes dependent upon notions of spatial and temporal distinctions between inside and outside. In this way Molloy emphasizes that, while there may be differences in the way these dynamics play out locally, responses to acts of terrorism globally can be said to follow and (re)produce certain common logics.

Louise Amoore's chapter brings the second part of the book to a close with a plea not to forget the 'war on terror', in the face of the UK government's decision to limit the use of this phrase. Amoore argues that an ethical response to events such as the London bombings must engage in remembering, reiterating and revealing the violence carried out and legitimized in the name of that War. Her insistence is that many of these violent practices are ultimately authorized by the routinization of norms and the identification of deviant practices that establish what is considered to be 'the norm' in the first place. What is necessary, in her view, is an ethical engagement with the politics of response by seeking to recover the forgotten aspects of our lives that allow for violent practices based upon a technologized and depoliticized algorithmic calculation of unknown futures. Amoore suggests that practices of artistic intervention offer a potentially valuable resource for rethinking political responsibility in the face of technical depoliticization.

Finally, Part III, 'Possibilities of response?', critically addresses the central animating concept of response as it relates to the study of terrorism, and draws on questions of politics, philosophy and ethics.

This part begins with James Brassett's chapter, which interrogates the relationship between cosmopolitanism and terrorism through the lens of the concept of response. Brassett argues that the disruption of the G8 Summit and the Make Poverty History campaign by the London bombings set up a dichotomy between cosmopolitanism on the one hand and terrorism on the other. He argues that this constituted a totalizing ethical discourse of possibility that foreclosed other responses beyond cosmopolitanism. The chapter finishes with a discussion of the need for an alternative ontology of the global beyond this discourse in order to recover a more critical moment in cosmopolitan thought.

Chris Rumford's chapter examines discourses of fear and risk in the aftermath of the events of 7 July 2005 in London. Rumford notes the highly emotional content of many responses to terrorist events by governmental leaders such as those displayed by Bush and Blair. He contrasts what he describes as emotional and rational responses to terrorist events but argues at the same time that these should not be understood as mutually exclusive. Rather, a focus on the politics of emotion can help offer us a critical analysis of the way in which meaning is produced in meaningless times. In the final part of this chapter Rumford turns to contemporary novels to engage his themes and to offer ideas on avenues for further research in this field.

Chapter 10, written by Madeleine Fagan, offers a critical interrogation of the concept of response that animates this volume throughout. Fagan highlights some of the major difficulties of this concept and the implications of these for any attempt to understand what the politics of response might mean. She argues, drawing primarily on the work of Emmanuel Lévinas, that any politics of response is also always already an ethics of response, and that response is inseparable from ideas of responsibility. Following on from this key insight, the chapter explores how the way we conceptualize otherness impacts on the possibilities of a politics, and an ethics, of response. It does so via an analysis of forms of identity captured in the general context of the war on terror and also the 'One London Campaign' instigated in the aftermath of the 7 July bombings in London.

The final chapter of the book is written by Costas Douzinas. This chapter offers a bold examination of the 'Live 8' event and the London suicide bombings as representing two dominant types of metaphysics which both correspond to forms of 'post-politics'. He argues that the moralistic humanism displayed at the Live 8 concert abandons a search for the good and sees its purpose as combating evil. The London bombings were driven by a different pursuit, of a politics in the service of the good but with this truth being only available to certain members. These two types of post-political politics, moralistic humanism on the one hand and terror on the other, share a basic metaphysical structure. Douzinas explores the general characteristics of this metaphysical structure, through a study of different conceptions of the self, otherness and community. He engages the endless struggle over meaning that forms such an important part of political life, using the work of Jean-Luc Nancy in particular. He concludes by attempting to rework the relationship between sovereignty, sacrifice and politics and proposes an alternative imaginary for forming political communities.

Notes

1 The idea that a terrorist attack of some sort was bound to take place in a city like London was quite widespread. This is revealed in the *Guardian*'s editorial on 8 July 2005 for example, which claims: 'This was, we have repeatedly been warned by police and security chiefs, an event which was likely to happen one day' ('In the face of danger'). While other debates deal with questions about the preparedness of the UK in general, and with the question of why Britain's threat level was lowered in advance of the events (this is addressed in the Intelligence and Security Committee's 2006 'Report into the London Terrorist Attacks on 7 July 2005'), we are more interested in the general framing of the events of 7 July 2005 as events that were always going to happen, and in questions about the politics of pre-emption and prevention raised by this assumption.

2 This approach borrows from David Campbell's citation of Michel Foucault's maxim: 'Practicing criticism is a matter of making facile gestures difficult', Foreword to Campbell 1992.
3 There are important exceptions however, including Tulloch 2006; Gilroy 2006; MacCabe *et al.* 2006.
4 'Home Office Rules Out Inquiry into July 7 Bombs' *Guardian*, 8 September 2007. Available online at www.guardian.co.uk/uk/2007/sep/08/politics.july7 (accessed 6 March 2008).
5 For a more detailed argument on the way in which this temporal indication masks an analysis of the spatial framings of the 'War on Terror' see Elden 2007; Gregory 2004.

References

BBC News Online (2005a), 'London Beats Paris to 2012 Games', 6 July. Online. Available at: http://news.bbc.co.uk/sport1/hi/front_page/4655555.stm (accessed 1 March 2008).

BBC News Online (2005b), 'London blasts: At a glance', 7 July. Online. Available at: http://news.bbc.co.uk/1/hi/uk/4659331.stm (accessed 7 March 2008).

Brown, W. (1997), 'Time and the Political', *Theory & Event*, 1(1). Online. Available at: http://muse.jhu.edu/journals/theory_and_event/ (accessed 27 November 2007).

Butler, J. (1999), *Gender Trouble: Feminism and the Subversion of Identity*, New York; London: Routledge.

Butler, J. (2004), *Precarious Life: The Power of Mourning and Violence*, London: Verso.

Campbell, D. (1992) *Writing Security: United States foreign policy and the politics of identity*, Manchester: Manchester University Press.

Campbell, D. (2002), 'Time Is Broken: The Return of the Past in Response to September 11', *Theory & Event*, 5(4). Online. Available at: http://muse.jhu.edu/journals/theory_and_event/ (accessed 27 November 2007).

Derrida, J. (2003), 'Autoimmunity: Real and Symbolic Suicides – A Dialogue with Jacques Derrida', in G. Borradori (ed.), *Philosophy in a Time of Terror: Dialogues with Jürgen Habermas and Jacques Derrida*, Chicago and London: University of Chicago Press.

Edkins, J. (2003), *Trauma and the Memory of Politics*, Cambridge: Cambridge University Press.

Elden, S. (2007), 'Terror and Territory', *Antipode: A Journal of Radical Geography*, 39(5): 821–45.

Gilroy, P. (2006), 'Multiculture in Times of War: An Inaugural Lecture Given at the London School of Economics', *Critical Quarterly*, 48(4): 27–45.

Gregory, D. (2004), *The Colonial Present*, Malden MA; Carlton, Victoria; Oxford: Blackwell.

Guardian (2005), 'In the face of danger', Editorial, 8 July.

Intelligence and Security Committee (2006), *Report into the London Terrorist Attacks on 7 July 2005*, London: The Stationery Office. Chaired by The Rt Hon. Paul Murphy MP.

London Assembly (2006), *Report of the 7 July Review Committee*, London: Greater London Authority. Chaired by Richard Barnes AM.

MacCabe, C. Ali, M., Carlin, P., Gilroy, P., Hext, K., Kureishi, H., Rushdie, S., Serret, N. and Young, S. (2006) 'Multiculturalism after 7/7: A CQ Seminar', *Critical Quarterly*, 48(2): 1–44.

Massey, D. (2005), *For Space*, London/Thousand Oaks, CA/New Delhi: Sage.

Massumi, B. (2005), 'The Future Birth of the Affective Fact', proceedings of the 'Genealogies of Biopolitics' conference, Online. Available at: http://radicalempiricism.org (accessed 10 September 2006).

Report of the Official Account of the Bombings in London on 7th July 2005 (2006), London: The Stationery Office.

Tulloch, J. (2006), *One Day in July: Experiencing 7/7*, London: Little, Brown.

Walker, R. B. J. (1995), 'International Relations and the Concept of the Political', in K. Booth and S. Smith (eds), *International Relations Theory Today*, University Park, PA: Pennsylvania State University Press.

Wolin, S. (1997), 'What Time Is It?', *Theory & Event*, 1(1). Online. Available at: http://muse.jhu.edu/journals/theory_and_event/ (accessed 27 November 2007).

Part I
Cartographies of response

1 Biopolitics, communication and global governance
London, July 2005[1]

Jenny Edkins

'Where is he, someone tell me, where is he?'

(Marie Fatayi-Williams 2005)

Contemporary biopolitical forms of global governance entail the instrumentalization or commodification of life, or the production of what Giorgio Agamben has aptly called 'bare life' (Agamben 1998; 2005).[2] The treatment of life as bare life entails a disregard for aspects of personhood and involves protocols of communication and administration that treat people as objects. In parallel with the global spread of states of exception described by Agamben we can track a global spread of forms of social interaction, governance and communication that produce life as bare life. Examples are numerous and widely discussed: the humanitarian interventions of the 1990s and the famine relief efforts of the 1980s, where life was something that was to be 'saved', nothing more – victims were not given a political voice – and the terrorist attacks and arbitrary detentions of the present decade, where once more life is disqualified politically and seen as an appropriate if maybe regrettable target of attack without warning or incarceration without trial.[3] One critique levelled at Agamben has been that he takes too grim a view of contemporary life: while it may be true that there are instances where life has been subject to the arbitrary whims of authority, this is not generally the case. The argument is that we are not all reduced to bare life, as Agamben claims (Laclau 2007: 11–22).[4] However, as this chapter seeks to demonstrate, when we look at small-scale, local practices we find in the detail of what happens – in the protocols of communication and the bureaucracies of governance – precisely that reduction or commodification of life of which Agamben warns.

This chapter examines one instance of the instrumentalization of life characteristic of global governance: the way in which people were treated by the British authorities in the aftermath of the London bombings of July 2005.[5] In particular, I am concerned here with the way in which communication with those searching for missing relatives or friends was one-way or non-existent. This treatment, it seems to me, provides an instructive example of what Michael Dillon has called 'governing terror' and what Giorgio Agamben called 'sovereign power', the practices and processes characteristic of contemporary forms of global liberal governance (Dillon 2007a; 2007b: Dillon and Lobo-Guerrero 2007; Agamben 1998; 2005). Although clearly it would be good if people were treated better in the terrible circumstances following what we call traumatic loss, and in particular if communications with those traumatized by the events could be managed more appropriately, this is not the central argument the chapter is making. The argument is rather that the way people are treated at such times is symptomatic of and plainly reveals 'the contingent instrumentality of pure operationality' (Dillon 2007a: 19). In other words, it is not a small local failure, which could be put right within existing frameworks; rather it is the inevitable product of the form of global governance to which we are apparently now subject. My purpose is to elucidate ways in which governance of this type, a form of governance that has been called biopolitics or sovereign power, works, how it can be traced through local practices, and how it is being and can be challenged or contested.

Biopolitical instrumentality does not reflect all there is to life, and traumatic events such as the 7 July bombings make this apparent.[6] Such events are dangerous for any form of authority that relies on a supposed ability to master contingency, to manage disaster, to provide security or to govern terror, for its authorisation. Events like this, traumatic events, threaten to reveal that governing contingency is impossible (Edkins 2003a). They provoke a recognition of the horrors of the ways we are governed and the extent to which these forms of governance not only fail in what they set out to do but miss the point. There is a contingency beyond the contingent that forms the object of contemporary governance, and it is this contingency that counts.[7] Events we call traumatic are precisely those that reveal that whatever systems we set up to reassure ourselves that terror is governable it isn't. Although after 11 September 2001 it began to seem as though the state, or whatever we call the place where authority resides, has taken charge of the traumatic, it has not (Edkins 2003a: 233). Despite all the talk of the inevitability of terrorist attacks and the existence of 'unknown unknowns', sovereign power's attempts to respond to and to 'govern' what we call trauma remain inept and ineffectual as inevitably they must. The contingent that can be governed is not the same as the contingency that cannot: governing terror, to use Dillon's phrase again, is not the same as governing trauma.

One of the most prominent protests against the way in which people were handled in the aftermath of the bombings in London came from Marie Fatayi-Williams. Her 'public display of grief and anger' had been a response to 'frustration at the lack of communication from the authorities' who had failed to confirm her son Anthony's death despite her pleas for information (Laville 2005: 1). Not only was there silence from the authorities as to naming the dead, there was a demand for detailed information from those searching for their friends and relations. Everyone was treated as a suspect: the priority was the search for the 'perpetrators', not the needs of the 'victims'. Families were plunged into a world of Disaster Victim Identification Forms, Police Liaison Officers, and stonewalling by officials. Any communication outside the protocols of disaster was disallowed.

In the aftermath of what we call disaster, communication – in this case the circulation and exchange of dead or dying bodies and information about them – has to conform to a certain discipline: it has to accept certain protocols or parameters.[8] In a similar way, academic communication – writing in the social sciences – is forced into a particular format in order to be heard: it has to be rational and referenced, for example. In both cases, communication that falls outside these disciplinary constraints is not acceptable. It is not heard, or is at best reduced to an incoherent murmur, reverberating faintly from the margins. Its voice is 'excommunicated', and only reluctantly permitted to protest in the role of 'traumatized victim', or to present alternative ways of writing in the role of 'marginalized dissident'.[9]

There can be a double silencing when we find academic writers joining forces, or attempting to join forces, with those who are produced as 'victims' or as 'traumatized' in an attempt to render them voiceless and excommunicated. The ways in which relatives of the missing caught up in the bureaucracies of disaster find alternative ways to perform and communicate their anguish lets us see how they are marginalized or 'disappeared' by the biopolitics or sovereign power that governs the exception or the emergency. Our attempts as academics to make their voices reappear can often, however, remain trapped within the disciplinary practices of International Relations.[10] This is not only a question of academic writing, important though that is, but also a question of the relation between academic life and political action, between scholars and 'practitioners' (Edkins 2005). Once we become or take on a certain role as 'academics', we are forced into certain protocols: our writing has to have an argument; we have to provide references; we have to write in a way that is relevant to the context in which we publish. In accepting our authorization as academics, we have a certain obligation. Moving outside those protocols, and using our academic authorisation to perform our work, to move our audience to tears, perhaps, and to influence but not through the force of the better argument, renders us uncomfortable.[11]

Occasionally, academics themselves become 'traumatized victims'.[12] And, even more occasionally, they find the courage to write from this tortuous and tortured perspective. One example is Susan Brison, who has written movingly and informatively about her experience as the survivor of a violent attack during which she was left for dead (Brison 2002). In the aftermath of the events of 7 July 2005 in London, two people who were caught up in the events in different ways and who beforehand had been inhabitants of the world of academia, wrote of their experiences to great effect: Marie Fatayi-Williams and John Tulloch (Fatayi-Williams 2006; Tulloch 2006).[13] Their writings help me raise some of the questions about communication, excommunication and biopolitics that interest me in this chapter.

I was asked to present a piece in the opening roundtable at a conference held in London in December 2006 under the rubric 'London in a Time of Terror: The Politics of Response.' I presented some of my work for this chapter. The conference was open to non-academics as well as academics, and people registering included survivors of 7 July as well as relatives of people killed that day. This meant that all the 'academics' presenting were very aware that they were not able to speak (should they have wished to) in what would have been a fairly common academic way: in abstract, theoretical terms, for example. It was also obvious that a performative presentation designed to provoke an emotional response would not be appropriate either. For once, it seemed more as if we were all in this together. We weren't outsiders and insiders, academics and practitioners. We all travelled on public transport, we all visited London; many of us lived there. There were clearly, as the organizers said in their opening address, sensitive issues at stake. There were people present for whom the questions we were to discuss would never be abstract theoretical concerns. During one of the discussions one question raised was why academics had had so little to say, why had they not spoken up more. Was it perhaps that the very academic conventions that give their voice authority can make them powerless to speak in such a context?

In the aftermath of the explosions on the London underground and in Tavistock Square in Bloomsbury on Thursday 7 July 2005, relatives of the missing were kept waiting for up to or over a week for information about where their sons and daughters, friends and family members might be. They were put through a bureaucratic process, the requirements of which were applied apparently without regard for the distress they would cause. In the first part of the chapter I trace some of the ways people on the streets responded to the aftermath, and look briefly at how responses to what we call traumatic events might be thought about in more general terms. I then focus on the search for the missing, and draw out how those involved attempted to express or communicate their 'trauma' in the face not only of the bombings themselves but of the bureaucratic processes of disaster management that were put in place by the authorities. The official processes, in particular the Disaster Victim Identification system, are detailed, and the way they set out to seek information – and the type of information they require – explored.

The abstract rationality of these official practices and the objective forms of communication they entail contrasts sharply with the requirements of those we call the traumatized for a personal response to their grief and suffering. The chapter attempts to align itself with the latter: it tries to communicate to its readers the emotional turmoil and anger afoot in London that July among those most directly affected. It argues that the response to trauma taken by officialdom, the attempt by the authorities to overcome trauma by a demonstration of their authority and competence in the production of safety and security – by focussing entirely on tracking down the 'perpetrators' at the expense of paying attention to the 'victims' – is not the only possibility. It is reflective of a particular form of biopolitical sovereign authority that is increasingly prevalent but that may well not be one whose ethos we would want to endorse, were we asked. Other forms of communication, other ways of being in relation to traumatic events, were demonstrated that summer.

The aftermath

Following the 7 July bombings in London in 2005, tributes were left at King's Cross and gathered together in a small memorial garden next to the station, temporarily supplanting what had been a cycle park. When I visited the garden on 16 July, a notice announced:

> A constant memory to
> all who lost their lives
> near this place on
> 7th July 2005.
> 'Peace is now theirs'
> We shall never forget.

A book of condolences was available just outside the garden. In the garden itself, the space surrounding a small tree was lined with flowers, flags and messages. It was possible for visitors to enter and make a circuit of the area to read the messages, though there would not have been room for more than around two or three dozen people at a time in the garden. Instructions at the entrance asked that people refrain from taking photographs. The garden was separated from its surroundings by metal railings, and messages and flags were attached to the railings too.[14]

From outside the garden it was possible to photograph those visiting the interior, and to take shots of some of the messages that were orientated to the outside. The garden – later returned to its familiar role of cycle park – is situated at a corner of the façade of King's Cross Station, adjacent to a very busy traffic crossroads, with signals for pedestrians and traffic. There is and was a continual flow of people past the area: the pavement outside would regularly be dozens deep with people weaving to and fro. The small area of contemplation was somewhat incongruous among the city bustle, apparently unnoticed by most passers-by. Visitors were however thoroughly absorbed.

The messages in the garden were interesting. Prominent among them were messages from other cities or different national or religious groups offering sympathy and understanding: messages from the Turkish community, the Afghan community in Walsall, from religious groups, from visitors to the city. 'We are with you: All Indians in UK & all over'; 'Our heart is with you just like your heart was with us'; 'America stands united with London against terrorism'; 'To you brave Londoners ... your friends from Norway'; 'Our prayers are with you. Keep the faith. From all South Africans'; 'We fought together in the last war and we will always be with you till the end. Maltese Community'; 'We are all Londoners: Christian, Muslim, Jew, Hindu, Sikh, Buddhist'; 'London: Madrid's heart is with you: Be Brave'. A message in Japanese from someone called Katahira, from Sayama City Fire Station, Saitama Prefecture near Tokyo reads: 'I pray for the souls of the dead and for the speedy recovery of the injured, for peace in the UK and the world. 7 July 2005'. One message summed up the general feeling: 'It wasn't necessary to have been born here to feel sadness for what happened in London'. It seemed at first glance different from New York after 11 September:[15] less insular, perhaps, with messages from all over the world offering support. There was little condemnation and no asking for retaliation: 'only one race is harmed by this: the human race'.

A little further along the same stretch of road, on the other side of the station entrance, was a hoarding on which details of missing persons were posted, behind clear plastic:

> Missing: James Mayes. White, slim build, 5' 11". Hazel eyes and short curly brown hair. Last seen or heard from before London Bombings. Was travelling on the Piccadilly line from King's Cross at 8.30–9am on Thursday 7 July. If you see him please call us urgently on ....
>
> Have you seen this man or his car? Christian Small (Age 28). Black male. Athletic build. 5' 01" Short black hair. Brown eyes. He left home at 7.55am on Thursday 7 July 2005. Car: Mitsubishi Colt Hatchback (silver). Stations: From Blackhorse Road or Walthamstow Central via King's Cross and Finsbury Park to Holborn. Contacts...

Other posters appeared in nearby parks, attached to gate posts: 'Missing: Neetu Jain. Last seen at Euston/Tavistock Square on the morning of 7th July. Please contact...';

> Karolina: Her appearance ... White female, short blond hair, distinct blue eyes, 1.6m (5ft 4ins), belly-button piercing, Polish nationality (speaks very good English). She was wearing ... Black trouser suit, with long-sleeved round neck black jersey, several silver rings on both hands, silver fine-medium linked chain, black heeled shoes. Personal belongings .... Black handbag (keys with London Olympics 2012 key ring, pack of cigarettes, Sony Eriksson mobile phone (silver, with falling autumn leaves screen saver). Karolina is still missing!!! Karolina is still missing and if anyway can help please contact anyone of us on the following contact details ....[16]

In the face of the bombs, people were posting notices on hoardings and lamp-posts in the desperate hope that passers-by would have information. They took snapshots from albums or computer files, family photos never intended for public display, and put together descriptions of distinguishing marks, height and weight, age and colour. One can only imagine the agony of waiting that relatives and friends went through in the days before details of the identities of those killed in the explosions were released.

These missing persons posters, and the distress of people searching, hopelessly, for their family members, are familiar from New York in 2001 (Edkins 2007a). After the fall of the World Trade Center Twin Towers, relatives and friends of the missing took to the streets with photographs of those they were searching for. Later, they produced photocopied sheets carrying a photograph alongside the same personal details: age, height, weight, distinguishing marks. Occasionally the posters would give full details of where the person was when they were last heard from: 'Edward Pullis. Aon Insurance. 101 Floor. Please call .... Last seen 78th Floor waiting for elevator. Anyone from AON who knows Edward please call'. Always there was the appeal for information, any information, and the list of contact names, numbers and email addresses. The London posters were very similar, noting when people were last seen or heard from, appealing for help and evoking sympathy. The scenario is familiar to us from other disaster sites, too; in the Asian tsunami the previous December people in a different part of the world posted notices describing those lost (SBC Baptist Press News).

In London, the missing posters put up by relatives were taken down as missing people were identified as among the dead. In New York this didn't happen. The missing posters remained on walls in Manhattan for a long time – several years – after the names of those killed had been more or less established. *This is a person, a missing person*, they seemed to be saying. *You have found their DNA, a finger tip, other body parts, maybe. But this person is still missing: they did not come home.* The posters became memorials in themselves: what had been intended as temporary flyers designed to track down missing family members became in the end unusual shrines – memorials carrying distinguishing features, scars, weight and height, memorials still protesting the disappearances (Edkins 2007a).

The placing of a bunch of flowers, the writing of a message: these are the ways in which people communicate with others who visit memorials, with the dead who are commemorated, and with the authorities – those supposed to be 'in charge'. It is communication and witnessing that bypasses the mass media or the official channels. It takes a more direct route. Visitors like myself take photographs of these memorial sites – photographs of the photographs, in the case of the missing posters. Many people take photographs of other people at the memorial sites: a mirror of repetition to infinity of testimony and witnessing.

Is what we have here nothing more than a commemoration, the remembering of lives lost, and the paying of respects to those who died, important as that might be? A cultural process, a process of communication, that enables us to come to terms with traumatic events, a process that is now global in its reach and in the tropes and symbolic capital it invokes? There seems to me to be much more at stake than this. There always was in the memory of trauma in any case.

The commemoration of what we call traumatic events bears a particular relationship to politics and political struggle.[17] Those who have experienced such events have been brought face to face with the vulnerability of life and the fragility of all forms of social and political community. Events that we call traumatic are events that reveal that there is no way round this vulnerability. There are only solutions that enable life to go on, that enable us to forget the pressing uncertainties of life and death for the time being. Remembering traumatic events can be a way of refusing a language that forgets the essential vulnerability of flesh in its talk of the importance of state, nation and ideology, a way of refusing a language that pretends that certainty and security is attainable. We can never quite know who we are, or who anyone else is: once we try to pin it down, something always escapes us: we are always both more and less than what we claim to be. There is a lack at the heart of subjectivity, and, though we imagine wholeness or completeness as attainable, it is not. The social order of which we are part – what we call social reality – is fragile and incomplete too. The form of biopolitical authority that originated in the sovereign state but is increasingly becoming globalized tackles this inherent incompleteness or lack of closure in a number of ways, including through two processes that are particularly relevant here. First, through the production of what it calls failure, disaster or emergency, this form of authority sustains the fantasy that were it not for this temporary hiccup, all would be well.[18] Second, through processes of exclusion, sovereign power or state authority produces an inside and an outside: a group of people to whom certain standards apply and another group to whom they do not. Through exclusions a social order is produced that appears bounded, complete and safe.

However, what we call traumatic events change this picture. The pretence that there are solutions to be found, security and certainty to be had, is seen as just that: a pretence, a fantasy. Often those who survive traumatic events find their world has changed and they want to bear witness, to remember and in particular to remember how trauma unsettles everything. They feel compelled to bear witness to what I have called trauma time, a form of temporality involving the unsettling juxtaposition of past and present as opposed to the smooth, homogeneous linear time of the state (Edkins 2003a). Those 'in charge' on the other hand – the authorities, sovereign power – have to remember traumatic events in different ways. There seem to be two options. Either they have to remember by scripting those events into a heroic history of the nation, of civilization or of humanity, a story of progress towards certainty and the overcoming of doubt: a linear narrative. Or alternatively, and this seems to be a more recent strategy or one that has gained prominence recently, they have to attempt to govern terror, to take control of the contingent: they have to put in place practices of disaster management that normalize emergency and institutionalize trauma time (Dillon 2007a).[19] One or other of these strategies is necessary. Otherwise authority would cease to be authorized. What we call social reality would be revealed as the fantasy that it is – and this is crucial – *all the time*, and not just in a 'time of terror' (Borradori 2003). Remembering trauma is then always a site of struggle, a political struggle over memory and forgetting. At stake is the form of biopolitics or sovereign power that underpins contemporary forms of governance.

According to Agamben, sovereign power works by producing forms of life as separate, distinct. In particular, it works, at least to begin with, through producing two forms of life: politically qualified life, the life of the inside, authorized life, life that can speak; and bare life, the life of the home, the life that is excluded from the political sphere, rendered mute. This distinction, like any distinction and the entities it claims to produce, is always fragile and unsustainable. Under this account, a traumatic event would be one that revealed this fragility and the impossibility of distinctions and called for a recognition of the radical relationality of existence.[20] What we have now, Agamben argues, is a zone of indistinction that has extended to the whole of the earth; all life has become bare life and 'politics is in a state of lasting eclipse' (Agamben 1998). A state of emergency is no longer confined to a short period of time or to a particular place but has extended to all places and all times.

In Dillon's account,[21] what we have is not a zone of indistinction or a state of emergency brought about by the sovereign suspension of the law. Rather, we have a state of emergency that arises once life is conceived as always emergent, always becoming, and hence always dangerous. Not 'a state of emergency born of a juridico-political analysis of sovereign subjectivities', but one 'born of a contemporary biopolitical analysis of emergent life' (Dillon 2007a: 18). What this state of emergency, or 'political emergency of emergence' then produces is 'a regime of exception grounded in the endless calibration of the ... ways in which the very circulation of life threatens life' (Dillon 2007a).

In both these accounts, the form of life that liberal governance sees and that it governs is produced, in a state of emergency/emergence, as a purely bare biological life of emergence that can be and is treated instrumentally. The goal of life, envisaged in this way, is nothing but the endless circulation and reproduction of life. There is no room in this vision, seen either way, for the person or for responsibility.

In London after 7 July the victims, the injured and those who survived were treated as bare emergent life by the police, the emergency services, officials and government ministers. They were thrown back on their own resources: they comforted each other, formed survivor self-help groups, and campaigned for changes. They watched appalled as the authorities ignored their needs. In the face of what we call traumatic events the limits of sovereign forms of power and authority and the biopolitical governance of terror are made clear, as we shall see.

The search for the missing

There was a palpable anger afoot that could be felt clearly in what we saw on the streets of London. An anger that was intensely political was communicated through the memorial site at King's Cross, and through the missing posters in particular. People were angry with those they held responsible for the deaths, of course, but they were also angry with those involved in the aftermath. People, ordinary people, had not been properly treated: not by the bombers, not by the emergency services, not by their political leaders. They were owed more.

This anger came across very clearly in an impromptu speech made on Monday 11 July by Marie Fatayi-Williams, the mother of one of those killed in Tavistock Square in London. Her speech was a compelling indictment of all those who use violence to try to change the world, and of the needless suffering this brings about: 'What inspiration can senseless slaughter provide? Death and destruction ... can never be the foundations for building society' (*Guardian*

2005a). It was also a moving lament at the added anguish caused when information about the missing is withheld – and a plea for that information.

Marie begins her speech by holding up a photograph of her son: 'This is Anthony, Anthony Fatayi-Williams, 26 years old, he's missing'. The photograph stands in for the person: 'This is Anthony'. *Here he is. He exists. I cannot find him, no one will tell me where he is, but he exists. I did not just imagine him.* Marie is an imposing, charismatic figure, powerfully emotional and hugely strong in her grief and her conviction. She stands surrounded by relatives and supporters and a press of media in the middle of the street leading to Tavistock Square itself, as near to the site of the explosion as she can get. Behind her are large photos of Anthony. She continues:

> We fear that he was in the bus explosion ... on Thursday. We don't know. We do know from the witnesses that he left the Northern line in Euston. We know he made a call to his office at Amec at 9.41 from the NW1 area to say he could not make [it] by the tube but he would find alternative means to work. Since then he has not made any contact with any single person.

And she, his mother, has been able to get no information whatsoever about where he is or what happened to him:

> My son Anthony is my first son, my only son, the head of my family. In African society, we hold on to sons.... This is now the fifth day, five days on, and we are waiting to know what happened to him and I, his mother, I need to know what happened to Anthony. His young sisters need to know what happened, his uncles and aunties need to know what happened to Anthony, his father needs to know what happened to Anthony. Millions of my friends back home in Nigeria need to know what happened to Anthony. His friends surrounding me here, who have put this together, need to know what has happened to Anthony. I need to know.

She enumerates the web of relationships in which Anthony is entwined. He is not just a statistic, an unidentified victim of a terrorist bomb. He is a person, someone with relatives, friends, sisters, uncles, aunts, a father, a mother, friends, his mother's friends. They all need to know what happened: this need is urgent, pressing. It is an entitlement, a right. It should not be suspended or held in abeyance.

Like other relatives, Marie Fatayi-Williams will have been told to wait. She will have been told that identification is 'a highly complex and sensitive process' (London Assembly 2006: 98), that it takes time, that she must go home and wait. As if this were something quite simple and easy to do. It is not. As Anthony's friend Amrit Walia said: 'We understand the police have a job to do, but it is agonising to sit and wait, which is all they have advised us to do' (*BBC News Online* 2005b).

Difficulties and delays started on the day of the bombings. To begin with, there had been unforeseen delays in opening the Metropolitan Police Service Casualty Bureau telephone lines. This service was designed for people to report relatives or friends as missing. According to the London Assembly Review of 7 July, delays in opening Casualty Bureau phone lines were due to an incorrect connection at the New Scotland Yard switchboard (London Assembly 2006: 84). This meant that the line was not working at all until after 4 pm on the day of the bombings. By then people were frantic with worry about those missing, and those with injured relatives had no means of finding out about them and getting to the right hospital other than contacting hospitals directly. When the phone lines did open, there were 42,000 attempted calls in the first hour. The system was hopelessly overloaded and it was taking people more than three hours to get through, even with their phone on automatic redial. According to one man whose wife was seriously injured, this was unforgivable:

> The thing that caused me absolutely unnecessary extra anguish and grief on the day, and I think many other people, was something that to me is incomprehensible and inexcusable, and that is the failure of the Central Casualty Bureau emergency number.... It took me slightly more than three hours, if my memory is correct, to register my wife as somebody who was missing and presumably involved. That needs to be addressed. It really really really does need to be addressed.
>
> (London Assembly 2006: 43)

The delay could have meant someone with a relative in a critical condition not getting to their bedside before they died. To add insult to injury, the Casualty Bureau number was not a free number.

However, delays, technical inadequacies and overload were not the chief problem in my view. The difficulty was that there was in fact no source of help for families in locating their friends and relatives. Neither the Casualty Bureau nor the ineptly named Family Assistance Centre set up two days later, was designed to help families locate missing relatives. The Casualty Bureau was the 'first stage in the criminal investigation and formal identification process' (London Assembly 2006: 84) not a mechanism for providing worried members of the public with information about relatives. Although counsellors and other advisors from voluntary organizations like the Salvation Army were present, the prime focus of the Family Assistance Centre was just as clear as that of the Casualty Bureau. Its focus was on 'gathering information: personal and forensic details of people who were potentially injured or killed in the attacks, to assist in the identification process' (ibid.: 99). The phrase 'gathering information' is crucial here. As the London Assembly Report points out, 'this met the needs of the Metropolitan Police in conducting their investigation and identification process' (ibid.: 99), but it was absolutely no help to those searching for family members:

> The Centre was not prepared to give out information, only to collect it. People searching for their loved ones have one primary need: information.

They may also have practical needs, but their main concern is to find out the whereabouts of their loved one. They may not need bereavement counselling in the first few days – the need for information is paramount.

(London Assembly 2006: 99)

Among other things, 'families and friends need a reception centre to provide a central contact point, when hospitals and other authorities identify survivors' (ibid.: 98). All that was provided were various under-staffed and difficult-to-access points with which families could register details of missing persons. Indeed, the families were more likely to get help and feedback by posting missing persons posters on park railings and standing outside stations pleading for information than from filing an official missing persons report, and they knew it. Outside King's Cross Station, a reporter spoke to Craig Laskey, whose friend Lee Baisden was missing:

My hope is that Lee is OK, is traumatised and is wandering around somewhere. We have tried the hospitals but they are very resistant to telling you everything. It has been very frustrating dealing with the authorities. The information flow is all one way. They are willing to take information but not to release anything at all.

(Gardham and Martin 2005)

At this point, according to the same report, the number of confirmed deaths in the bombings was 52, and there were still 56 people being treated in seven hospitals: 'Staff said they had all been identified, dashing the hopes of those clinging to the belief that their loved ones may be alive'. This was on Wednesday 13 July (Gardham and Martin 2005).

There is some confusion about exactly how long full identification of the bodies took; it was somewhere between seven and ten days before relatives were notified and the bodies of victims identified and released for burial. In one place the London Assembly report notes: 'It took ten days for all those who were killed on 7 July to be formally identified by the police' (London Assembly 2006: Para 9.1) In another comment on the same page, the report says: 'The correct identification of the deceased was a highly complex and sensitive task, and this was completed within 7 days' (ibid.: Para 9.3). Although, according to one report, Inner North London Coroner Dr Andrew Reid had said the bodies of the bombers would be treated in exactly the same way as those of the victims (*Guardian* 2005b: 7), their bodies were in fact held for much longer. All four were released in the last week of October 2005. The body of Shehzad Tanweer was buried in Pakistan; relatives of Mohammad Sidique Khan asked for the body to be kept in the mortuary pending another post-mortem (Rozenberg 2005). Anthony Fatayi-Williams' father and uncle (the latter a former Nigerian foreign minister) were informed of Anthony's death by two police officers on Wednesday 13 July; they were invited to identify him (Olaniyonu and Kintum 2005). When they saw the body, they noted remarkably few injuries and described the body as 'well-preserved'. According to the inquest opened on Thursday 14 July, identification had been made from dental records (*Daily Telegraph* 2005). There would seem to be no reason why the family could not have identified the body before 13 July. Why was this not attempted, when Anthony's mother was crying out for information?

According to Marie Fatayi-Williams' account, her first contact with the Metropolitan Police was when she was phoned in Nigeria on Friday 8 July by an officer asking whether she would be flying out to London and when, but saying nothing in response to her questions (Fatayi-Williams 2006: 38). When she arrived at Heathrow on the Saturday morning, she was met by another Metropolitan Police Officer. Again she got no response to her questions, though she later wrote

> it's obvious to me now that the tragic news could have been delivered straight away. Instead, his bureaucratic bosses had dispatched this man not to end my agony of uncertainty, but to ascertain that Mrs Fatayi-Williams had arrived as intended.
>
> (Fatayi-Williams 2006: 48)

Relatives of Samantha and Lee, a couple who both died as a result of the bombings, did not get a formal identification of Samantha until 16 July, nine days after she gave her full name to her rescuer at Russell Square. In the words of a letter from the family to the London Assembly Review, this is the story:

> Sammy was found alive and gave her name, Samantha _____, to her rescuer, and he then passed her on to the emergency staff in the ticket hall of Russell Square, where she died. When we were phoning every hospital in London, it came to one and we asked if there was a Mr Lee _____ or a Samantha _____ and they said there was a Miss Samantha _____ and they would find out more details for us. When she came back she said she was mistaken. If a person is found alive there needs to be a way of transferring their name with the person, i.e.: plaster, pen, anything. As this mistake built up our hopes so much. It then took until 16 July to be notified of her identification. We were never asked if we could or would like to see her or be with her. We do not know where her body was kept. Was it in every way being looked after humanly and with respect?
>
> (London Assembly 2006: 223)

Why was it not possible for this family to be with the body? Why was the information that she was dead withheld from them?

The story of another woman, this time someone who was killed at Aldgate, was similar (Dear 2006). During the 'identification process' prints and DNA swabs were taken from the victim's house; CCTV pictures were obtained of her on her way to London on the morning of the bombings. Finally, after ten days, an identification was made. This person too, like Samantha, was alive after the bombing: a fellow passenger sat with her waiting for the emergency services to arrive. When they did arrive she was still alive, and they treated her; she died a few minutes later. Surely her injuries cannot have been so horrific that her parents could not have identified her by sight? Why was it necessary to delay the identification by ten days?

Disaster victim identification

> 'Nobody in authority seemed to be thinking of us as people with emotions'
> (Marie Fatayi-Williams 2006: 86)

The London Assembly Report highlights some of these stories (London Assembly 2006: 157, 279, 296). The committee made a point of asking survivors and relatives for their views, in person, in public hearings or private, and by written submissions – the first time this has been done in the aftermath of a disaster, amazingly. The report stretches to 157 pages, with the second volume of 279 pages being devoted to transcripts of meetings and correspondence with organizations, and the third volume (296 pages) to views and information from individuals. It is an excellent report, which raises many questions and makes a series of important recommendations, as I will discuss later. However, on the question of the identification process, it seems to be the view of the committee that given that 'this was the first time a Resilience Mortuary had been set up in the UK' and that 'the Mass Fatalities Plan had only been completed a few weeks before 7 July': 'The establishment of the Mortuary by 10 pm on 8 July was a remarkable achievement. The correct identification of the deceased was a highly complex and sensitive task, and this was completed within 7 days' (London Assembly 2006: 98). The brief report known as 'Lessons Learned', published later by the Home Office and the Culture Secretary, runs to a much shorter 32 pages (Cabinet Office 2006) and can be seen as in many ways a response to some of the issues raised powerfully by the Assembly report. Some of the suggestions it makes are laughable – for example, it suggests that a recorded message should be made available for callers trying to get through to the Casualty Bureau. When it comes to the question of identification, the report suggests that more could be done to explain the process:

> It is essential to ensure absolute certainty before a family is told about the death of a loved one and this may take time. We hope that, by explaining the nature and complexity of the Disaster Victim Identification (DVI) process to families in full, and by improving the way the police communicate with families, we will be able to make the experience less distressing for them. We are working up a series of information sheets for victims of major emergencies that we will collect together in an online library. These will include a sheet about the DVI process, to be distributed by Family Liaison Officers and at Assistance Centres. In addition, the police are reviewing the training for Family Liaison Officers so that they are better aware of the DVI process and the issues for families.
> (Cabinet Office 2006: 12)

What then is the 'nature and complexity of the Disaster Victim Identification (DVI) process', and why was it used in London on 7 July?

The International Criminal Police Organization (Interpol) Manual on Disaster Victim Identification was first published in 1984 and later revised and circulated to all Interpol member countries 'to encourage the compatibility of procedures across international boundaries, which is essential in these days of ever-increasing world travel' (Interpol 1984).

As a process, the system of Disaster Victim Identification is eminently straightforward and clear. There are three forms to be completed: a yellow Ante-Mortem (AM) form, a pink Post-Mortem (PM) form and a white Comparison report. When all three forms are completed and an identification has been made, they are filed together under a set of cover pages provided, the AM and PM forms being interleaved to make comparison of data easier. The cover pages and the Victim Identification Report, on white paper, are the final parts to be completed. They are filled in by a panel of experts (police officer, pathologist, odontologist) before a death certificate can be issued or a body released for burial. The final stage links a particular 'DEAD BODY', identified by nature, place and date of disaster and number, with a particular 'MISSING PERSON' identified by name and date of birth.

The Ante-Mortem and Post-Mortem forms[22] each comprise 15 pages arranged in seven sections and covering: personal data (AM form only);[23] recovery of body from site (PM form only); description of effects (clothing, jewellery, etc.); physical description and distinguishing marks (tattoos etc.); medical information that may assist identification; dental information; and 'other'. The assumption here is clearly that we are dealing with dead bodies: there is no provision for people who die during the rescue process, only for those who are already dead. The two forms are completed separately. The AM form is completed by those interviewing the relatives, and the PM form by those recovering bodies from 'the disaster site'. The instructions ask that the AM forms be completed and forwarded as quickly as possible and that full and detailed information is obtained since 'it is impossible to know what data will be found from the disaster site'. The onus is on the relatives to put down everything they can think of. And the AM form is extremely detailed. For personal effects details of all clothing, shoes, jewellery, watches, glasses, personal effects and identity papers carried must be given, down to details of keys carried, purse/wallet, etc. This section covers three pages. Then a full physical description is needed beginning with height, weight, build, race, hair. The description required includes great detail. For example, the nose: Is it small, medium or large? Pointed, Roman or alcoholic's? Is it concave, straight or convex? Turned down, horizontal or turned up? Are there marks of spectacles or not? Any other peculiarities? The same details are required for other facial features: forehead, eyes, eyebrows, ears, facial hair, mouth, lips, teeth, smoking habits. And it goes on: chin, neck, hands, feet, body hair, pubic hair, scars, skin marks, tattoos/piercings, malformations, amputations, circumcision. Finally, it asks for a full list of medical conditions: AIDS? Addictions? Pregnancies? IUD?

This type of information, in this amount of detail, was presumably being collected from relatives in the London bombings, perhaps even over the phone to the Casualty Bureau.[24] It is recognized that there will be a far greater number of people reported missing in the early stages than there are casualties in the end, so that it doesn't make sense to complete AM forms in great detail at an early stage. In London, the total was 7,823 (Travis 2006). Even if the information was collected later, one has to ask how necessary the detail was in all cases, when it appears that the majority of victims were in the end identified by dental records. Much of the information included in the form would not be regarded anyway as satisfactory confirmation of identity. According to a report in the *Independent*, 'primary' evidence, sufficient on its own for identification, includes fingerprints, dental records, DNA, or 'a unique identity feature, say, a pacemaker with a serial number of it'. If none of these is available, then some combination of 'secondary' forms of evidence may be acceptable: 'marks and scars, blood group, jewellery, X-ray, and deformity' (Bennetto 2005).

As relatives spotted, the collection of data through the Casualty Bureau or the Family Assistance Centre as part of DVI is a very one-sided process. Relations of the missing complete more or less exhaustive details of their family member on the AM forms, which are immediately passed to the police. The primary role of the family liaison officer allocated to relatives of the missing is as part of the investigation: the liaison officer works on behalf of the police, specifically to assist in the gathering of information. The police and forensic experts working with the bodies of victims also collect information and complete forms. However, these PM forms are not made available to relatives. Indeed relatives are not given any details, even of the most general sort, of the bodies recovered. They are kept very much in the dark until they need to be contacted for further information. A matching process takes place behind closed doors, as it were, and it is only when a positive identification has been made that family members are informed. Remains are released for burial and death certificates issued at this point. Before then, the bodies belong to the Coroner not to the next of kin. The information belongs to the Coroner too. There is no provision for identification of the body by relatives as part of the process. The rationale for this is that 'visual recognition' is 'unscientific' and prone to inaccuracies. The face has disappeared as a means of identification: tattoos can be used, but face recognition by someone who knows the person is not allowed (Bennetto 2005).

There has been a longstanding battle by survivors and relatives bereaved in 'disasters' of all types to ensure that the authorities dealing with the aftermath pay attention to their needs (Hare 2005). The group Disaster Action, whose members are all survivors or people bereaved in disasters – including, as they note on their website,[25] the Zeebrugge ferry sinking, King's Cross fire, Lockerbie air crash, Hillsborough football stadium crush, Marchioness riverboat sinking, Dunblane shootings, Southall and Ladbroke Grove train crashes, the 11 September attacks in the United States and the Bali bombing – produces guidance on issues related specifically to disaster victim identification. This stresses the importance to the bereaved, both relatives and friends, of knowing the cause of death, in some detail, and the need to be with the person after death or to view the body, whatever its condition. In the case of missing persons, Disaster Action stresses that

> friends and family members may go to great lengths to find them themselves, regardless of other efforts or advice by the authorities. This may include travelling to disaster zones, temporary mortuaries, hospitals, etc. It is important that their families feel reassured that all that could be done is being or has been done to find, recover and establish the identity of all the victims.
> (Disaster Action 2005: 3)

The production of emergency

But is all that could be done being done? Why are relatives of the missing, like Marie Fatayi-Williams and many others, left to wander the streets, distraught and helpless?

In the case of the London bombings of 7 July, a convincing argument can be made and was made – the London Assembly enquiry found it convincing – that *in the circumstances* all that could be done was being done. However, we need to pay much more attention to what these 'circumstances' were, and how they came to be defined as such. In the end it was the treatment of what happened on 7 July as a disaster that led to the invocation of the DVI process for the identification of the bodies of those killed. To what extent was that appropriate? It may seem obvious that what happened was a disaster, an outrage, 'a terrible and tragic atrocity that has cost many innocent lives' in the words of Prime Minister Blair (*BBC News Online* 2005a). The Government's Emergency Committee met without hesitation that morning. There is no doubt that a large number of people were affected by the bombings: 56 people died, including the bombers, 700 were injured, '1,000 adults and 2,000 of their children ... suffered from post-traumatic stress as a result of their experiences on 7 July [and] 3,000 others are estimated to have been directly affected' (London Assembly 2006: Para 11.6).

However, what counts as an emergency or a disaster is not largely a question of numbers. In the bombings at Aldgate and at Edgware Road taken separately the numbers of fatalities were no greater than a bad road traffic accident. There is a choice as to whether an incident should be treated as a 'disaster' and whether, for example, all the intricacies and complexities of the Disaster Victim Identification processes need to be invoked. This is, or rather should be, a political choice. As such, it needs to be justified; delays in the identification of bodies cannot be argued to be the result of the circumstances when those circumstances (the treatment of what had happened as 'a disaster') were not an automatic result, but a political decision. What had happened on 7 July was appalling; it was arguably made worse by invoking the bureaucratic apparatus of disaster management.

In a number of cases clearly there will have been reasons why under no circumstances could identifications have been made more quickly. On the other hand, there are several cases where an immediate identification could almost certainly have been made. And in most cases, with a different approach to the identification process – that is, under different circumstances, under circumstances not defined as 'a disaster', under circumstances not scripted by the biopolitical practices of 'governing terror' – there is no reason why families should have been kept in limbo for seven to ten days.

What is called 'sovereign power' and the production of states of exception or 'disaster' are closely interrelated. The type of politics that leads to the invocation of a 'disaster' or 'emergency' affects not only how the tracing of missing persons is handled, but also the treatment of survivors, and, more broadly still, the treatment of people in general 'in a time of terror' (Borradori 2003). This returns us to the questions of forms of authority and power that were broached at the start of this essay.

Sovereign power is a type of governance that normalizes the emergency, the disaster, by setting out rules and procedures for dealing with it. This has not only been the case since 7 July or 11 September; it can be found in attempts to set out rules for humanitarian intervention in conflict zones, to 'do no harm', to deal with famines and other events perceived through the discourses of sovereign power as exceptional, as failures of the system, as disasters. Exceptions were always, as Agamben has shown so clearly, intimately related to the norms they serve to instantiate. When the state of emergency and its accompanying zones of indistinction spread to encompass the terrain of politics in its entirety, all life becomes bare life. Such a form of life is seen by sovereign power as worthy of being saved, but of little else. As we have seen, it is not worthy of respect or of dignity, in life or in death.

What we saw in London after 7 July can also be read as a prime example of how the 'general economy of the contingent' that liberal biopolitics puts in place works (Dillon 2007a). Governing terror, in the sense of attempting to govern the contingent, leads to an approach to policy making and management that is 'comprehensively technologised', and where 'biopolitical government begins to find its nihilistic rationale and ultimate test in the operational competence it displays as a service provider of emergency relief and emergency planner of emergence' (Dillon 2007a: 15, 18). As a form of governance it is not something that has been brought about by the 'War on Terror' which it predates it by a long way, though it is amplified by it. The technologization to which it gives rise works to the detriment of those caught up in it: the form of life that the governance of terror recognizes as life is 'a continuous process of complex, infinitely contingent, circulatory transactional emergence'. According to Dillon, what is at stake, and what must be contested if biopolitics itself is to be contested, is this account of life, a 'life of pure operationality [that] renders the state of emergency normal' (Dillon 2007a: 24).

The traumatic events surrounding the sudden deaths of partners, friends and relatives on 7 July made it quite clear that 'there is more to life than meets the molecular biopolitics of contemporary biopower' (Dillon 2007a: 20). The lack at the heart of the hypersecuritization to which biopower is driven in its attempts to govern the dangers of emergent life is revealed. 'Governing terror' cannot pause to respond to those suffering loss: it has to rush around madly trying to secure emergent life as if that were the only game in town.

Conclusion

> 'I would like once again to express my sympathy and sorrow for those families that will be grieving so unexpectedly and tragically tonight.'
> (Tony Blair, *BBC News Online* 2005a)

Condolences communicated in advance of the fact are a danger sign: a sign of an attempt to govern trauma, to appropriate it, take charge of it and normalize it through rituals of memory and grief. George Bush expressed his condolences on the morning of 11 September at around 9.30 am – before the buildings had fallen in Manhattan and before the plane had crashed in Pennsylvania. Those to whom Blair offered his condolences on 7 July 2005 could not have been grieving that night, though they would undoubtedly have been distraught. Families were still trying desperately to find out what had happened: ringing round friends, trailing round hospitals, trying to get through to the Casualty Bureau, taking the first flight to London. They couldn't get any news of their missing sons, daughters, mothers, fathers, brothers, sisters, friends or partners. They could not possibly begin to mourn. No one could or would tell them whether the people they were looking for were dead or alive.[26]

What I have argued in this paper is that the distress they suffered is a symptom of a more deep-seated problem. The reason for the appalling delay in letting families know what had happened can be traced back to the automatic invocation of a state of emergency and its attendant bureaucracies. This state of emergency or exception also involves the production of life as bare life: life with no political say, life as nothing but emergent biological life. To the bureaucracies of biopower the lives at stake in a disaster are merely lives to be saved; the quality of life is of little importance, and neither are the wishes and needs of the individuals involved. The forms of life that go along with a politics of exception entail the absence of proper political life. People are no longer seen as important in themselves, each for what they are or might be. They are only either bare life – life that can go home and carry on, walk away from the disaster, or dead bodies that can be matched in due course with names and dates of birth of missing persons and filed away. If what went wrong after 7 July is to be put right, this is what needs to change. It is a major change. As the London Assembly report put it:

> There is an overarching, fundamental lesson to be learnt from the response to the 7 July attacks, which underpins most of our findings and recommendations. The response on 7 July demonstrated that there is a lack of consideration of the individuals caught up in major or catastrophic

incidents. Procedures tend to focus too much on incidents, rather than on individuals, and on processes rather than people. Emergency plans tend to cater for the needs of the emergency and other responding services, rather than explicitly addressing the needs and priorities of the people involved.

(London Assembly 2006: 9)

Their conclusion is that 'a change of mindset is needed to bring about the necessary shift in focus, from incidents to individuals, and from processes to people' (ibid.: 9). What is being suggested here is a rethinking of how we expect our policing and emergency services to behave in relation to us, and by extension, how we would like our governments to behave.

This is a change that is not only needed at a time of emergency or in a 'time of terror'; it is needed all the time. Indeed the argument is that our politics has become little more that a permanent state of emergency or exception, where the respect owing to each and every life has disappeared. Life becomes nothing more than bare life, to be used instrumentally. If life dares to disagree, if people challenge the government or the processes of governance, then the solution is to persuade, to educate, to patronize, not to listen and debate. If people don't like the Disaster Victim Identification process, for example, if they want to make sure the bodies of the dead are 'treated humanly', then all we need apparently is a library of online information sheets that explain the DVI process to them and a fully trained Family Liaison Officer to make sure they go along with it.

What has been isolated here, in the aftermath of the bombings of 7 July, is a collision between the global liberal biopolitical governance of terror and the incalculable, the traumatic, that which escapes governance. Relatives do not just accept what they are told. They do not just go home and wait. They walk the streets, they put up missing posters, they protest the injustice to anyone who will listen. However, the form of biopolitical governance that was exemplified by the particular forms and practices of official communication that were evident after the London bombings is not unique to these circumstances. It is both emblematic and symptomatic of the treatment of all life as bare life or as the emergent life of the global biopolitical governance of terror, in a situation where the state of emergency is rapidly becoming the norm. We need to take note before we all become nothing more than a list of physical characteristics and distinguishing marks, dead bodies in all but name.

Notes

1 This chapter has benefited from many different conversations and discussions. First, I would like to thank Costas Constantinou, Oliver Richmond and Alison Watson for a very productive workshop in St Andrews, Scotland, where the argument of this chapter was first presented and for their encouraging and challenging comments. Participants in the workshop – Roland Bleiker, Kevin Dunn, Stephan Stetter and Cynthia Weber – were very supportive, and I am grateful to Emma Hutchinson for detailed and perceptive comments afterwards. Some of the research for this chapter was presented at 'London in a Time of Terror: The Politics of Response', an inter-

national conference held at Birkbeck College in London. Thanks are due to the convenors, Angharad Closs Stephens and Nick Vaughan-Williams for the invitation to take part in the opening panel of the conference and for their comments afterwards, and to other participants, among them Costas Douzinas, Vivienne Jabri, Patricia Molloy, Mustapha Pasha, Julian Reid, Emily Trahair and Rob Walker, for interesting discussions. I would like to thank Marie Fatayi-Williams especially, and not just for the conversations we had but for her work more generally. Last but not least, I am much indebted to Mick Dillon for his comments on a draft of the chapter and the wonderful conversation, fortified beautifully by a metaphorical whiskey or two, that followed.

2 For detailed discussions of Agamben's work in relation to the concerns here, see Edkins (2007b); and Edkins and Pin-Fat (2005).

3 See, for example, Korf (2007); Lentin (2006); Sylvester (2006); Laustsen and Diken (2005); Edkins, Pin-Fat and Shapiro (2004); Huysmans (2004); Van Munster (2004); Rajaram and Grundy-Warr (2004); Diken and Laustsen (2002); Edkins and Walker (2000).

4 Examples of international relations scholars critical of Agamben in various ways, including the argument that he dismisses sovereignty too easily, include: Aradau (2007); Ojakangas (2005); Prozorov (2005); Neal (2004); Prozorov (2004); Walker (2004); Connolly (2004). See also Calarco and DeCaroli (2007).

5 For other discussions of events in London in July 2005 as part of a globalization of the localized state of exception see Minca (2006) and Vaughan-Williams (2007). These authors pay particular attention to the spatial aspects of the events, whereas I focus here on communication and the production of subjectivities.

6 Or, in Dillon's phrase, there is 'more to life than meets the molecular biopolitics of contemporary biopower' (Dillon 2007a: 20).

7 Although 'life, especially the life of populations, is characterised by contingency', in this context 'contingency is not arbitrary chance' (Dillon 2007b: 45). The contingency of the traumatic (the contingency beyond the contingent) is precisely a demonstration of the absolutely arbitrary; it is the reduction of population to a singularity: a population of one, the level at which statistics no longer apply.

8 'Communication' is used here not with any connotations of the transference of previously formulated thoughts or images or events from one person to another or several others, but rather as 'encompassing the multiple circuits of exchange and circulation of goods, people and messages' (Mattelart 1996: xiv).

9 'Excommunication' is Mattelart's term. See Constantinou (2008); for 'dissidence' in international relations writing see Ashley and Walker (1990); Campbell (1992): 4.

10 I capitalize to indicate the academic discipline, following convention for once.

11 The term 'performative writing' is gaining currency in the humanities and social sciences. See Pelias (2005).

12 More frequently perhaps, 'traumatized victims' become academics. There are numerous examples – in 'Holocaust Studies', for example, many people now writing as academics have reached that position via a family or personal history of involvement.

13 Tulloch's book is most notable to me for the postscript in which he addresses the bomber, Mohammad Sidique Khan, directly, as a fellow person.

14 The London authorities had obviously learned the lessons of the aftermath of Diana's death in 1997 and the street memorials in Manhattan in 2001: by July 2005 memorial activities were allowed but closely circumscribed, in this case by iron railings. See Kear and Steinberg (1999).

15 For discussions of memorial practices in New York after 11 September see, for example, Simpson (2006); Edkins (2004); and Edkins (2003b).

16 The *Guardian* later reported that 'Magda Gluck, whose 29-year-old twin sister, Karolina, was killed at Russell Square, said the aftermath was a "big mess. It took us more than a week to find out that she was killed. It was too long to find out that kind of information". The family received compensation of £11,000' (Travis 2006).

17 This argument is presented more fully in Edkins 2003a.
18 For an account of the production of famine as 'disaster' see Edkins and Walker (2000).
19 Of course, neither of these practices can succeed: both are impossible.
20 For a more detailed development of this argument, see Edkins (2006).
21 There is much more to be said about the distinctions between the two ways of developing Foucault's thinking proposed by Agamben and Dillon, but I do not have space here. The state of emergency is of course a feature of the work of Carl Schmitt as well (Schmitt 1996). For another reading of contemporary biopolitics that develops Foucault's thinking, see Massumi (2005).
22 The forms are available at www.interpol.int/Public/DisasterVictim/Forms/Default.asp (accessed 15 November 2006).
23 The fact that there is no space for name on the form that the authorities recovering bodies use, could explain why even when the victim had given a name before they died, it did not link with the body.
24 Marie Fatayi-Williams confirms that this is the case: she was asked repeatedly whether Anthony was wearing a watch. Since she had not been staying with him on the morning of the bombings she did not know. Personal communication 7 December 2006.
25 See www.disasteraction.org.uk (accessed 15 November 2005).
26 For the development of a similar idea about how 'responding to threat requires the time of government to be politically corrected' see Massumi (2005). Thanks to Nick Vaughan-Williams for drawing my attention to the similarities here.

References

Agamben, G. (1998), *Homo Sacer: Sovereign Power and Bare Life*, Stanford, CA: Stanford University Press.
—— (2005), *State of Exception*, Chicago and London: University of Chicago Press.
Aradau, C. (2007), 'Law transformed: Guantanamo and the 'other' exception', *Third World Quarterly*, 28: 498–501.
Ashley, R. K. and Walker, R. B. J. (eds) (1990), 'Speaking the language of exile: dissident thought in international studies', *International Studies Quarterly*, 34 (Special Issue).
BBC News Online (2005a), 'In full: Blair on bomb blasts. Statement from Downing Street, 1730 BST 7 July 2005'. Online. Available at: http://news.bbc.co.uk/1/hi/uk/4659953.stm (accessed 12 November 2006).
—— (2005b), 'Missing people sought after bombs'. Online. Available at: http://news.bbc.co.uk/1/hi/england/london/4666679.stm (accessed 18 October 2006).
Bennetto, J. (2005), 'Terror in London: police identifying victims of Asian tsunami switch', *Independent*, 12 July. Online. Available at: www.findarticles.com/p/articles/mi_qn4158/is_20050712/ai_n14719312 (accessed 12 November 2006).
Borradori, G. (2003), *Philosophy in a Time of Terror: Dialogues with Jürgen Habermas and Jacques Derrida*, Chicago: University of Chicago Press.
Brison, S. J. (2002), *Aftermath: Violence and the Remaking of a Self*, Princeton, NJ, and Oxford: Princeton University Press.
Cabinet Office (2006), 'Addressing the lessons from the Emergency Response to the 7th July 2005 London Bombings: What we learned and what we are doing about it', John Reid (Home Secretary) and Tessa Jowell (Culture Secretary), 22 September.
Calarco, M. and DeCaroli, S. (eds) (2007), *Giorgio Agamben: Sovereignty and Life*, Stanford, CA: Stanford University Press.

Campbell, D. (1992), *Writing Security: United States Foreign Policy and the Politics of Identity*, Manchester: Manchester University Press.
Connolly, W. E. (2004), 'The complexity of sovereignty', in J. Edkins, V. Pin-Fat and M. J. Shapiro (eds), *Sovereign Lives: Power in Global Politics*, New York and London: Routledge, pp. 23–40.
Constantinou, C. M. (2008), 'Communications/excommunications: an interview with Armand Mattelart', *Review of International Studies*, 34: 21–42.
Daily Telegraph (2005), 'Inquest into oil executive opens', 14 July. Online. Available at: www.telegraph.co.uk/news/main.jhtml?xml=/news/2005/07/14/uinquest.xml&sSheet=/portal/2005/07/14/ixportaltop.html (accessed 14 November 2006).
Dear, Paula (2006), 'Don't wait for me tonight, Mum'. *BBC News Online*. Online. Available at: http://news.bbc.co.uk/1/hi/uk/5098448.stm (accessed 12 November 2006).
Diken, B. and Laustsen, C. B. (2002), 'Zones of indistinction: security, terror and bare life', *Space and Culture*, 5 (3): 290–307.
Dillon, M. (2007a), 'Governing terror: the state of emergency of biopolitical emergence', *International Political Sociology*, 1: 7–28.
—— (2007b), 'Governing through contingency: the security of biopolitical governance', *Political Geography*, 26: 41–7.
Dillon, M. and Lobo-Guerrero, L. (2007), 'Biopolitics of security in the 21st century', unpublished paper.
Disaster Action (2005), 'When disaster strikes – disaster victim identification: issues for families and implications for police family liaison officers (FLOs) and coroner's officers (COs)'. Online. Available at: www.disasteraction.org.uk/guidance.htm (accessed 6 February 2007).
Edkins, J. (2003a), *Trauma and the Memory of Politics*, Cambridge: Cambridge University Press.
—— (2003b), 'The rush to memory and the rhetoric of war', *Journal of Political and Military Sociology*, 31: 231–51.
—— (2004), 'Ground Zero: reflections on trauma, indistinction and response', *Journal for Cultural Research*, 8: 247–70.
—— (ed.) (2005), 'Ethics of engagement: intellectuals in world politics', *International Relations*, 19, Special Forum Section.
—— (2006), 'Remembering relationality: trauma time and politics', in D. Bell (ed.), *Memory, Trauma and World Politics: Reflections on the Relationship between Past and Present*, Basingstoke and New York: Palgrave, pp. 99–115.
—— (2007a), 'Missing persons: Manhattan, September 2001', in E. Dauphinee and C. Masters (eds), *The Logics of Biopower and the War on Terror: Living, Dying, Surviving*, New York and Basingstoke: Palgrave Macmillan, pp. 25–42.
—— (2007b), 'Whatever politics', in M. Calarco and S. DeCaroli (eds), *Sovereignty and Life: Essays on Giorgio Agamben*, Stanford, CA: Stanford University Press, pp. 70–91.
Edkins, J. and Pin-Fat, V. (2005), 'Through the wire: relations of power and relations of violence', *Millennium: Journal of International Studies*, 34: 1–24.
Edkins, J. and Walker, R. B. J. (eds) (2000), 'Zones of indistinction: territories, bodies, politics' *Alternatives* 25(1).
Edkins, J., Pin-Fat, V. and Shapiro, M. J. (eds) (2004), *Sovereign Lives: Power in Global Politics*, New York: Routledge.
Fatayi-Williams, M. (2005), Speech given near Tavistock Square, London, Monday 11 July.
—— (2006), *For the Love of Anthony: A Mother's Search for Peace after the London Bombings*, London: Hodder & Stoughton.

Gardham, D. and Martin, N. (2005), 'How much blood must be spilled, a mother asks', *Daily Telegraph*, 13 July. Online. Available at: www.telegraph.co.uk/news/main.jhtml;jsessionid=V1AYTHXQSP1ZVQFIQMFCFF4AVCBQYIV0?xml=/news/2005/07/12/nvict12.xml (accessed 14 November 2006).

Guardian (2005a), 'Straight from the heart'. 13 July. Online. Available at: www.guardian.co.uk/print/0,,5237594-117079,00.html (accessed 10 November 2006).

—— (2005b), 'Bomb victim IDs may take weeks – Coroner', 15 July: 7.

Hare, D. (2005), *The Permanent Way or La Voie Anglaise*, London: Faber & Faber.

Huysmans, J. (2004), 'Minding exceptions: the politics of insecurity and liberal democracy' *Contemporary Political Theory*, 3 (3): 321–41.

Interpol (1984), 'Disaster victim identification'. Online. Available at: www.interpol.int/Public/DisasterVictim/Default.asp. (accessed 6 February 2007). The manual is available at www.interpol.int/Public/DisasterVictim/guide/default.asp. The forms are available at www.interpol.int/Public/DisasterVictim/Forms/Default.asp (accessed 15 November 2006).

Kear, A. and Steinberg, D. L. (1999), *Mourning Diana: Nation, Culture and the Performance of Grief*, London and New York: Routledge.

Korf, B. (2007), 'Antinomies of generosity – moral geographies and post-tsunami aid in Southeast Asia', *Geoforum*, 38: 366–78.

Laclau, E. (2007), 'Bare life or social indeterminacy?' in M. Calarco and S. DeCaroli (eds), *Giorgio Agamben: Sovereignty and Life*, Stanford, CA: Stanford University Press, pp. 11–22.

Laustsen, C. B. and Diken, B. (2005), *Culture of Exception: Sociology Facing the Camp*, London and New York: Routledge.

Laville, S. (2005), 'Mother's fury at "slaughter of the innocents"', *Guardian*, 12 July: 1.

Lentin, R. (2006), 'Femina sacra: gendered memory and political violence', *Women's Studies International Forum*, 29: 463–73.

London Assembly (2006), 'Report of the 7 July Review Committee', chaired by Richard Barnes AM, London: Greater London Authority.

Massumi, B. (2005), 'The future birth of the affective fact', in *Sinues of the Present: Genealogies of Biopolitics: Proceedings of the Colloquium* (Workshop in Radical Empiricism). Online. Available at: www.radicalempiricism.org/biotextes/anglais_index.html (accessed 26 September 2006).

Mattelart, A. (1996), *The Invention of Communication*, Minneapolis, MN, and London: Minnesota University Press.

Minca, C. (2006), 'Giorgio Agamben and the new biopolitical nomos', *Geografiska Annaler, Series B: Human Geography*, 88: 387–403.

Neal, A. (2004), 'Cutting off the king's head: Foucault's "society must be defended" and the problem of sovereignty' *Alternatives: Global, Local, Political*, 29 (4): 373–98.

Ojakangas, M. (2005), 'Impossible dialogue on bio-power: Agamben and Foucault' *Foucault Studies*, 2: 5–28.

Olaniyonu, Y. and Kintum, F. (2005), 'Anthony Fatayi-Williams body recovered', *Online Nigeria*, 15 July. Online. Available at: http://nm.onlinenigeria.com/templates/?a=3831&z=12 (accessed 15 November 2006).

Pelias, R. J. (2005), 'Performative writing as scholarship: an apology, an argument, an anecdote', *Cultural Studies, Critical Methodologies*, 5: 415–24.

Prozorov, S. (2004), 'Three theses on "governance" and the political', *Journal of International Relations and Development*, 7 (3).

—— (2005), 'X/Xs: toward a general theory of the exception', *Alternatives: Global, Local, Political*, 30 (1): 81–112.

Rajaram, P. K. and Grundy-Warr, C. (2004), 'The irregular migrant as Homo Sacer: migration and detention in Australia, Malaysia and Thailand', *International Migration*, 42 (1): 33–64.

Rozenberg, J. (2005), 'Relatives of Tube bomber want another post mortem', *Daily Telegraph* 29 October. Online. Available at: www.telegraph.co.uk/core/Content/displayPrintable.jhtml? (accessed 15 November 2006).

SBC Baptist Press News, Southern Baptist Convention, Baptist Press. Online. Available at: www.bpnews.net/images/IMG2005249686HI.jpg (accessed 6 February 2007).

Schmitt, C. (1996), *The Concept of the Political*, Chicago: University of Chicago Press.

Simpson, D. (2006), *9/11: The Culture of Commemoration*, Chicago and London: University of Chicago Press.

Sylvester, C. (2006), 'Bare life as a development/postcolonial problematic', *Geographical Journal*, 172: 66–77.

Travis, A. (2006), 'Victims of 7/7 bombs were not given enough help, ministers admit', *Guardian*, 23 September.

Tulloch, J. (2006), *One Day in July: Experiencing 7/7*, London: Little, Brown.

Van Munster, R. (2004), 'The war on terrorism: when the exception becomes the rule', *International Journal for the Semiotics of Law*, 17 (2): 141–53.

Vaughan-Williams, N. (2007), 'The shooting of Jean Charles de Menezes: new border politics?', *Alternatives: Global, Local, Political*, 32: 177–95.

Walker, R. B. J. (2004), 'Sovereignties, exceptions, worlds', in J. Edkins, V. Pin-Fat and M. J. Shapiro (eds), *Sovereign Lives: Power in Global Politics*, New York and London: Routledge, pp. 239–49.

2 Security, multiculturalism and the cosmopolis*

Vivienne Jabri

The bombings of 7 July 2005, targeted as they were at London's public transport system and its population, and perpetrated as they were by a group of young British men of Asian descent, brought into sharp focus questions relating to social integration and the meaning of citizenship in a liberal multicultural society. That the attacks were aimed at London, a distinctly multicultural space, and above all, a city characterized by its cosmopolitan character, might suggest that the target was not simply the city itself, its complex infrastructure, but the worldly aspect of its inhabitants. While the bombers themselves hailed from northern English towns, their victims represented the world in all its constitutive difference, the world present in London, the paradigm global city. The distinctiveness of cities such as London and New York exactly derives from their capacities to draw in the global, so that the landscape of the city, economic, social, political, is one defined by the intersection of the global and the local. In the cosmopolis, every street, every neighbourhood, comes somehow to reflect this mixing of cultures and identities and yet the spaces they traverse remain strictly London in character, so there is, as Peter Ackroyd's *Biography of London* so clearly demonstrates, both fixity and mobility and each has historically relied on the other. While such complexity is celebrated in all the capacities it generates, at the same time it is drawn into practices of security that increasingly construct difference as a source of threat.

Multiculturalism has long been viewed as presenting a challenge to liberalism and the liberal state. Articulated mainly in normative discourses around the question of citizenship, the tension highlighted is between liberalism's primary attachment to individual autonomy and the question of group rights in multi-ethnic liberal societies. With the advent of the so-called 'war against terrorism', multiculturalism has increasingly been associated with insecurity; that cultural difference as such is potentially a source of threat and danger. The question is not however confined to how cultural difference comes to be securitized, but more significantly relates to conceptions of citizenship and the role of the state in practices of security. That such practices are now centrally defined in terms of 'social cohesion' is suggestive of the construction of particular modalities of culture as constitutive of an existential threat faced by liberal society at large.

This chapter explores the implications of practices of security centred on the government of social relations defined in terms of cohesion. The aim is to analyse the significance of the shift away from discourses of multiculturalism and towards those that emphasize terms such as 'community resilience' and community cohesion. It will be apparent that this shift in discourse and institutional practices can be located within the purview of security, but is, in addition, revealing of longstanding tensions within liberal society, between the universalism of liberal thought and practice, and the particularity of cultural affiliation based on tradition (Kymlicka 1996; Taylor 1994). While the events of 11 September 2001 and subsequent bombings in London, Madrid and elsewhere have been portrayed as the impetus behind this shift, looked at closely, culture is revealed to be a carrier of distinctly other political concerns the parameters of which are drawn variously from policies relating to migration, increasing racism and xenophobia, practices within particular communities deemed to be anathema to a liberal society, as well as a concern with evident transnational affiliations across the boundaries of the state.

That the bombings of 7 July 2005 were targeted at a distinctly global city, namely London, and before it New York, must be significant in developing our understanding of how distinctly late-modern social and political life responds to the claims of the other, claims that are in themselves enabled by the parameters of late modernity, those that insert the global into the local. In locating the tensions within liberalism in the global city, the spatio-temporal manifestation of late-modern politics should not simply be read in terms of tensions between the global and the local, but rather in the resources that the global city brings to a re-articulated notion of the political.

In thinking of security practices in terms of the 'government' of social relations,[1] and specifically social relations within the multicultural setting, what is being highlighted in this chapter is the question of how security practices come to be related to conceptions of political community and how such community is forged in the midst of difference. Placed in the temporality and spatiality of the global city, the cosmopolis, the intellectual provocations focus on what the relationship is between traditional conceptions of political community based on the territorial state and the distinctly different spatiality represented by the global city, where interactions and transactions appear to run in the imbrications of the local and the global. Locality in the context of the global city is a complex terrain of transnational movement and affiliation that seems to defy the conceptual fixities associated with the state or nation as containers of singular modes of citizenship or expressions of identity. The challenge to those who seek to govern social relations in the name of security is the production of political community despite the odds. I want to suggest speculatively that locating our deliberations on these matters in the global city can perhaps provide some indicators into a rethinking of political space and political community, so that fixity is not seen as the only way through which we might think through these matters.

The questions being addressed in this chapter are then focused on a number of concerns that seek to unravel the relationship between the politics of security, multicultural social space, and the global city. At the heart of this relationship is the idea of political community and how such community emerges in the context of difference, and specifically cultural difference. The chapter unravels the issues through focusing on the question of how cultural difference comes to be securitized, framed in a discourse of security, how such securitization feeds into the government of social relations in the form of concepts such as social cohesion and community resilience, the relationship between the government of social relations and conceptions of political community, and finally what these practices mean in the context of the global city, the spatiality and temporality of which appear to defy any fixed notions of citizenship and political community.

Practices of security and cultural difference

Contemporary discourses in the public sphere on multiculturalism, migration and the distinctiveness of cultural practices appear to represent difference in terms of an existential threat. The discursive formations, to use a Foucaultian term, rely on oppositional representations whereby particular forms of cultural articulation, when located into the public sphere, are signified as constitutively other, as existentially opposed to the prevailing order within the liberal polity, and hence as presenting an imminent danger to society. From the presence of the veiled woman on urban streets, to public statements relating to cultural affiliation across state boundaries, the articulation of difference when taken out of the private realm of cultural practices and placed into the public arena at large is in contemporary times seen not just in terms of cultural diversity and the benefits that might stem from such diversity, but is firmly located in a discourse of enmity and threat.

The genesis of the securitization of difference is certainly not a new phenomenon and indeed there has historically been an association of migration with some form of an existential threat to what is referred to as 'our way of life'.[2] As a number of scholars engaged in research on the securitization of migration have clearly indicated, the migrant other comes up against discourses and institutional practices that seek to primarily exclude rather than include, and such exclusions are often legitimized through discursive practices that perpetuate some notion of 'unease' (Bigo and Guild 2005; Huysmans 2007). The migrant, being constituted as other to the prevailing community, is hence perceived and constructed as a distinct source of threat, so that the 'securing' of borders is exactly a response to such constructions. The aim here is not to replay what has already been revealed in relation to the securitization of migration. Rather it is to suggest a background that in many ways provides the historical conditions enabling of the discursive practices that are currently in force when cultural difference as such is related to security threats. For it is the case that the securitization of migrants has always been imbricated with discourses of racism and xenophobia, so that migrants that hail from, for example, the white Commonwealth or North America, are not similarly subjected to the exclusions that state boundaries might bring into force.

What is significant in the present political context is the construction of the particular other as threat, so that it is the Islamic, the Asian, or he or she who hails from the Middle East, that is constituted in discourse as the existential threat and is hence subjected not simply to practices of exclusion, but to a whole panoply of interventions that seek to re-shape, re-form, re-design the very subjectivity of this other in the name of security. Any practice, any statement by government aimed at what is referred to as 'social cohesion', is primarily geared towards the government of the other and her/his behaviour, modes of expression and affiliation.

The interventions are hence corporeal and social; they cover self-expression as well as communal interaction. Representations are also corporeal and social, so that form of dress is as much represented as a source of threat as is community organization in the name of a distinct political cause or indeed a religion. When Dutch parliamentarians advocate banning the 'burqa' in public spaces, their language is imbued with references to terrorism, extremism, radicalization, so that the veiled woman is indeed represented as a potential source of threat to Dutch society.[3] Similarly, in proposals in the UK and elsewhere to 'map' geographical areas as being 'vulnerable' to terrorist mobilization, the methodology must by definition be based on ethnic/cultural profiling of distinct cities and regions based on the percentage of the population that is Muslim.[4] When the European Commission or the Economic and Social Research Council fund projects on so-called 'radicalization', interest is primarily in 'radicalisation and violence purportedly in the name of Islam' (Economic and Social Research Council 2007). The paradox for government is that, despite efforts in the form of published declarations or policy frameworks aimed at the elimination of racism and xenophobia, the substantial content of the government of social relations is targeted at the Muslim subject perceived and constructed as the potentially 'radicalized' other. Both categories, Muslim and radical, utilized in the identification of citizens, come to constitute those citizens exactly in these terms. The paradox of such interpellations is all too clear; governmental discourses aimed to combat 'radicalization' actually radicalize.

The corporeal presence of the other is formative of contemporary security practices. The racialization of cultural difference is one that sees the population not simply in the form of the citizen and migrant, but crucially in accordance to the caesura drawn through the social body at large; the body of citizens already in place, the 'born and bred' no longer seen as constituting a multicultural society gradually 'at home' with difference, but one that constructs 'breaks', again to use a Foucaultian term, or boundaries within. The border as such is hence no longer solely located at the boundaries of the state, but is carried by the racialized other (Jabri 2006; 2007a), so that borders have a presence in the street, in neighbourhoods, in the schools and colleges, in the health service, the prison system and so on. The border has shifted therefore; it is no longer at the geographic border of the territorial state, but is firmly located in the everyday and the routine. This shift away from the spatial to the temporal has profound implications, so that what is being achieved is the exact opposite of social cohesion. It is social fragmentation. In locating the enemy in the everyday and the routine, such practices create the caesura in society that divide the citizen body in terms of a cultural/racial profile.

That a population is racially profiled is, of course, not a new occurrence. The practice might indeed be seen as the defining moment of the colonial experience where populations were subjected not just to a racial division from those who ruled over them, but were, in addition, subject to ethnic and tribal division institutionalized as a mechanism of colonial government. The colonized was hence always a racially profiled subject (Gilroy 2004). Seen through the purview of the contemporary era, and in relation to the liberal democratic polity, what we observe is a racial profiling of the citizen, again in the name of policing. While such profiling has always been an instrument drawn up to fulfil 'equal opportunities' criteria and anti-discriminatory procedures, a significant factor in state action has centred upon the *policing* of ethnic/racial difference. As pointed out by a number of authors, and as the Scarman Report and the Macpherson Inquiry showed all too clearly in the aftermath of the Brixton riots and the inquiry into the Stephen Lawrence murder respectively, policing was then and continues to be now informed by a distinctly racialized approach to the population.[5]

If the liberal democratic state has, in the postcolonial era and in the era of migration, defined its citizens in terms of race and if the breaks in society are racialized, then what constitutes the meaning of political community and how is the membership of such community defined? In providing the following analysis, the premise throughout is that the government of social relations, practices that seek the management, through rationalized procedures, of population categories and their interactions, is related to but is nevertheless distinct from the emergence of 'political community'.

Political community and the government of social space

Understood in Foucaultian terms, the citizen, indeed all citizens of the liberal polity are subjected to surveillance as a technology of rule. All modern rationalized societies emerge from the gradual shift in relations of power, so that the governed are no longer subjected to the violence of sovereign power, but are rather incorporated into systems of control that are rendered gradually more subtle and indeed more all-pervasive.[6] Within such systems of control, the individual corporeal body is as much a target of rationalization, calculation and, significantly, practices that seek to shape and mould, as is the population conceived as mass. What is significant about this conception of the citizen as subject, the subject emergent from techniques of control and governmentality, is that it makes no assumptions about how such government forges political community; in other words, how the citizen as individual and as collective entity is produced in a relationship with the state. While we gain a picture of population in Foucault's analytics of power, the question of how a distinctly political community emerges is, within this framework of understanding, answered in terms of the government of social relations. Political community is somehow forged out of practices emanating from the state and its agencies, so that the creative moment is primarily driven by the state and its constitutive entities.

Security practices that seek to forge what is now referred to as social cohesion are suggestive of an underpinning assumption that social space is currently fragmented, that affiliation is somehow displaced away from the state, and that, within the multicultural setting, culture is no longer simply a matter of the private realm but has somehow acquired space deep into the public arena. The social body as such is hence constructed in the public sphere and in discursive interventions emanating from government as a location that has somehow shifted from unity to culturally determined division, from coherence to uncertainty, from a time in an imagined past where values could be nationally defined to a problematic time in the present where some in the multicultural space adhere to a different set of values.[7] Once again, such constructions must not be assumed to be formative of a new era, but are rather continuities from past practices; ones that have always been targeted at minority communities subjected to the test of loyalty. The difference now is that such interventions/constructions are related to security, while in the past they seemed to be the proclamations of a reactionary politics of the Right the remit of which was variously driven by opposition to immigration, particular readings of the nation, and racial domination.

In his analysis of prospects for liberal democratic citizenship, Gianfranco Poggi asks the question: 'What do citizens (as it were) *look like* when viewed from the vantage point of the state?' (Poggi 2003: 39) His response to this question reveals much that is currently in vogue in governmental circles. Government responses to the 7 July bombings can hence be understood in the context of how government *views* the citizenry and how in turn it has sought to re-shape and re-constitute the social space that constitutes this citizenry.

Poggi draws on Foucault, Giddens and Tilly in the suggestion that the age of political modernization constitutes citizens as 'surveillees', subjected to forms of rule that are increasingly rationalized and sophisticated to the degree whereby citizens are not simply seen as subjects, but are recognized as sources of revenue in an 'increasingly expansive and expensive state' wherein 'extraction' forms the citizen into the taxpayer, the soldier as an element in organized violence, and the loyal citizen engaged in the legitimization of the state's monopoly over such violence. The image that emerges in this formulation is one where the construction of citizenship results from unidirectional technologies of power where the resultant citizen is but a passive recipient of discursive and institutional interventions. Viewing the citizen through this lens clearly suggests to the state that the citizen might indeed be shaped, reshaped, and moulded in accordance with the requirements of the state and its historically contingent priorities. For Poggi, the state's paramount view of the citizen derives from a fundamental relationship of power between state and subject; even as other discourses on citizenship, those Poggi defines as 'normative', might place emphasis on rights and the inter-subjective state–citizen relation.

When read through the practices of government in the contemporary period, policies geared towards 'social cohesion' are informative of how government views the population in the aftermath of the 7 July bombings in London. Budgetary allocations through the Department of Communities and Local Government are geared at cities and towns with significant Muslim populations. The formation of an advisory committee of Muslim women by this same department of state is aimed not at the welfare of women generally, but seeks to make use of and help develop the potential of women in the Muslim communities, in the name of 'resilient communities'. The distribution of monies to mosques and religious groups is again geared towards gaining the input of such groups in the struggle against extremist practices and the 'radicalization' of young Muslims. Judging from this set of policies, 'social cohesion' as a governmental practice is not geared at the diversity of populations currently making up the UK, but is clearly focused on one particular community, namely the British Muslim community. Even as a number of the statements and policies aim to combat discrimination, it is nevertheless possible to read in these practices the ways in which the security state views a certain sector of the population and how it would wish to re-shape and re-design this sector, pedagogically or otherwise.

The modern self in the liberal democratic state is assumed to have the capacity, born of technologies of power, for self-rule and self-government within the limits of continuing and highly bureaucratized modes of governmental intervention into the lived experience of the individual self (Dean 2007). The government of social relations through the construct of 'social cohesion' suggests that the citizenry is no longer conceived as a coherent whole. Rather, the population, seen through the eyes of the security state, is divided exactly through a religious and cultural marker, between those considered governable and those who have somehow lost the trust of government to self-govern. The aim of social cohesion practices might be represented as geared benevolently towards aiding non-discrimination towards these communities; the fact that such practices are being articulated ethnically and culturally is productive of subjectivities deemed to be a danger to society. The singular act; an individual's violation of the law, their participation in proscribed organizations, or their complicity in terrorist acts come to be generalized to the community as a whole, so that the category problematized is the culture, and through such a culturalist move, the subject's 'externality'[8] comes to be defined in terms of culture or religion, and the problems of the multicultural setting.

How the state views the citizen has profound implications for the lived experience of the individual and their subjectivity as a member of a political community. The practice of social cohesion is hence not so much about the forging of a coherent unity wherein members define their identity as citizens in terms of some common purpose, but is rather about the teaching of a particular sector of the population the tricks of *self-government* within the wider modes of governance structures that give shape to the social sphere conceived territorially in terms of the state. Such practices should not be read through the repressive model, as Michel Foucault argues with respect to the government of sexuality, but rather as practices that seek to govern through the 'conduct of conduct', through the re-design of communities in the shape of modern subjectivities that have a primary relationship to the secular state.

With the increasing securitization of the multicultural space has come the emergence of 'social cohesion' conceived as an alternative approach to the government of social relations. Where multiculturalism assumes a common juridically and bureaucratically defined citizenship irrespective of difference, social cohesion and practices thereof foreground identity and relocate difference from the private sphere of cultural practices to the public sphere of policy and the governmentality of social space. Such relocation is defined as an imperative of security whereby recipient communities a) are primarily defined in terms of cultural markers, b) where such markers are read as signifiers of potential risk, and c) where the aim of governmentalizing practices is the re-design of the minority community in the shape of what is perceived to be representative of the dominant culture. The aim is not to repress cultural articulations of identity, but rather to create the conditions of possibility wherein Muslim communities come to self-govern within the modalities of rule created by the state.

The multicultural space that is the global city presents particular challenges to the model of political community and citizenship assumed by practices of social cohesion. While the global city shares much in common with any multicultural space, its temporality and spatiality both depend on while defying the fixities associated with the territorial state or limited conceptions of political community. The final section of this chapter places the lens on the global city and its implications for the securitization of cultural difference.

The cosmopolis and subjects of security

The bombings of 7 July 2005 brought the conflicts of the Middle East to the streets of London. Within the space of the morning rush hour, they signified the global spatiality of the invasion of Iraq and the Palestinian issue; that those affected are not simply communities in the immediate vicinity of occupation, or even their ethnic and national kith and kin, but a far wider transnational network of affiliation that proclaims its place in relation to these territories and their populations. The bombers were not of the Middle East, nor were they of London, but hailed from northern English towns, were of South Asian origin, and accrued to themselves a right of response in the name of the Middle East and their view of this geographic space as Islamic.

There is a simplification to renditions that seek a direct causal relationship between the bombings and the events in the Middle East. The simplicity of such explanations is also apparent in the discourses of the Blair government, which sought exactly to deny such a connection. The affirmation of the link is as complicit in simplicity as its denial.

The Middle East conflict has always been part of London's political landscape, its distinct international politics. London has not, however, functioned as that other arena to the conflict, where the different affinities involved, Arabs of various origins and the Jewish community confront each other in claim and counter-claim. Rather, London's place, its distinctive role has been to act as host to these communities. Significantly, both are historically exile communities, both appreciative of London as a place of sanctuary. While each articulates, in many different ways, a distinct sense of history, identity, and affiliation, and might in the present declare support for each side in the Israeli–Palestinian conflict, they nevertheless recognize that London somehow has the capacity to accommodate both. Those who committed the atrocities of 7 July were not of these communities or of the complexities of the Middle East and its multicultural, multi-religious, and multi-linguistic character. Those who proclaim a unitary identity to that region and its history deny this complexity, this rich inheritance just as their representations of London as the symbol of imperial power in contemporary times is itself a denial of this city's complexity, its cosmopolitan mix.

Similarly, responses to the 7 July bombings, in the form of stop-and-search operations sanctioned through anti-terror legislation, constitute a moment of danger to London's character as a city that accommodates the stranger, even as such accommodation is often reluctant, grudging, exclusionist in its official manifestations. But once here, the stranger traverses spaces occupied by strangers, all strangers to themselves, to each other; a form of conviviality of strangers (Gilroy 2004). However, the government's responses to the 7 July bombings, and to the events of 11 September, risk undermining exactly this conviviality of strangers, so that the stranger is rendered a foreigner, always suspected, searched, targeted, vilified, rendered the subject of surveillance, ethnically and racially profiled. In 2005, Asian young men were five times more likely to be stopped on London's streets and transport system than whites. The securitization of the cultural other renders the cosmopolis an impossibility, and yet, it is this very cosmopolitan character of the global city that in turn resists such a politics of security. Communities may be profiled, they may be subjected to differential targeting, but the exiled will always seek the cosmopolis.

The 'international' as a location of politics, economics and culture is a constitutive part of what confers London its status as a global city. But there is something more to London than the formal transactions that move through the global institutions located here. The international and the global are manifest in lived experience, in the everyday interactions and practices that take place on our streets, in the neighbourhoods, and in the distinctiveness of London's geographic identities, East, West, North and South. Each of these locales, or postcodes, is at one and same time multicultural, international and cosmopolitan, mixes of populations across culture and class, always connected somehow, in the present and in the past, with the local and the global, so that articulations of locality and globality come to acquire their own distinctive London character. Multiculturalism has come under increasing scrutiny, as I indicate above, often hostile, since the events of 7 July, so that even the Chair of the Commission for Racial Equality, Trevor Philips, has talked of multiculture as a danger to the character of this country, that the different communities constituting our multicultural space live parallel lives, never interacting. Philips argues for a greater emphasis on assimilation. The multicultural city enables the articulation of cultural difference in the absence of fear. To render the multicultural a location of fear, just as Philips does, is to be complicit not just in the securitization of the cultural other, but in every act of violence targeting those whose cultural difference is outwardly and therefore visibly apparent.

However it would be a mistake to think of London simply as a multicultural space. Its multiculturalism is but one aspect of its international and cosmopolitan character. The presence of the distinctly 'international' in the global city suggests spaces of interaction that invoke relations between states as national entities that paradoxically are at once suggestive of fixed spatialities as well as mobilities characteristic of a globalized era, wherein the circulation of people and material capacities are exactly enabled by the resources of the city that has global reach. The global city, as Saskia Sassen has argued, should not be read as a denationalized space, but rather as representing a dynamic intersection of the local and global, so that the mobilities associated with the global are enabled by the very fixed resources and infrastructures contained in the administrative unity that is the territorial state. However it is the 'insertion' of the global into the national that constitutes the city as distinctly global, so that it is not every capital city that achieves this distinctive status. As Sassen points out:

> Global processes are often strategically located/constituted in national spaces, where they are implemented usually with the help of legal measures taken by state institutions. The material and legal infrastructure that makes possible the global circulation of financial capital, for example, is often produced as 'national' infrastructure – even though increasingly shaped by global agendas.
>
> (Sassen 2000: 218)

The 'insertion of the global into the national' is described by Sassen as a 'partial and incipient denationalisation of that which historically has been constructed as the national or, rather, of certain properties of the national' (ibid.: 219). For Sassen, as the global is inserted into the national, what takes place is a 'temporal and spatial unbundling' of the national, so that what is constructed as the national is substantially transformed.

The global and its insertions in the form of material and people come to constitute the global city while the global itself comes to be articulated differently in relation to the spaces it comes to intersect. The movement and circulation of people through the global city, when viewed from the perspective of the state, represent at one and the same time both resource and a challenge, and whether a resource or a challenge comes to depend on how government profiles a population in terms of public services and the various provisions associated with infrastructure. However, as the evidence of the recent past indicates, the movement and circulation of people as a manifestation of the presence of the global in the city is also constructed in terms of security, and in the context of the 7 July bombings in London, subsequent policing operations, and the revelation of other attempts aimed at various metropolitan centres, this becomes the primary element in defining the challenges of the global. While the public discourse might focus on issues relating to migration and its infrastructural implications, what is of interest in the present context is the association of a security threat with the movement of people and specifically those whose 'profile', as read and constituted by the state, might suggest a source of danger. While the presence of new migrant communities presents particular policing challenges; for example, in relation to communicating unfamiliar aspects of law, this is substantively different from the specificity of security operations where the objects of policing are considered in terms of an immediate and existential threat, to the city and the movement and circulation of all who dwell within it.

When transnational spaces are viewed from the point of view of the territorial state, what appears are temporalities and spatialities that are indeterminate, unpredictable, defiant of fixity and suggestive of uncertainty and fragmentation. Movement and circulation through the transnational are suggestive of the absence of borders, and indeed the defiance of state boundaries and the authority that such boundaries assume – in the control of subjects allowed in and those excluded, in the definition of citizenship and the rights associated with such, and in the symbolic aspects of statehood, all of which are territorially bound. However, transnational spaces appear to defy the temporality of the state, so that the state's authority in determining the limits of political community is increasingly confronted by the emergence of transnational spaces of political community where affiliation and loyalty are no longer place-bound, but virtual in their immediacy and historical in their definition. Identities expressed in transnational, and indeed global spaces, reframe the meaning of political community, away from the limited spaciality of the state and its symbolic order.[9] The articulation of political identity, when apparently so distant from the state, when seemingly so out of the remit of control that the state assumes is within its bounds of authority, immediately brings to the fore issues relating to the capacity of the state to shape, mould, survey, the citizen as subject of control. No longer is the citizen the subject surveyed, but the subject open to the inscriptions of the global, so that such inscriptions are not simply apparent in relation to the national, but more importantly, in relation to the very subjectivity of the citizen.

When the global comes to be inscribed not simply into the institutions of the state or the state's relationship with global institutions, but comes to occupy a place in the very subjectivity of the citizen, the reach of the state in its capacity to constitute the limits of political community is challenged. The implications for identity are described above. However, read in relation to the politics of security, the presence of the global in the political subjectivity of the citizen suggests a political landscape distinctive to the global city and indeed constitutive of the global city as a distinctly cosmopolitan political space. The policing, or indeed the government, of this space cannot simply be reduced to the problem of 'social cohesion' and the pedagogy of 'national values', as it is constitutively defined in terms of the global arena and the political contestations, divisions and consequent affiliations, constitutive of this arena. Distant conflicts in this terrain are no longer distant, but of the everyday and the routine, having a presence in the immediate, subject to judgement not simply by the political class, but by the subject globalized, the citizen whose lived experience is no longer determined simply by local concerns.

The political landscape of the global city is a complex one and cannot be reduced to the politics of diaspora affiliations, even as these form a significant feature of it. As I indicate above, the global city has the fixities of place that enable the very movements and circulations constitutive of all that is global in a city such as London. The landscape of the city is one that has deep roots, but it is also transient, suggestive of the perpetual circulation of the population through its spaces. However, communities constitutive of the city at the same time seek to lay down roots, to place their cultural imprint on the city, and in many ways to assert cultural difference while recognizing full well that the imprint is itself of hybrid identity, reflective of the city's own imprint on the multiplicity of communities resident within its limits.[10] Global cities confer their own city-based articulations of identity, so that the iteration Londoner or New Yorker is immediately evocative of a sense of identity that is at once both place-bound *and* transnational; local *and* global. The city itself transforms those who reside in it, so that even the most culturally bound are impelled to negotiate the complexity of the city and the diversity of its populations. The political landscape of the global city is not cosmopolitan by intent, as might be suggested by forms of moral cosmopolitanism that assume uniform subjectivities and ontologies. Rather, the political when given temporal and spatial form through the global city emerges through the intersections of the global, the national, and the distinctly local. As argued by Nicholas Rose, 'citizenship is multiplied and non-cumulative: it appears to inhere in and derive from active engagement with each of a number of specific zones of identity – lifestyle sectors, neighbourhoods, ethnic groups – some private, some corporate, some quasi-public' (Rose 1999: 178).

In calling for a reposing of the citizenship question, Rose's following words should perhaps be sent to the Home Office and the Department for Communities: citizenship 'is no longer a question of national character but of the way in which multiple identities receive equal recognition in a single constitutional form. We have moved from "culture" to "cultures"' (ibid.: 178).

There is at the same time a disjuncture created by the presence of the global in a political landscape that can no longer be contained within national boundaries.[11] This does not, however, mean that boundaries disappear or are somehow irrelevant. Borders are rather being created and recreated, they are social, economic, and political, and in the present context of population profiling as policing practice, they are corporeal. The shooting of Jean Charles de Menezes is not simply one indicative of policing malpractice or indeed a serious error in operational leadership, but is reflective of exactly the constitution of boundaries corporeally. That the source of danger is identified in terms of the body is suggestive of policing practices that are, despite protestations to the contrary, primarily defined in terms of racial and cultural markers – colour of skin, gender, mode of attire – coupled with the surveillance of discursive affiliations expressed over virtual space, in neighbourhoods, bookshops, places of religious worship and so on.

When the source of threat is corporeal then technologies of surveillance must in themselves be corporeally defined. The total security state is one defined by contingency, as I state above, and the foremost contingency is a practice that develops a capacity to 'read' every citizen, every resident, corporeally. The transience of the global city, the very presence of the global in the subjectivity of those who inhabit this distinctive terrain, suggests practices of government that aspire to know the movement and location of every resident, citizen and non-citizen. However, the disjuncture between aspiration and practice reveals the aporias contained in the practice of social cohesion as security policy. For here it is the case that the constitution of the population into a 'people' or 'political community' defined in terms of the national, while targeted at communities constitutively defined as a problem is suggestive of the constitution of political community not defined in relation to an external enemy, but is rather directed at the internal other.

The political landscape of the global city appears to defy national containment. However, what must be stressed is that the global city, the cosmopolis, also defies the fixities of culture. That the discourse of 'social cohesion' appears to be inscribed ethnically and culturally is indicative of how practices of government can be complicit in the reiteration of fixed notions of identity. Such a culturalist understanding of subjectivity appears to seek a diminution, somehow, of global influences upon the subject citizen. Just as the colonial practices of the past sought to contain anti-colonial struggle through the empowerment of communal and religious leaders (and you can see this again manifest in post-invasion Iraq), so too now it is 'Islamic leaders', community organizations, and so forth that are invited into government deliberations about how to contain Islamic dissent. The pedagogical exercise is all too clear; it is about the government of conduct aimed at the management of communities. The parochialism of community is in consequence reinforced by the very practices that seek its transformation.

How does the cosmopolis resist? It resists through a rejection of the communal and the neighbourly. Londoners do not, on the whole, make for good neighbours, though they are conscious of sharing neighbourhoods, and indeed express strong affiliations in this sense. Orhan Pamuk argues that the idea of neighbourliness has two sides to it, one desirable and the other to be rejected. He states: 'for me, living in a modern city essentially means being free from the pressure that comes from having neighbours' (Pamuk 2006). The neighbour, according to Pamuk, is the person we should love and if we don't 'informs on us, polices us, denounces us for faults in our attitude and behaviour' (ibid.). The communal society for Pamuk is one that gets along with the state, with the police, with the army, so that dissent is suppressed. Modernity, for Pamuk, the global city as a distinctly modern phenomenon, is the 'yearning to escape from provincialism': the 'wish to avoid the neighbour, to avoid the prying and controlling eyes of the community' (ibid.). Of course, we remain friendly to the neighbour, we exchange pleasantries, we go to the local pub, buy bread from the local patisserie, but, according to Pamuk the darker side of neighbourliness is that we open our doors to what he refers to as the 'control mechanisms of society' (ibid.).

So I want to argue that the global cosmopolis is a hospitable place, it accommodates the stranger, but it resists by refusing the communal and the neighbourly, so that we all remain strangers to ourselves (Kristeva 1991). It is exactly this cosmopolitan ethos that the bombers of the 7 July and the politics of security that so dominates the discourses of the present seek to undermine, for the cosmopolis is the only remaining space where governmentality fails to fully capture the subject, to fully name self and other, just as it is the only space that rejects the violence of reactionary modes of representation and forms of affiliation that seek to reduce lived experience to religiosity. The constitutive element of London is the seeing and hearing we associate with it, the seeing and hearing of the world. For some, this worldliness of global cities constitutes them as 'CITIES OF PANIC that signal, more clearly than all the theories about urban chaos, *the fact that the greatest catastrophe of the twentieth century has been the city*, the contemporary metropolis of the disasters of Progress' (Virilio 2005: 90). Note the upper-case lettering of 'cities of panic'. The words convey Virilio's parochial anxieties relating to complexity and difference in all their articulations.

For others, global cities are the apotheosis of creative forms of expression, ones that defy the simplicities of categorical conceptions of subjectivity or fixed readings of 'culture' or affiliation. The global city presents a political landscape that is disjunctural by definition, but it is only so when 'political community', indeed community as such, is conferred an impossible fixity.

Notes

* This work forms part of ongoing research on the politics of security conducted within the project 'CHALLENGE: The Landscape of Liberty and Security in Europe', funded by the European Commission's Framework 6 programme.
1 The concept of 'government' is used throughout in Foucaultian terms, namely the idea that power in complex modern societies works in terms of practices of government aimed at the shaping and control of the life of individuals and populations. Foucault's understanding of 'governmentality' encompasses technologies of control aimed, in disciplinary terms, at the individual, and in biopolitical terms, at the population, its life, welfare, its distributions and categories. See Foucault (2001).
2 Gilroy (1987) exactly reveals the discourses of racism and xenophobia that historically met Caribbean migrants into the UK.
3 The former Dutch immigration minister, Rita Verdonk, referred to the 'burqa' as a matter of security: 'From the security standpoint, people should always be recognisable and, from the standpoint of integration, we think people should be able to communicate with one another.' See Castle (2006).
4 Recent proposals emanating from the Association of Chief Police Officers seek the mapping of every area in terms of its potential for extremist recruitment. See Dodd (2008).
5 See Scarman Report (1982). On race and policing, see, for example, Bowling (1999).

6 Michel Foucault's analytics provide such a temporal trajectory of power in modern societies. See, for example, Foucault (2003). For a critical engagement with Foucault's analytics of power and their implications for our understanding of the government of populations, race and culture, see Jabri (2007a; 2007b). Dean (2007) again draws on Foucault in an analysis of liberal modes of government and their implications for individuals and populations.
7 See, for example, Home Office Community Cohesion Unit (2003); a report 'Community cohesion: an action guide' published by the Local Government Association in 2004; and many reports from the Department for Communities and Local Government, including the most recent, 'Preventing extremism: winning hearts and minds', 2007. I am thankful to my research assistant and PhD student, Jorg Speiker, for his work on these reports.
8 I borrow the term, 'externality', from Gilroy (1987) and his discussion of the policing of the Black community in Britain.
9 For an analysis of the intersection of the transnational with the local in the context of 'political Islam' see Mandaville (2004; 2007).
10 The concept of 'hybridity' in postcolonial discourse is especially developed in Bhabha (1994).
11 See Appaduri (1996) for an interpretation of the disjuncture between globalized identity formations and 'national' articulations of citizenship.

References

Appaduri, A. (1996), *Modernity at Large: Cultural Dimensions of Globalisation*, Minneapolis, MN: University of Minnesota Press.
Bhabha, H. K. (1994), *The Location of Culture*, London and New York: Routledge.
Bigo, D. and Guild, E. (eds) (2005), *Controlling Frontiers: Free Movement into and within Europe*, Aldershot: Ashgate.
Bowling, B. (1999), *Violent Racism: Victimisation, Policing and Social Context*, Oxford: Oxford University Press.
Castle, S. (2006), 'Dutch Muslims condemn "populist" burqa ban move', *Independent* 20 November. Online. Available at: www.independent.co.uk/news/world/europe/dutch-muslims-condemn-populist-burqa-ban-move-425035.html (accessed 10 March 2007).
Dean, M. (2007), *Governing Societies*, Milton Keynes, Bucks: Open University Press.
Dodd, V. (2008), 'New strategy to stem flow of terror recruits', *Guardian*, 28 February.
Economic and Social Research Council (2007), 'New security challenges: radicalisation and violence – a critical reassessment'. Online. Available at: www.esrc.ac.uk/ESRCInfoCentre/Images/Specification_tcm6-18574.pdf.
Foucault, M. (2001), 'Governmentality', in J. D. Faubion (ed.), *Power: The Essential Works*, Vol. 3, trans. R. Hurley *et al.*, London: Allen Lane.
—— (2003), *Society Must Be Defended*, trans. David Macey, London: Allen Lane.
Gilroy, P. (1987), *There Ain't No Black in the Union Jack*, London and New York: Routledge.
—— (2004), *After Empire: Melancholia or Convivial Culture*, London and New York: Routledge.
Home Office Community Cohesion Unit (2003), 'Building a picture of community cohesion: a guide for local authorities and their partners'. Online. Available at: www.local-pi-library.gov.uk/documents/communityCohesionIndicators.pdf.
Huysmans, J. (2007), *The Politics of Insecurity*, London and New York: Routledge.
Jabri, V. (2006), 'War, security and the liberal state', *Security Dialogue*, 37(1): 47–64.

—— (2007a), *War and the Transformation of Global Politics*, London and New York: Palgrave.

—— (2007b), 'Michel Foucault's Analytics of War: the social, the international, and the racial', *International Political Sociology*, 1: 67–82.

Kristeva, J. (1991), *Strangers to Ourselves*, trans. L. Roudiez, New York: Columbia University Press.

Kymlicka, W. (1996), *Multicultural Citizenship: A Liberal Theory of Minority Rights*, Oxford: Clarendon Press.

Mandaville, P. (2004), *Transnational Muslim Politics*, London and New York: Routledge.

—— (2007), *Global Political Islam*, London and New York: Routledge.

Pamuk, O. (2006), 'Neighbourhoods', Opening address, 18th European Meeting of Cultural Journals, Istanbul. Published in *EUROZINE*, 13/10/2006. Online. Available at: www.eurozine.com/articles/2006–10–13-pamuk-en.html (accessed March 2007).

Poggi, G. (2003), 'Citizens and the state: retrospect and prospect', in Q. Skinner and B. Strath (eds), *States and Citizens*, Cambridge: Cambridge University Press.

Rose, N. (1999), *Powers of Freedom: Reframing Political Thought*, Cambridge: Cambridge University Press.

Sassen, S. (2000), 'Spatialities and temporalities of the global: elements for a theorization', *Public Culture*, 12: 215–30.

Scarman Report (1982), *The Brixton Disorders 10–12 April 1981*, London: Penguin.

Taylor, C. (1994), *Multiculturalism*, Princeton, NJ: Princeton University Press.

Virilio, P. (2005), *City of Panic*, Oxford and New York: Berg.

3 Seven million Londoners, one London

National and urban ideas of community

Angharad Closs Stephens

The political responses to the bombings in London on the 7 July 2005, the subsequent 'failed' bombings on 21 July, and the shooting of Jean Charles de Menezes by anti-terrorist officers on 22 July, show us that the idea of a community in unity continues to be the overwhelmingly dominant model we have available for how we might organize political communities. This is the idea that a community must be formed around the foundational principle of unity, representing a shared essence that goes beyond people's membership in a society or state.[1] It is the image of community that underpins nationalist discourses, the kind that were circulating at full speed in the aftermath of the London bombings. This chapter will explore the idea of a community in unity through the case of political responses to the London bombings. In doing so, it will seek to reveal the tremendous capacity of this idea in steering out ability to conceive of possible alternatives. It will also offer a contribution to studies in international political theory that are specifically interested in exploring what might be involved in the task of forming different ideas of community, and what might be done to avoid reproducing the familiar impasses.

The former British Prime Minister Tony Blair's immediate response, delivered within three hours of the bombings in London, was a characteristic affirmation of a British community in unity. He stated that these events must be understood as attacks on the 'British way of life' (Blair 2005). This narrative worked very successfully in creating a binary logic between the 'British people' and 'those people [that are trying] to cow us, to frighten us out of doing the things we want to do' (ibid.). People were asked to choose: either they were with the British people, and the British government representing 'our way of life', or they were with the people who acted through terrorism. This consolidation of British identity worked well insofar as it silenced any seriously threatening criticism of the British government in the aftermath of the bombings. Unlike in Madrid, where the bombings on the 11 March 2004 led to sharp political divisions, and a change in government following the general election three days later, nothing as remotely subversive or disturbing happened to the social order in London and the UK: calm was quickly restored, leaders of government and the police remained in their positions, and Prime Minister Blair maintained his authority.

An alternative idea of community circulated alongside this declaration of British unity in the aftermath of the London bombings however: this was the idea of London as an urban, multicultural community, organized around the principle of difference rather than unity. This message was most powerfully supported and disseminated by the then Mayor of London, Ken Livingstone. And it was summed up in many high-profile and well-sponsored advertising campaigns that the Mayor's Office and Transport for London ran in the aftermath of the bombings.[2] These included posters and banners displayed across the London Underground, at bus stops, train stations and along various streets, declaring the slogan, '7 Million Londoners, 1 London', and then later, 'We are Londoners, We are One'. This response, led by the Mayor of London, sought to celebrate the plurality and diversity of the city, in contrast to British identity and unity. This cosmopolitan ethos was largely seen as a preferable substitute for those who felt critical of Prime Minister Blair and his government's role in the war in Iraq especially.[3] Yet, it is significant that the multicultural message promoted by these poster campaigns is also firmly underpinned by an insistence on unity: We are Londoners, but we are also One. This raises some questions: to what extent did the idea of London as a multicultural community represent a notably alternative understanding of community to the nationalist narrative? Did the multicultural narrative provide an opportunity to disturb or disrupt the binary between Britishness and Terrorism? Or, did the idea of a multicultural community work more in tandem with narratives of British identity, providing a more progressive undertone to them? In this chapter, I explore two different ideas of community that circulated in the aftermath of the London bombings and ask what effect these had on opening up or closing down our ability to ask critical questions about these events. This discussion will raise broader questions for political geography and international relations theory, insofar as it will address the possibility of imagining community without reproducing oppression.

I begin by focusing on the dominant idiom we have for understanding community, as principally based around unity. This is the idea that a community is formed around some sense of commonality, and that members of the community draw their identity from a *thing* that they share in common.[4] This *thing* can be language, culture, traditions, customs or habits; it can also, in its most pernicious forms, become 'race', superiority, biology, or an elusive 'way of life'. I examine the different ideas of community deployed in the aftermath of the bombings by looking at the way in which they lay claim to a different understanding of origins. I ask, what are the foundational claims that underpin these ideas of community? How does the focus on a common culture or on multiculturalism work to different effects? In this comparison, I don't assume that the multicultural narrative is necessarily a preferable alternative to a nationalist narrative. Although the former may seem to have to come to supplant the latter, as a more 'enlightened' version of it, it is worth remembering that both developed more or less together in the history of ideas.[5] Furthermore, neither is in essence a progressive or a reactionary narrative: both can work to either effect in different historical, political and economic contexts. Both can therefore be oppressive. Furthermore, nationalist and cosmopolitanist narratives can work in alliance and in opposition (Cheah 1998: 22). Consequently, we need to trace the ways in which they are invoked in different, shifting contexts, to various political effects.

This focus on the question of origins will inevitably lead to a discussion of how different ideas of community are also framed through particular understandings of space and time. For example, the idea of a community in unity, such as that which we find under nationalism, is formed according to a very particular, linear trajectory of time. The assumption is that we were once united in the past, and that we must work to restore this sense of unity in the future. This principle of unity forms what Zygmunt Bauman has called the *focus imaginarius* of a modern idea of community (Bauman 1991). As such, it sets us off in pursuit of an impossible task. The *focus imaginarius* represents the idea of harmonious unity and order, which forms both the point of origin of the community, and the point of perfection that we hope to reach. Acting as both origin and limit, it propels the forward march of time. It is significant that Bauman calls it an 'impossible' task, because this sense of perfect stability, through unity, is of course a fantasy. But this fantasy has formed part of a relatively consistent and prevailing response to the experience of life under modern conditions. In a world that seems radically open to change, flux, fortune and chance, figures from Rousseau to Marx to Weber to Wagner have pined for a time when everything can once again be solid and secure (Nancy 2004: 10). In line with Bauman's description of this nostalgic yearning as a fantasy, Jean-Luc Nancy has argued that it is important to understand that the community in unity has not 'lost' anything: it is simply constituted through the idea of loss. There wasn't a time of green pastures or a common language but the *idea* of this 'loss' is fundamental and foundational to the idea of a community in unity (ibid.: 13).

While it is fairly straightforward to appreciate that the idea of a community in unity informs nationalist ideas of British identity, I want to suggest that the idea of a community in unity might also be deployed in the city. Narratives of unity are frequently circulated to support the state, but this language can be borrowed by sub-state governmental organisations, as well as by movements that might be trying to resist the state. Thus, I will address two points. First, I want to show how what might appear as an alternative idea of community, one that celebrates difference rather than unity, might nevertheless work to reproduce nationalist principles. The insistence upon unity is never innocent, and it is rarely innocuous. More specifically, I will argue that Mayor Livingstone's celebration of urban multiculturalism provides a compelling variation on the theme of a community in unity, but doesn't necessarily offer us much of an alternative to it. Second, I want to argue that we might nevertheless find in the city, and in urban writings, some material for developing a critique of the idea of a community in unity. In exploring how urban *and* national narratives can work to affirm the logic of a community in unity, I will suggest that the city might nevertheless provide us with an interesting motif for imagining different forms of community, that don't rely upon unity.

London as a British community

One of the key ideas through which this myth of a 'resilient' British community was constructed in the aftermath of the bombings was through the historical narrative of the Blitz (Manthorpe 2006: 21–2). The story of the Blitz was consistently told across almost all the British national newspapers, together with the bombing campaign of the Provisional IRA, as proof of the enduring 'calm and courage' of Londoners (Manthorpe 2006: 21–2). The *Guardian* newspaper's Editorial on the 8 July 2005, the day following the London bombings, opened by quoting from George Orwell writing at the time of the Blitz: 'As I write, highly civilized human beings are flying overhead, trying to kill me' (*Guardian* 2005a). This is a line that seems somewhat hyperbolic when we consider that at this point, the violence was largely understood as an isolated event, and not part of a continuous process. Some of the tabloid newspapers are more excited in their comparisons: 'Adolf Hitler's Blitz and his doodlebug rockets never once broke London's spirit' and 'We survived the Blitz. We lived through 30 years of IRA outrages.... Once again the British people will triumph over evil' being prime examples (*Guardian* 2005b).[6] But this narrative is not the prerogative of the tabloids: it is recounted by Prime Minister Blair and Sir Ian Blair, head of the Metropolitan Police Commission, and it is further deployed across the British newspapers on the first anniversary of the bombings (Manthorpe 2006: n. 12; Freedland 2006). It is well established that national narratives produce a story of origins that can account for the idea that we are a common community, travelling together through history. By invoking the Blitz as a story of origins, the history of London is recounted as the history of Britain. By tying the people living in London today into a direct relationship with those who lived in London at the time of the Second World War, this linear national narrative produces a certain idea of British culture. Given the constant movement of people in and out of cities, it is at best difficult to draw such direct histories of straightforward descendants in the city. But the Blitz invokes a distinctly national history of London as Britain.

Paul Gilroy has rightly pointed to the astonishing endurance of the Blitz narrative in providing an image of British culture at its alleged best. It is still widely circulated, together with the narratives of the war against Hitler and the battle of Britain, as the model of commonality to which people should aspire (Gilroy 2004: 95–8). Of course, the Blitz paradigm also provides a good reminder that history is written by the victors. It's the dominant that stipulate a point of origin from which we are deemed to have emerged as a community. In this context, Gilroy is right to say that the Blitz narrative must be seen in part for its role in mourning a certain whiteness, and a 'long-vanished homogeneity' (ibid.: 95). Although London at the time of the Blitz was a cosmopolitan city, this is not the image conjured by the Blitz narrative. Rather, it evokes the image of a distinctly white, wartime Englishness.

The Blitz narrative also worked well in introducing a dichotomy of good guys and bad. It was useful in so far as it enabled the government, and other authorities, to explain the bombers as people who belonged to the 'outside' of the community. This is of course one of the prevailing tricks of all nationalist narratives, to distinguish simply and unabashedly between 'us' and 'them'. Three of the bombers were second-generation British citizens who grew up on the outskirts of Leeds, England; the fourth was born in Jamaica but grew up in Huddersfield, England. They were all young, with varying degrees of further and higher education; they were mostly not from poor backgrounds (relatively at least); they were, according to the *Report of the Official Account of the Bombings in London on 7th July 2005*, of 'unexceptional background' (*Report of the Official Account* 2006: 13). Nevertheless, in order to conform to a nationalist dichotomy, these young men needed to be portrayed as exceptional. The construction of the bombers as different, as un-British, and as radically 'other' would have taken some effort. But the decision to draw a sharp and absolute distinction between the bombers and British society more generally, was quickly and forcefully enacted by Prime Minister Blair in his statement following the bombings:

> When they try to intimidate us, we will not be intimidated, when they seek to change our country, our way of life by these methods, we will not be changed. When they try to divide our people or weaken our resolve, we will not be terrorised.
>
> (Blair 2005: n. 2)

The problem with a British 'call to arms' such as this one is that it is not automatically clear who counts as members of 'our country' and who gets to decide what signifies 'our way of life'. Rarely is such language deployed without some people deciding to take it upon themselves to declare violently who is not properly 'British'. Muslim communities, or those *assumed* to be Muslim, now regularly experience the full force of these casual and sovereign judgements. On 7 July 2005, the Islamic Human Rights Commission in the UK took the exceptional step of instructing Muslim people not to travel, or go out unless strictly necessary, for fear of reprisals (*Independent* 2005).

In asserting the importance of British unity, former Prime Minister Blair made a concerted effort to bring Muslims in to this 'British identity' and to disassociate 'extremists' from Muslims at large. The British government, and Blair in particular, have become unlikely spokespeople on the teachings of Islam, and regularly instruct us that the majority of Muslims abhor terrorism.[7] But in a double move, while 'bringing Muslims in', Blair's framing of terrorism also works to construct Muslims as another community – who are not quite British, and not quite terrorist either:

> I welcome the statement put out by the Muslim Council who know that those people acted in the name of Islam but who also know that the vast and overwhelming majority of Muslims, here and abroad, are decent and law-abiding people who abhor this act of terrorism every bit as much as *we* do.
>
> (Blair 2005: n. 2; emphasis added)

This is a striking statement, and it is worth noting the timing of it. Released on the day of the bombings, it makes a very definite assumption that the perpetrators 'acted in the name of Islam' *before* the police and the intelligence authorities had been able to gather any facts (at least, if we believe the official government reports of what they knew, and when). But the most revealing thing about the statement is the way in which it skilfully distinguishes between Muslims who abhor terrorism and 'we' who also do. Muslims are therefore left hanging between an authentic British culture into which they are not fully invited, and a 'terrorist' community that Blair has constructed to differentiate the bombers from anything to do with British society. Muslims are 'decent and law-abiding people', Blair says. But he also firmly establishes that all 'Muslims' belong to a community that is not quite the same as 'ours'.

What we find is that Blair affirms three distinct communities: the British, the Muslims and the terrorists, and these three communities are disassociated from one another through their organization along a temporal scale. According to this progressive order, the 'British way of life' lies closest to the top, as that community that doesn't have to explain itself. The Muslim community, being British and yet not quite British, lies further down the scale, and will be called upon to demonstrate its enlightenment, and its allegiance to the 'British way of life', or else risk being branded as terrorist.[8] The terrorists are, crucially, off the scale: they are simply unable to acquire the kind of values that make us British and civilized, and will therefore never become enlightened. In an arresting move that carries with it great consequences, Blair shifts the burden of responsibility for the bombings from the terrorists, and from British society more generally, and places it squarely with the 'Muslim community'.

The politics of origins

Because appeals to a community of unity work by projecting from a 'lost' point of commonality, events such as the London bombings come to be seen as something that happened *to* the (British) community, which was settled and secure in its identity before these events came about to disturb it. This temporal framing needs to be challenged if we are in any way interested in exploring alternative responses to the bombings, and furthermore, different ideas of community. Rather than understand communities as always already constituted, we might instead adopt an idea of communities as constitutive, as created over and over again.[9] The motif of the city might be helpful in this respect, in suggesting the idea that communities are less something we inherit, and more of a politics.[10] The nationalist idea of communities as organisms, travelling steadily and linearly through history, doesn't rest easily with the idea of the city. In the city, communities are fragile, improvised and shifting; their creation often involves violence, and communities often find themselves together having been forcefully shifted from another area of the city, or, from another country or region. Being in the city often means bearing witness to massive-scale building works as well as significant devastation and ruin. It rarely involves stable and orderly development. Thus, cities represent key sites that illuminate the idea that violence isn't something that happens to resting communities, but rather, there is a constitutive relationship between community, power and violence.

Urban theorists argue that cities, warfare and organized political violence have always had a mutual relationship. As Stephen Graham has pointed out, cities continue to be key sites of conquest in war, and the symbol of national defeat or survival (Graham 2004: 1–25, 31–53). This might be demonstrated by the occupation of Baghdad in the most recent Iraq war, the fall of Kabul in November 2001, the attacks on New York's twin towers and the Pentagon in Washington, and the violence witnessed in recent years in Mumbai, Istanbul, Madrid, Casablanca, Delhi, Beirut, Grozny, Fallujah and so on. Thus, just as cities require immense effort, toil, labour and energy to build, a similar effort is regularly deployed to take them apart. Therefore, writers who study the city are perhaps more inclined to understand communities through a different temporal prism. Rather than assume communities as sites of continuity, solidity, order and progress, communities in the city are perhaps better understood as constructed, fleeting and moving. The unpredictable and contingent aspect of city life might be demonstrated in Marshall Berman's writings on the massive reconstruction of nineteenth-century Paris and the aggressive 'modernization' of New York, led by Baron Haussmann and Robert Moses respectively (Berman 1983). Both projects involved the forced expulsion of thousands of people, the displacement of entire communities, the wrecking of hundreds of buildings, the mass coordination of hundreds of workers, and the creation of some sublime but spectacular urban sculptures and landscapes. Berman shows us that urban life, and indeed modern life, involves a dialectical relationship of construction and destruction, brilliance and disaster. Following Berman and Graham, perhaps we shouldn't understand urban planning and urban destruction, as different phenomena in kind, but as part of a continuum, which connects urbanity, violence and modernity:

> All of which means that the division between urban planning geared towards urban growth and development, and that which focuses on attempts at place annihilation or attack, is not always clear. It is certainly much more fuzzy than urban planners – with their Enlightenment-tinged self-images of devoting themselves to instilling urban 'progress' and 'order' – might want to believe. In fact, it is necessary to assume that a continuum exists connecting acts of building and physical restructuring, on the one hand, and acts of all-out organized war and place annihilation on the other.
>
> (Graham 2004: 33)

How might this understanding of community, as foundationally intertwined with force and violence, alter our reading of London in the aftermath of the bombings, and our capacity to imagine communities more generally? First, it suggests a different relationship between community and time. Rather than assume that the British community is a longstanding, bounded fixture that was 'attacked' in the bombings, we might instead trace the way that this British community was constructed through, and in response to the bombings. The language of British unity, and the dichotomies of civilized men and barbaric ones, good guys and bad were of course available – and dominant – before the bombings. But this narrative formed the governing framework through which responses to the bombings were formed. Second, it suggests that narratives that invoke a community of British unity involve their own forms of violence. Commonality can only be produced through exclusion, after all, and in order to determine what 'we' are, it will be necessary to establish who is not the same. This might help us in enquiring into the power processes through which the idea of a community in unity is produced. Who does it claim to represent? And who does it exclude in its assertion of a common community?

London as a multicultural community

The Blitz narrative was not the only account of commonality invoked in the aftermath of the bombings however; it was tied to the stipulation of contemporary London as a cosmopolitan city, recounted through the case of London winning the bid to host the Olympics in 2012. The International Olympic Committee announced that London had won the bid on the 6 July, a day before the bombings in London. Subsequently, the Olympics played a large part in the dominant narrative through which the 7 July bombings were explained. London's Olympics bid had been built on a platform selling the idea of London's diversity, and as a city of multiple communities. In the event of the bombings, it served as an ideal model to refer to in order to affirm the idea that London, and through it Britain, were tolerant communities, at ease with their multicultural, postnational selves. This is demonstrated in the *Guardian*'s leading commentary on the day following the bombings:

> Less than 24 hours before the bombs went off, London won a golden accolade from the rest of the world because it offered them an Olympic Games based on hope and inclusiveness towards all races, creeds and nations.... London has won the Olympics because it is an open and tolerant city. The way Londoners responded to the vicious attacks on them has vindicated the Olympians' confidence.
>
> (*Guardian* 2005a)

The narrative of the Olympics quickly dispersed as another example of Londoners at their best, and as the form of community that we should desire. There is nevertheless a difference in ethos between the Blitz narrative and the Olympics one. Whereas the Blitz conjures an image of British unity, the Olympics narrative was mainly deployed to affirm London – and through it Britain – as a multicultural, multiethnic community. Traditionally, under nationalism, difference represents a threat to the common identity of the community; the Blitz narrative conformed to this idea by suggesting an image of the British holding off the enemy 'outside'. In the Olympics narrative however, difference is celebrated as part of the community's postmodern identity. Yet although these two narratives present two seemingly very different agendas, they are more similar than we might at first glance suspect.[11]

Mayor Livingstone was widely seen as presenting a more progressive response to the bombings: leaders of civil liberties organizations and Muslim associations seemed to be more willing to speak alongside Ken Livingstone in order to try and contain the violence, than with the British government. This was demonstrated in a statement released by the Mayor and representatives from a range of community organizations and pressure groups following the bombings, and which was turned into a poster that was displayed across the London transport network. It claimed that, 'Only united communities will defeat terrorism and protect civil liberties'.[12] This message sought to provide a collective show of solidarity, across communities, faiths and organizations against the use of violence; but it also announced to the government that it would be ready to resist any suspension of civil liberties. Yet in order to deliver the statement, it effectively borrowed the statist-nationalist language of unity as the most important ordering principle. The theme of unity is persistent. Yet why must a united identity be a condition for organizing to defend civil liberties? And what are the risks involved in reproducing this principle?

The Mayor's statement that, 'This was not a terrorist attack against the mighty and the powerful.... It was aimed at ordinary, working-class Londoners, black and white, Muslim and Christian, Hindu and Jew, young and old', worked well in bringing many different community leaders and pressure groups together (Livingstone 2005b). The full statement affirms London's status as a multicultural community. But as I have noted, this promotion of difference is curiously, and yet firmly supported by an insistence on unity. Thus while the Olympics narrative presents difference as something to be celebrated rather than feared, it is also accompanied by an appeal to a foundational unity:

> That isn't an ideology, it isn't even a perverted faith – it is just an indiscriminate attempt at mass murder and we know what the objective is. *They seek to divide Londoners.* They seek to turn Londoners against each other. As I said to the International Olympic Committee, the city of London is the greatest in the world, because everybody lives side by side in harmony. Londoners will not be divided by this cowardly attack. They will stand together in solidarity alongside those who have been injured and those who have been bereaved and that is why I'm proud to be the mayor of this city.
> (Livingstone 2005b; emphasis added)

Even while celebrating London's diversity, the greatest threat to the community is nevertheless understood to lie with 'division'. Wittingly or unwittingly therefore, this statement seems to tie into a nationalist narrative that values unity above all else. Only in this case, difference appears as both something that can be valued *and* a threat.

It is important to understand that the two narratives of the Blitz and the Olympics were often deployed together. Thus in many of the British broadsheets, including the *Independent*, the *Guardian* and the *Daily Telegraph*, the affirmation of a specifically British wartime history is accompanied by the proud declaration that London is a multicultural city. It is significant that the Olympics narrative works in a very similar way to the Blitz narrative. It also focuses on a lost moment of harmony, which we must now, in the face of the bombings, seek to recover. We find a classic juxtaposition, organized according to a linear trajectory, between a time when we were deemed to be great and a time when we are now low: 'The contrast between triumph and sudden vulnerability could hardly be greater' (*Daily Telegraph* 2005). The longing to achieve greatness again abides by the classic formula through which the idea of a community in unity is produced. Only in this case, it is a community of diversity that is mourned, and appears as that which we must recoup. Winning the Olympics bid gains currency as another *focus imaginarius*, or as a 'high point' of multicultural solidarity from which we have now been plunged. In both the Blitz and the Olympic narratives however, it is the disorder of the present that we really cannot live with, and the idea that we are faced with differences that seem beyond our understanding. The multicultural narrative doesn't so much present an alternative to a triumphant account of British identity, as a variation on it. Sport, in particular, becomes the site around which a 'soft' and 'benign' form of nationalism is cast.

Of course, nationalist discourses of belonging are incredibly appealing; this is just one reason, quite apart from the massive institutional and financial support they receive, why they continue to circulate as the most dominant idiom through which we can imagine being together. But the idea of a community in unity also has its pernicious aspects: nationalism is Janus-faced. After all, our united identity is constructed in opposition to an 'other' that doesn't share it: in this case, the 'terrorists'. This is why the question of who decides who belongs to the community, and who doesn't, is a serious problem. This might be explored through another massive poster campaign that was launched by Transport for London in the later aftermath of the bombings, and in early 2007, continues to be displayed at a vast number of tube and bus stations. This campaign, aimed at boosting safety and security on London transport, urges that, 'It's up to all of us'. The press release that accompanied the launch explains what, exactly, is up to us in more detail:

> The poster campaign, titled 'It's up to all of us', is supported by the Mayor of London, the British Transport Police (BTP), the Metropolitan Police Service (Met) and the City of London Police.
>
> Jeroen Weimar, TfL's Director of Transport Policing and Enforcement, said: 'The safety of our passengers and staff is our over-riding priority.
>
> 'We continue to invest in a range of measures to maintain the security of London's transport system, including the dedicated deployment of BTP and

Transport Operational Command Unit officers undertaking visible patrols across London's Tubes, buses and DLR.

'One of the best security measures we have is the eyes of our customers. We are asking everybody to remain vigilant.

'Do look after your own luggage and belongings when travelling...

'Don't be afraid to speak up...

'If you spot something suspicious, don't be afraid to tell a member of staff or a police officer. It's up to all of us to keep London secure.'[13]

The theme of 'all of us' produced in this poster campaign provides further support to the idea that we are a united community. When this poster campaign was launched, it was often to be found placed next to a poster declaring '7 Million Londoners, 1 London', thereby multiplying the message of a community in unity. The shift to the word 'us' sets off warning bells for those who know well the capacity of nationalist language to stir violence. The bold black writing on the bright, warning-coloured red poster is contrasted by white writing that highlights the word 'all'. This emphasis on the word 'all' is interesting, for it seems to imply that part of the problem presented by terrorism is that not *everyone* is playing by the rules. In response, we *all* have to pull our weight to be on the lookout for those who threaten the community. And so we are effectively invited to police our fellow passengers. The problem is that we're not told what it is that we should be on the lookout *for*, apart from 'something suspicious'. Londoners, especially tube and bus travellers, had their reasons to be anxious in returning to their everyday journeys in the aftermath of the bombings. The many survivors caught up in the blasts, some more severely injured than others, had more reason still. But this poster introduces another reason why we might be anxious: we have all become suspicious of one another, even by city standards, in the wake of the bombings. The response offered to such apprehension however, is not to build relations, or to keep prejudices in check, but 'to speak up' against our fellow passengers. Although we have nothing specific to be monitoring, we are nevertheless called upon to monitor. What is at stake in cultivating suspicion towards an ultimately mysterious object? Which communities and which peoples will mostly find themselves at the receiving end of this suspicion? How violent might some people's attempts at community level policing become? This poster demonstrates that some people will be singled out as part of the process of establishing a single community.[14]

Community and the city

In some ways, Ken Livingstone uses the opposite logic of Tony Blair to make his case for London as a community in unity. Tony Blair cleverly pushes the bombers out of British identity, by portraying them as representing everything that decidedly isn't the 'British way of life'. This smart, and yet utterly inaccurate formulation was delivered in a speech roughly eight months after the bombings, in which Blair commented on a video of what we are told to be Mohammad Sidique Khan, the deemed ringleader of the group's pre-recorded statement of intent to cause terror: 'There was something tragic, terrible but also ridiculous about such a diatribe. *He may have been born here. But his ideology wasn't.* And that is why it has to be taken on, everywhere' (Blair 2006; emphasis added).

Leaving aside for now the potentially terrifying implications of the plan to 'take' these views 'on', 'everywhere', I want to note the way in which Blair distinguishes so absolutely between 'us' and 'them'. In contrast, Ken Livingstone brings the whole world into the community: 'London United: One City, One World' (Livingstone 2005a).

Everyone is welcome in Ken Livingstone's world city. In contrast to the temporal construction of Britishness as enlightened and in no need of justification, Livingstone presents a spatial account of a community that can stretch out to include all differences. Yet, again, although Livingstone welcomes all faiths, ideologies, colours and creeds in his city, the terrorists must be portrayed as barbaric and fundamentally incapable of acquiring the values that Londoners represent: 'That isn't an ideology, it isn't even a perverted faith – it is just an indiscriminate attempt at mass murder and we know what the objective is. They seek to divide Londoners.'

This approach radically excludes the bombers from the community, in a similar way to Blair. In doing so, Livingstone presents us with similar problems: who decides on this limit between the community and the terrorists? Who decided which differences will not be included in the community of differences?

Uniquely, in his statement of response, Ken Livingstone chooses to address the bombers directly. While Blair addresses them in the third-person plural, as 'they' who have tried to frighten 'us', projecting a sense of distance between him and the bombers, Livingstone chooses to 'speak directly to those who came to London to take life', and says to them:

> [People] choose to come to London, as so many have come before because they come to be free, they come to live the life they choose, they come to be able to be themselves. They flee you because you tell them how they should live. They don't want that and nothing you do, however many of us you kill, will stop that flight to our city where freedom is strong and where people can live in harmony with one another. Whatever you do, however many you kill, you will fail.
>
> (Livingstone 2005a: n. 35)

Livingstone's speech represents an interesting fluctuation between nationalistic and cosmopolitan discourses. First of all, it is striking how Livingstone addresses the bombers as 'you ... who *came to London* to take life' (ibid.: n. 35; emphasis added). We may assume that Livingstone also didn't know at this point that the bombers were British citizens. More significantly, he surely couldn't have known that the bombers were *not* British, and not Londoners. Yet, here, he skilfully distinguishes between a community of Londoners and these people who came in to the city from 'outside'. He firmly depicts them as foreigners to the city. This process of 'othering' seems similar to the one that Blair operated. What is significant, and indeed clever about it, is that it immediately constructs the bombers as people who are alien to British (and London's) society. Although this idea might seem appealing when the horror of what happened seems beyond our capacity to understand the events in any meaningful way, it is nevertheless unhelpful. In upholding the idea that the perpetrators and their violent actions are radically 'other' to 'our' community, we disassociate ourselves from any responsibility towards understanding the wider social inequalities and unrests from which such rage may develop, and we excuse ourselves from any critical exploration of how these events may relate to London's position as a global power and to British foreign policy more generally. Livingstone's idea of a multicultural community seems to reproduce the language of nationalism.

Some aspects of the Mayor of London's campaigns go a long way to try and affirm a different, non-nationalistic understanding of community, however. This is exposed in the attempt to draw on the fabric of the city, as a site that is composed of radical difference. Nevertheless, a residual nationalism continues to haunt these campaigns, in that unity, as a rule, is still fundamentally necessary. How might the city present us with a different understanding of community to one that is based on unity? Homi Bhabha has suggested that the metropolis presents a radically different understanding of time and community to the one assumed by nationalism's 'homogenous, empty-time', in which we are all imagined to be travelling together, through history (Bhabha 2004: 199–244). Bhabha claims that the city, in its radical cosmopolitanism, disturbs the narrative of national, linear time, by presenting the 'return of the postcolonial migrant to alienate the holism of history' (ibid.: 241). Whereas British narratives of solidity and continuity might portray London as the capital of a British organism's development in time, Bhabha suggests that the city disturbs that narrative, by exposing the way in which London, and Britishness, have both been constructed through global power games. The figure of the postcolonial migrant in the city reminds us of those multiple, trans-national histories. As Paul Gilroy deftly puts it: 'The immigrant is now here because Britain, Europe, was once out there' (Gilroy 2004: 110).

However, Livingstone's presentation of London as a multicultural city doesn't present a rupture of the national narrative. The community of '7 million Londoners, 1 London' is decidedly flat, and omits mentioning that the presence of so many different people in the city might be somehow linked to Britain and London's role as a colonial and imperial power. This doesn't help us appreciate how 'others' in the city are here *because* of British history, and that they cannot be understood in a separate relationship to it. It also doesn't help us understand how differences get treated differently.[15] However progressive we might find Livingstone's approach to be, it chooses to ignore the critique of British nation-

National and urban ideas of community 73

alism that could lie with the idea of a cosmopolitan society, and specifically, in the figure of the migrant in the city. This symbolic figure stands as a historical witness to British colonial and imperial history and to the pernicious effects of nationalist ambitions to secure historical legacies:

> Cultural pluralism recognizes difference so long as the general category of the people is still fundamentally understood within a national frame. Such benevolence is well intentioned, but it fails to acknowledge the critique of modernity that minoritarian cosmopolitans embody in their historic witness to the twentieth century.
>
> (Breckenridge *et al.* 2002: 6)

Yet in balance to the nationalist spin, Livingstone does seem to touch upon a tradition of urban thought in which he understands the city as presenting a significantly alternative understanding of community. In his statement, the city represents a space to possibly escape determinist or fundamentalist ideas about identity and community. It is a place where people 'come to be free', to 'come to live the life they choose', to 'come to be able to be themselves'. Of course, this description, and the idea that *Stadtluft macht frei* is overly romantic. People often come to the city because they are fleeing for their lives, or struggling to avoid absolute poverty. The city presents its own risks of violence. As Thrift and Amin suggest, the city is as much a means of shutting down possibility, as it is a means of opening up some alternative encounters (Thrift and Amin 2004: 105). There is no 'escape' from determinations, from the force of the law, or from a capitalist and statist system. Yet, nevertheless, Livingstone touches upon an important cultural tradition that is as inherent to the experience of modernity as is the yearning for a lost community of unity. For a flood of figures in music, art, film and writing have sought to respond to the contingency, the chaos, the risks, and the volatile experience of everyday life under modern conditions by refusing to rely on nostalgia, or to live according to a *focus imaginarius* in which we can all look forward to a day when differences will be phased out and a stable order will be restored. This tradition might be represented by figures as diverse as John Cage, Rohinton Mistry, Orhan Pamuk, Susan Sontag, Luce Irigaray and Jacques Derrida. This is the idea of a city that those most fond of a community in unity have often struggled against. Fran Tonkiss expands on this contrast:

> The life of community is the vanishing counterpoint to urban life, and the longing for community carries an implied critique of the city. As a social form that is always receding from view, continually at a point of crisis, community might be seen as much as the stuff of political fantasy or sociological romance as a matter of social actuality.
>
> (Tonkiss 2005: 9)

This is not to say that there is no community in the city. Rather, the city offers us a symbol through which we might imagine a different way of understanding community. If this longing for commonality is largely a fantasy, and city life displays the very impossibility of it to an extreme, how then might the city landscape offer us an alternative way of conceiving what it might mean to be and to live in common?

Drawing from urban theory and writings on the city, Tonkiss makes the point that many people don't come to the city to celebrate their difference; rather, people also come to the city to be indifferent. She remarks on the tradition of urban writing represented by figures such as Georg Simmel, who have explored the paradoxical quality of anonymity in the city. While the idea of walking in the crowd, of being surrounded by a thousand faces and not knowing any of them, of touching and pushing past people in the busy street or metro carriage while carefully refraining from getting too close, represents an art of city life that some might understand as alienation, loneliness and a *lack* of community; for others, this is the culture that has enabled them to be indifferent, to be private, to walk and travel 'unhindered, unremarked and unbothered' (ibid.: 9–10). Various feminists have associated this experience with being in the city. It might also apply to spaces sought out in the city by lesbian, gay, bisexual and transgendered communities. It might be seen in the underground spaces and the squats rooted out by musicians and artists. It could be seen in the figure of the young migrant – in London to earn a better living and enjoy the life of the city.

Jean Charles de Menezes is a figure that reminds us that escape and being indifferent is never, however, guaranteed. Jean Charles was a Brazilian working in London as an electrician, and was shot eight times at close range on 22 July by British anti-terrorist officers in a case of mistaken identity. Although the Metropolitan Police Commissioner Sir Ian Blair initially announced that the decision to shoot was 'directly linked' to their search for those who allegedly attempted and failed to detonate four bombs across the transport network on 21 July, it quickly emerged that he had no connection to the events at all.[16] Perhaps this young man experienced the full terrifying stakes of what is legitimized to protect the British community and London from 'division'. What happens if we persist with Homi Bhabha's approach, refusing to understand the figure of the migrant in the city as that which temporarily disrupts a pre-constituted community, and rather, think of him as he who illuminates, for a moment, the terror that is the condition of constituting the community? How does this sort of terror compare to that which was unleashed by the bombers? Or as Jacques Derrida asked in relation to the tragic loss of life in Washington, New York and Pennsylvania on 11 September 2001:

> How does a terror that is organized, provoked, and instrumentalized differ from that fear that an entire tradition, from Hobbes to Schmitt and even to Benjamin, holds to be the very conditions of the authority of law and of the sovereign exercise of power, the very condition of the political and the state?
> (Borradori 2003: 102)

The deeper implications of this study of political responses to the London bombings for political geography and international relations theory is that the idea of

National and urban ideas of community 75

a community in unity continues to provide the overwhelmingly dominant framework for imagining what it might mean to be in common, or to form political coalitions. But why is unity necessary for effective political action? I have explored how particular accounts of community work in relation to a story of original unity and a narrative of linear time, and how that trope is often reproduced when we examine claims to alternative notions of community more closely. I have sought to reveal the violence involved in claims to origins and how they work to reify a dichotomous understanding of the possibilities for identities and differences. I have also suggested that the task of avoiding this reification of a community in unity might lie with exploring a different idea of origins, as something other than a shared essence, and with it different ideas of time that might prompt other forms of imagining communities. At its core, this task will involve disputing the experience of modernity as one of yearning for a snatched unity. I have suggested that this aspiration might be pursued in the motif of the city. But, as I have argued, the city might equally lead us to the familiar impasses involved in an insistence upon unity. The question of how we pursue the possibility of community without reproducing oppression remains a challenge.

Notes

1 For more on the idea of a community in unity, see Corlett (1989), and the opening chapters of Nancy (1991).
2 In this chapter, I refer to the following poster campaigns: '7 Million Londoners, 1 London' sponsored by London advertising and media organizations (launched by the Mayor's Office 1 August 2005); replaced in Autumn 2006 by 'We are Londoners, We are One', funded by British Gas and Capital Radio (www.london.gov.uk/onelondon, accessed 26 April 2006 and 6 December 2006); a joint statement, and poster, see Mayor and representatives (2005); and a poster aimed at boosting safety and security on London transport, Transport for London (2005). At the time of writing, in early 2007, 'It's up to all of us' posters continue to be displayed across the London Underground.
3 Tulloch (2006) offers both a fascinating personal account of 7 July 2005 and the months following, and an excellent critical analysis of the media coverage of the events. Tulloch points to Ken Livingstone as someone who offered an alternative response to the Blair line (p. 196).
4 For more on how nationalism involves a relationship toward the Nation *qua* Thing, see Žižek (1993), pp. 200–37.
5 For more on how nationalism and cosmopolitanism developed together in the history of ideas, see Cheah (1998), pp. 20–44.
6 *Guardian* 2005b. The first quotation is from the *Sun*, the second is from the *Daily Mirror*, two British tabloid newspapers.
7 For more on the radical dispersion and globalisation of authorities on Islam, see Devji (2005).
8 For a brilliant analysis of the way in which the burden of responsibility was laid with Muslim communities in the Werenotafraid.com internet campaign, following the London bombings, see Weber (2006).
9 For more on constitutive ideas of identity and community, formed around the notion of performativity in particular, see Butler (1999).
10 I borrow this phrasing from Clifford (1997), p. 46.

11 For more on how the national and the post-national accounts of community work according to the same principle whereby difference is seen as a threat, see Honig (2001).
12 Initial signatories included the Mayor of London Ken Livingstone; Director of Liberty, Shami Chakrabarti; Sir Iqbal Sacranie, Secretary General of the Muslim Council of Britain; the Muslim Association of Britain; politicians from the Labour, LibDem, Green and Scottish National parties; writers and journalists; the General Secretaries of four national trade unions; representatives of a range of community organizations and faith groups; civil liberties lawyers and student leaders.
13 A similar message is repeated by Chief Superintendent Paul Crowther, of British Transport Police and Mike Bowron, Assistant Commissioner of City of London Police in the full press statement.
14 This responsibility placed upon 'all of us' coincided with an intensification in 'stop and search' police operations, which had been reduced following criticism in the UK context for the way in which the policy grossly discriminated against young Black men.
15 For more on how certain differences are treated differently, see Crosby (1992), pp. 130–43.
16 For more see Chapter 5 by Nick Vaughan-Williams in this volume.

References

Bauman, Z. (1991), *Modernity and Ambivalence*, Cambridge: Polity Press.
Berman, M. (1983), *All That Is Solid Melts into Air*, London and New York: Verso.
Bhabha, H. (2004), *The Location of Culture*, London and New York: Routledge.
Blair, T. (2005), 'We will hold true to the British way of life', Statement to the Press Association, 7 July. Online. Available at: www.guardian.co.uk/print/0,, 5233964-111274,00.html (accessed 23 November 2006).
—— (2006), 'Not a clash of civilisations, but rather a clash about civilisation', 21 March. Online. Available at: www.number10.gov.uk/output/Page9222.asp (accessed 26 April 2006).
Borradori, G. (ed.) (2003), *Philosophy in a Time of Terror: Dialogues with Jürgen Habermas and Jacques Derrida*, Chicago: University of Chicago Press.
Breckenridge, C. A., Pollock, S., Bhabha, H. K. and Chakrabarty, D. (2002), 'Cosmopolitanisms', in C. Breckenridge, S. Pollock, H. K. Bhabha and D. Chakrabarty (eds), *Cosmopolitanism*, Durham, NC and London: Duke University Press.
Butler, J. (1999), *Gender Trouble. Feminism and the Subversion of Identity*, 2nd edn, New York and London: Routledge.
Cheah, P. (1998), 'Introduction Part II: the cosmopolitical today', in P. Cheah and B. Robbins (eds), *Cosmopolitics. Thinking and Feeling Beyond the Nation*, Minneapolis, MN and London: University of Minnesota Press.
Clifford, J. (1997), *Routes. Travel and Translation in the Late Twentieth Century*, Cambridge, MA, and London: Harvard University Press.
Corlett, W. (1989), *Community without Unity: A Politics of Derridean Extravagance*, Durham, NC, and London: Duke University Press.
Crosby, C. (1992), 'Dealing with differences', in J. Butler and J. W. Scott (eds), *Feminists Theorize the Political*, New York and London: Routledge.
Daily Telegraph (2005), 'A dark day from which we will emerge stronger', Leader, 8 July.
Devji, F. (2005), *Landscapes of the Jihad. Militancy. Morality. Modernity*, London: Hurst & Company.

Freedland, J. (2006), 'How London carried on', *Guardian*, 7 July. Online. Available at: www.guardian.co.uk/print/0,,329523471-117079,00.html (accessed 11 July 2006).
Gilroy, P. (2004), *After Empire*, Abingdon, Oxon: Routledge.
Graham, S. (2004), 'Introduction: cities, warfare, and states of emergency' and 'Cities as strategic sites: place annihilation and urban geopolitics', in Stephen Graham (ed.), *Cities, War and Terrorism. Towards and Urban Geopolitics*, Oxford: Blackwell.
Guardian (2005a), 'In the face of danger', Editorial, 8 July.
—— (2005b), 'What the papers say', 8 July.
Honig, B. (2001), *Democracy and the Foreigner*, Princeton, NJ and Oxford: Princeton University Press.
Independent (2005), 'Muslims told not to travel as retaliation fears grow', 8 July.
Livingstone, K. (2005a), *Fifty-fourth Mayor's Report to the London Assembly*. Online. Available at: www.london.gov.uk/mayor/mayors_report/200509.jsp (accessed 23 November 2006).
—— (2005b), 'London will not be divided'. Online. Available at: www.london.gov.uk/londoner/05aug/mayors-message.jsp (accessed 23 November 2006).
Manthorpe, R. (2006), 'Spirit of the Brits', *Guardian*, 1 July: 21–22. (Winner of the Ben Pimlott prize for political writing.)
Mayor and representatives from a range of community organizations (2005), 'Only united communities will defeat terrorism and protect civil liberties', launched 26 August 2005. Online. Available at: www.london.gov.uk/view_press_release.jsp?releaseid=5795 (accessed 26 April 2006).
Nancy, J. (2004), *The Inoperative Community*, Minneapolis, MN: University of Minnesota Press, ed. Peter Connor, trans. P. Connor, L. Garbus. M. Holland and S. Sawhney.
Report of the Official Account of the Bombings in London on 7th July 2005 (2006), London: The Stationery Office.
Thrift, N. and Amin, A. (2004), *Cities. Reimagining the Urban*, Cambridge: Polity Press.
Tonkiss, F. (2005), *Space, the City and Social Theory*, Cambridge: Polity Press.
Transport for London (2005), 'It's up to all of us', poster campaign launched by Transport for London and supported by the Mayor of London, the British Transport Police (BTP), the Metropolitan Police Service (Met) and the City of London Police, launched 28 November 2005. Online. Available at: www.tfl.gov.uk/tfl/press-centre/press-releases/press-releases-content.asp?prID=603 (accessed 26 April 2005).
Tulloch, J. (2006), *One Day in July. Experiencing 7/7*, London: Little, Brown.
Weber, C. (2006), 'An aesthetics of fear: the 7/7 London bombings, the sublime, and Werenotafraid.com', *Millennium. Journal of International Studies*, 34 (3): 683–712.
Žižek, S. (1993), *Tarrying with the Negative. Kant, Hegel, and the Critique of Ideology*, Durham, NC: Duke University Press.

Part II
War on terror/war on response

4 'Foreign' terror?
Resisting/responding to the London bombings[1]

Dan Bulley

Introduction

The facts of the bombings in London on 7 July are well known: four bombs; 56 people killed; around 700 injured. But such facts take on meaning when they are placed in discourse, when they are interpreted, mediated and constructed; used *by* someone and *for* some purpose. This paper looks to examine one way in which the events were discursively constructed: the way the terrorism was made 'foreign'. Despite the attacks being carried out by Britons, in Britain and primarily on Britons, two months after the event, Prime Minister Tony Blair stressed that '[t]he terrorist attacks in Britain on 7 July have their origins in an ideology born thousands of miles from our shores' (Blair 2005a). Inspired by the work of Jacques Derrida, this chapter asks how the London bombings were made 'foreign', to what end, and it explores the unintended consequences of such a construction.

The British public's response has been encouraging, especially when compared to the way the US government managed to silence and de-legitimize any response to their own insecurity other than the violent assertion of securitized nationalism (Butler 2004). As Jonathan Freedland has observed, '[i]n this sense, the politics of 7/7 has played strangely. It has not led to a new hawkishness in the British public.' While the American public were apparently 'ready to forgive any excesses in the name of combating terror', the same has not been the case in Britain (Freedland 2006). Yet this response should not be taken for granted, and it remains important to question the British government's attempt to make terror 'foreign'.

The aim of this analysis is to show that, although the government's interpretation may have looked to de-politicize and control the response to the London bombings, the opposite, a politicization of response, can be the unintended outcome. Rather than close debate and avenues for response, the making foreign of this terror provides numerous sites for resistance: domestically, in the clampdown on human rights; internationally, in Britain's foreign policy; and conceptually, in terms of breaking down the inside/outside spatial imaginary of the domestic and foreign. To produce such resistance, this article reads the government's totalizing representation of the bombings against itself.

82   *D. Bulley*

The first section below argues that exteriorizing threat and insecurity fulfils a need to construct terrorism as unusual, contingent, part of the uncontrollable 'otherness' of the 'foreign'. However, this draws the governmental description of the bombings into the arena of its foreign policy, where the 'failing state' has been the dominant conceptualization of insecurity and terrorism, especially since the attacks of September 2001. The significance of the 'failing state' in British foreign policy is outlined in the second section. When the London bombings are examined alongside, and through, the conceptual framework of the 'failing state', we see the former deconstructing the latter, revealing that Britain itself is a 'failing state' according to its own description, but also producing a generalization of state 'failure'.

Exteriorizing terror

Ostensibly the London bombings were a domestic matter. Of the four bombers, Mohammad Sidique Khan, Shehzad Tanweer and Hasib Hussain were all born in Britain as second-generation British citizens, raised and educated locally in West Yorkshire (*Report of the Official Account* 2006: 13). Germaine Lindsay, while born in Jamaica, moved to Britain when he was five months old, and was also raised and educated in West Yorkshire (Campbell and Laville 2005). The radicalization of these men is largely unaccounted for, but appears to have taken place almost entirely in Britain. Certainly, as the official report observed, '[t]heir indoctrination appears to have taken place away from places with known links to extremism' (ibid.: 26). Indeed, with the exception of Lindsay, they were all apparently well integrated into British society (ibid.: 26). The BBC's website profiles of the bombers specify that Tanweer and Khan both spoke with unmistakeably Yorkshire accents (BBC 2006a).

Evidence of a foreign influence is largely limited to Kahn and Tanweer's two-and-a-half-month trip to Pakistan between November 2004 and February 2005. Far from exceptional, this was one of 400,000 visits by UK residents to Pakistan in 2004 (*Report of the Official Account* 2006: 20). During this time, they *may* have met key figures in Al-Qaeda, travelled to training camps in Afghanistan, or made contact with international terrorist groups (Harding and Cowan 2005). However, most of these claims have since been falsified (Townsend 2006). Indeed, there is no evidence of support from Al-Qaeda or any other 'foreign' group (*Report of the Official Account* 2006: 21). Email contact was made with someone in Pakistan prior to the attacks (ibid.: 26), but no evidence corroborates the theory that this was an Al-Qaeda 'fixer' (Townsend 2006).

In fact, almost everything about the attacks appears 'domestic' rather than 'foreign.' The attacks were financed by a British bank loan procured by Khan (*Report of the Official Account* 2006: 23). The know-how to produce the bombs appears to have been gleaned from the internet (BBC 2006b) rather than Afghan camps. The bombings took place on the British mainland and the bombers journey from their homes to central London did not once take them outside the territorial borders of the UK. By May 2006 an immense police investigation had produced over 12,500 statements and over 26,000 exhibits (*Report of the Official Account* 2006: 26), the vast majority of which was within Britain.

Yet despite its 'domesticity', Blair insisted upon the 'foreignness' of the bombing's ideological origins two months after they happened. In fact, the process of exteriorising this terrorism began earlier. On the day of the attacks Jack Straw, the *Foreign* Secretary, was called upon to conduct a range of media interviews (Straw 2005). This was peculiar as a bombing on the British mainland, indeed in the nation's capital, remains primarily the terrain of the *Home* Secretary. The prominence was further emphasized when Straw was the only Minister to be included with the main party leaders in a meeting with Muslim community heads after the bombings.

Later, Blair made this exteriorization explicit. By 2006 he was emphasizing the distinction between the bombers' nationality and the nationality of their ideology. Focusing on Khan (the 'ringleader'), Blair asserts that '[h]e may have been born here. But his ideology wasn't' (Blair 2006a). Approaching the anniversary of the bombings, Blair used a keynote foreign policy speech to widen the context. Rather than the ideology alone being 'foreign', the bombings are tied in with a range of other international issues: regional unrest, environmental concerns and mass migration. All these require pre-emptive action, and 'often ... intervention far beyond our boundaries' (Blair 2006b). British-based terrorism is no exception.

> The terrorism we are fighting in Britain, wasn't born in Britain, though on 7th July last year it was British born terrorists that committed murder. The roots are in schools and training camps and indoctrination thousands of miles away, as well as in the towns and cities of modern Britain. The migration we experience is from Eastern Europe, and the poverty-stricken states of Africa and the solution to it lies there at its source not in the nation feeling its consequence. What this means is that we have to act, not react; we have to do so on the basis of prediction not certainty; and such action will often, usually indeed, be outside of our own territory.
>
> (Blair 2006b)

The coupling of migration and terrorism is itself troubling. However, Blair argues beyond the 'foreignness' of the ideology, towards the 'foreignness' of the solution. Just as with migration, the solution to terrorism lies 'at its source not in the nation feeling the consequence' (ibid.). And where is the source of this terrorism? 'The terrorism that afflicts [Iraqis] is the same that afflicts us. Its roots are out there in the Middle East, in the brutal combination of secular dictatorship and religious extremism' (ibid.).

Blair here moves away from semi-exteriorization, which involved noting that the terrorists were born in Britain, but their ideology was not, that the roots of this terrorism exist in the towns and cities of modern Britain, as well as thousands of miles away. By the Iraq section of his speech, the roots of all terrorism are foreign, they are in the Middle East, in a form of government and a form of religion which is also deeply foreign to British sensibilities. The way this shift is made begs the question: why is the issue so vehemently constructed as foreign? What is threatened by the possibility of 'domestic' terrorism?

This chapter suggests that a primary motivation was to emphasize the contingency of the bombings, their extraordinary nature, their uncontrollability and 'otherness'. The discourse is repeating the move made throughout international relations (IR) theory, of differentiating an 'inside' from an 'outside' (Walker 1993). Richard Ashley designates this a realist 'double move' (Ashley 1987: 413). First, a spatial relation of *difference* is invoked: domestically the state's internal autonomy is maintained and thus we have the potential for community, progress, justice and ethics; outside the state, the 'foreign' is considered different however, discernible by different forces, (dis)orders and anarchy. This spatial move of *difference* then justifies the second move: a temporal relation of *deferring* the domestic community's 'essential project for a universal and timeless national unity' (ibid.: 412–13).

Thus the community possible 'inside' the state always has its *historical* margins despite its universal aspirations; beyond these its project must be deferred. Without the authority possible within, the 'international' and 'foreign' are always different, uncontrollable, and dangerous. As Walker has it, the lack of community *outside* the state was 'taken to imply the impossibility of history as a progressive teleology' in the international (Walker 1993: 63). This Labour government has certainly continued to trumpet the possibility of morality, justice, progress and community in international relations (see Cook 1997a; Blair 2003a; 2004b). However, when disaster struck, refuge was sought in the discursive separation of 'inside' from 'outside, 'domestic' from 'foreign', and the realist double move which such separation institutes.

This move is made more understandable through an exploration of how the 'foreign' is conceived in the government's schema: the vagueness of the 'international community' not entirely mitigating the de-securitizing impact of 'failing' states. This move to presenting the terrorism in London as a 'foreign' issue takes us directly into the government's foreign policy. A fundamental aspect of this foreign policy has been the concept of the 'failing state', a state marked by instability which subsequently 'exports' its problems. As the next two sections illustrate, this designation of the terrorism on 7 July as a matter of 'foreign' policy is both fundamental and detrimental to the success of the government's response.

The 'failing state' and British foreign policy

The concept of the 'failing state' has played a key structuring role in British foreign policy, especially since 11 September. However, it is important to consider the context in which this idea rose to prominence, how British foreign policy developed, and how the 'failing state' fitted into this general discourse. Especially significant, in this respect, is the 'doctrine' of international community, and its structuring rights and responsibilities. It is only by outlining this logic that it will become clear how it undermines itself, as well as the exteriorization of the terror in London.

The doctrine of international community – rights and responsibilities

Blair fleshed out the British idea of international community in 1999. 'Our task is to build a new doctrine of international community, defined by common rights and shared responsibilities' (Blair 1999a). The emphasis upon states having rights and responsibilities becomes a refrain (see Blair 2000). By March 2004 he was still making the same point (Blair 2004b). As Foreign Secretary, Jack Straw added steel to this discourse, observing that '[t]he rights of members of the global community depend *exclusively* on their readiness to meet their global responsibilities' (Straw 2002a; emphasis added).

The rights that come with this membership are never systematically listed. However, they appear to include the right to development aid and debt relief, to an unpolluted environment, to trade in free markets (Blair 1999a), and to enter into international treaties and organizations (Blair 1999c). The *central* right, however, is 'the right to live free from the threat of force' (Blair 1999a). As a member of the international community, one's sovereignty and territorial integrity is respected. If not part of the international community, this right is relinquished. Initially this is played down: the 'principle of non-interference' remains valid, but it 'must be qualified in certain respects' (Blair 1999b). For Mark Wickham-Jones this demonstrates the 'quiet burial of the doctrine of non-intervention' (Wickham-Jones 2000: 17).

Later, the burial is emphasized. The new doctrine is represented as breaking from the 'traditional' philosophy of international relations which has 'held sway since the Treaty of Westphalia in 1648' (Blair 2004b). It is no longer the case that 'a country's internal affairs are for it and you don't intervene unless it threatens you, or breaches a treaty, or triggers an obligation of alliance' (Blair 2004b). Denis MacShane, then a Junior Foreign Office Minister, thus declared that '[t]he Westphalian era of inter-state relations is over. The days when what happened inside a state was of no interest to other nations is over' (MacShane 2002b).

As stated, these rights are dependent upon the fulfilment of a state's responsibilities, of which there is also no definitive list. However, respect for human rights form the 'rules of membership' of the international community (Cook 1997b). Bill Rammell, a Junior Minister at the Foreign Office, observed that '[t]he core role of any state is to guarantee basic human rights: life, security, the rule of law. But some fail in this responsibility' (Rammell 2003). Other general responsibilities involve: not threatening international peace and security, either by committing acts of genocide and producing refugees (Blair 1999b), or by threatening one's neighbours (Blair 1999a); not supporting terrorism (Blair 2004a); and neither developing nor proliferating weapons of mass destruction (Blair 2003b). A range of other responsibilities link directly to some of the rights above, but these are generally only applied to African states (see Blair 1999a).

If others fail in their responsibilities, the international community itself has a responsibility to act (Blair 2003b). Thus, in 2004, the principle of non-interference was dug up and re-buried by Straw.

> States have the right to non-interference in their internal affairs; but they also have responsibilities, towards their own people, and towards the international community and their international engagements. Where those responsibilities are manifestly ignored, neglected or abused, the international community may need to intervene: the cost of failing to do so in Rwanda or in Bosnia still haunts us today.
>
> (Straw 2004)

There is, of course, a name for these states who manifestly ignore, neglect or abuse the responsibilities they owe: after 11 September they are increasingly called *failing states*.

Failing states, foreign terror

The primary, though unspoken, responsibility of any member of the international community is the responsibility to be *successful*. This is the nodal point, the master signifier which all other responsibilities refer back to, even if silently. State failure, however, only became central to British foreign policy after Straw became Foreign Secretary. His definition of 'success' was heavily premised on the value of human rights. '[T]he key measure of a state's success is the extent to which it guarantees the human rights of its population' (Straw 2002b). He also highlights three other characteristics of state success – 'democracy, good governance and the rule of law' – without which 'human rights cannot be enjoyed' (Straw 2002b). A more precise definition is given a few months later.

> How do we define a failed state? In general terms, a state fails when it is unable: to control its territory and guarantee the security of its citizens; to maintain the rule of law, promote human rights and provide effective governance; and to deliver goods to its population (such as economic growth, education and healthcare).
>
> (Straw 2002c)

Examples of failed and failing states include Somalia and Liberia, which even resemble Hobbes's state of nature. However, there is another type of state failure, which fits the above definition but does not match the Hobbesian 'chaos' of some African states. The best example is pre-intervention Iraq.

> in Iraq it is an all too powerful state – a totalitarian regime – which has terrorised its population in order to establish control. From one perspective, totalitarian regimes and failed or failing states are at opposite ends of the spectrum. But there are similarities: one is unable to avoid subverting inter-

national law; the other is only too willing to flout it. And in failing to secure widespread popular support, both have within them the seeds of their own destruction.

(Straw 2002c)

The metaphor – seeds of destruction – is important and shall be called upon later. Straw's point is clear: failing states do not live up to the responsibilities required of them in the international community; for some, such as Somalia, this is because they cannot; for others, such as Iraq, this is because they refuse to.

Perhaps it is still unclear why successful members of the international community should be concerned about failing states. This is where the crucial discursive link between failing states and the 'foreignness' of terrorism is made. While there are human rights fears, 11 September revealed 'a more particular and direct reason for concern', as a state's failure and 'disintegration' impacted the lives of people 'at the heart of the most powerful democracy in the world' (Straw 2002c).

Here we have the key to the exteriorisation of terror. Already, in 2002, four years before the London bombings, Straw has made the attacks of 11 September 'foreign' – the result of another state's failure and disintegration. Purely and simply, the terrorism of that day was a 'foreign' problem, produced by 'chaos' in Afghanistan. This is why the international community must act, pre-emptively if necessary, to prevent states from failing. The terror is foreign, so it demands a pro-active foreign policy. Straw sums this up superbly, linking the three themes: failed/failing states – terrorism – foreignness: 'the dreadful events of 11 September have given us a vision of one possible future. A future in which *unspeakably evil acts* are committed against us, coordinated from *failed states* in *distant parts of the world*' (Straw 2002c; emphasis added).

This link is underlined by the description of failing states *exporting* their problems. Shortly after 11 September, Blair argued that the attacks had 'shattered the myth' that the West can ignore the rest of the world. 'Once chaos and strife have got a grip on a region or a country trouble will soon be exported' (Blair 2001). As MacShane starkly put it, '[t]he Westphalian era came to an end when states behaving badly exported their tensions and hates to our shores' (MacShane 2002b). Describing the situation in more offensive terms, '[i]f we fail to help Africans on to help themselves on their own continent they will come and help themselves on ours' (MacShane 2002a).

Now we can more fully understand how it was possible for the British government to exteriorize and 'make foreign' the terror of London. When Blair places this terror in the same bracket as mass migration, he is talking about the exportation of problems. These attacks were not domestic, they were a matter of Britain importing, shipping in, a 'foreign' ideology from the Middle East. To combine MacShane and Blair, the London bombings were a product of importing foreign 'tensions and hates to our shores', from failing states and their 'brutal combination of secular dictatorship and religious extremism'.

To understand how it was possible for the British government to construct the

London bombings as a foreign issue, we must understand the discourse, the chain of references, from which it arose. An examination of British foreign policy illustrates how the exteriorization of terror makes more sense when examined alongside concepts of 'international community' and failing/failed states. These states, who are unable to control their territory, guarantee security, human rights and the rule of law, export their 'foreign' problems to states like the US (on 11 September 2001) and the UK (on 7 July 2005). Of course, this discourse rests on two crucial points: first, that Britain is not a failing state (if it were, its primary responsibility would be to its own citizens, not those of other states); and second, that failure is the exception and not the general rule. If either of these are problematic, so is the government's response to terrorism, domestically and internationally.

Autoimmunity: deconstructing the failing state

A simple response to the discourse of 'foreign' terror would be merely to re-state the facts of the suicide bombers, their and their crime's 'Britishness', and then assert that this insecurity was not imported. The London bombings were a matter of 'domestic' terror. However, there are several advantages to a Derridean analysis. First, the bald statement of 'domestic' terror does not place the government discourse in its wider context. Instead of helping *explicate* the government's response, it is merely rejected. In contrast, Derrida's focus upon 'autoimmunity' reveals that the government's understanding of 7 July breaks down under its *own* logic; it does not require a separate version of events. Second, an assertion of 'domestic' terror would merely invert the hierarchical binary (domestic/foreign) within which the government is already working. In other words, it would change which element of the opposition is given primacy, but it would not displace the opposition, the fundamental difference between the domestic and foreign itself.

A deconstructive critique works back from the government's representation of terrorism and enacts a form of resistance, not only to this representation, but to the dominant system of thought in which its conceptualization is captured. As well as criticizing the description of the bombings as 'foreign', a product of 'failing states', deconstruction also undermines the possibility of a 'domestic' explanation. This is not to say that a 'domestic' terror argument is not important, and it will be stated below, but such an inversion of the binary opposition is only one gesture in the double-move of deconstruction (Derrida 1988: 21). To intervene in, and respond to, the descriptions of 7 July, it is important to overturn the inside/outside logic upon which they are built. As we have seen above, the 'domestic/foreign' opposition is founded upon an opposition in the government's foreign policy discourse, between 'succeeding/failing' states.

The diseased/autoimmune state

In a 2002 speech, Straw included a section entitled 'Diagnosing State Failure' (Straw 2002c). 'Diagnosis' implies that state failure is a disease or medical condition to be *treated*. After 11 September, Straw says, he asked officials at the Foreign Office to 'look more closely at the underlying causes of state failure and identify a broad "at risk" category' (ibid.). Those at risk could easily slide towards failure. Thus, the medical analogy is extended:

> In medicine, doctors look at a wide range of indicators to spot patients who are at high risk of certain medical conditions – high cholesterol, bad diet, heavy smoking for example. This does not mean they ignore everyone else nor that some of those exhibiting such characteristics are not able to enjoy long and healthy lives, against our expectations. But this approach does enable the medical profession to narrow down the field and focus their efforts accordingly. We should do the same with countries.
>
> (Straw 2002c)

Straw recommends that, with sharpened criteria and weighting, we can and should be able to *intervene before states fail*. 'Returning to my medical analogy, prevention is better than cure. It is easier, cheaper and less painful for all concerned.'

The fundamental test of such disease/failure is the health of human rights. As stated, the 'key measure of a state's success is the extent to which it guarantees the human rights of its population' (Straw 2002b). Thus, human rights and the rule of law should be used as an 'early warning system' of future crises and state failure. We could say that human rights are the immune system of the international community. They reveal signs of disease and can be used to fight against this disease both by those within the state and, if need be, by the international community. As demonstrated, to establish failure, the British discourse advocates asking if there are areas of a state's territory the government cannot control, significant ethnic or religious tension or terrorist activity (Straw 2002c). Fundamentally, a state's success depends on whether it is strong enough to control such tension and maintain the safety, security and human rights of its citizens.

Derrida used a similar medical analogy, that of 'autoimmunity', to explain the contradictory, even suicidal, nature of democracy. Democratic states, he argued, essentially work against their own 'success'. 'Autoimmunity' is a 'strange illogical logic by which a living being can destroy, in an autonomous fashion, the very thing that is supposed to protect it against the other' (Derrida 2005: 123). It describes a biological process in which an organism's immune system turns on itself, on its own cells, thus destroying its own immunity. Hence it is 'quasi-*suicidal*' as it 'works to destroy its own protection, to immunize itself *against* its "own" immunity' (Derrida 2003: 94).

Democracy, for Derrida, is not just a system of government confined to the state. Following Plato's portrait of the democrat in the *Republic*, Derrida associates democracy with freedom/liberty (*eleutheria*) and licence (*exousia*), which is also whim, free will, ease, freedom of choice, the right to do as one pleases. Thus, from Ancient Greece onwards, 'democracy' is conceived on the basis of such freedom (Derrida 2005: 22). This liberty and licence associates itself with the concept of human rights, the rights which protect one's democratic freedoms. However, the point of 'autoimmunity' is to show that these democratic freedoms attack their own defences from within.

This can happen in at least two ways. First, the very openness of democracy, the free speech, the right to stand for election to public office, and so on, can allow a party intent on ending democracy to triumph legitimately by election. For example in 1992, the Algerian government decided 'to suspend, at least provisionally, democracy *for its own good*, so as to take care of it, so as to immunize it against a much worse and very likely assault' (Derrida 2005: 33). Democracy always has this quasi-suicidal possibility within itself – it may commit suicide (impose authoritarian rule and end democracy) to prevent its murder (the democratic end to democracy).

The second autoimmune reaction is more applicable to the current deconstruction: that of terrorism. The attacks of September 2001, the March 2004 train bombings in Madrid, and the London bombings of July 2005 all attest to how the openness and freedom of a successful, democratic, state can literally be seen as 'contain[ing] the seeds of its own destruction' (as Straw says of failing states in 2002c). Those who flew planes into the World Trade Center were armed and trained to fly in the US (Bennett 2004); similarly, the Madrid bombings were mainly perpetrated by resident Moroccans and some Spanish (Hamilos 2007). In Britain, as stated, the bombers were British nationals, educated in extremist views, armed and trained almost entirely in Britain. They were allowed to travel to, and through, a capital city carrying deadly bombs without let or hindrance.

The apparently successful, democratic state is here caught in a double bind. On the one hand, the very openness of Britain's democratic culture of freedom and rights, which signify precisely its success as a state, are *the very source of its own failure*. Britain can no longer claim to protect the human rights, freedoms and security of their own citizens (the definition of a successful state), and specifically *because of the human rights it seeks to protect*. On the other hand, however, what is represented as the necessary solution to this suicidal openness is a strengthening of the invasive powers of the state and a basic suspension of human rights and democratic freedoms. This itself will produce a self-imposed state failure, similar to, though less severe than, the imposition of authoritarian rule in Algeria.

This was revealed in the starkest terms on 22 July 2005 after the Metropolitan Police implemented its 'shoot-to-kill' policy towards suspected suicide bombers. The Brazilian electrician Jean Charles de Menezes was shot seven times in the head and once in the shoulder as he boarded a train at Stockwell underground station (see Walker 2006). Britain, as a state, was not only incapable of protecting human rights on 7 July; two weeks later it was *actively attacking* them, attacking its own immune system.

The immune system continued to be attacked with proposals and measures instituted by the Labour government, presented precisely as a *necessary* curb on human rights. Primary among these was the ability to detain suspects without charge for up to 28 days (contravening Article 5 of the EU Convention on Human Rights), the attempt to increase this period to 90 days and the successful increase in June 2008 to 42 days. Those who opposed and eventually defeated this measure were branded 'irresponsible' for their defence of human rights by Blair (Blair 2005b). In June 2006 a further high-profile instance saw the police raid two houses in Forest Gate, London, arrest two men, shooting one of them. The lawyer for one family involved highlighted the state's failure, declaring that this action 'was as lawless as the wild west' (Gareth Pierce, in Gillan and Muir 2006).

One could easily dispute the severity of this failure. Yet, whatever the *severity*, the point remains that failure is inherent. Framing these issues as marginal, or operational 'mistakes' specifically avoids a critical response (see Chapter 5 by Nick Vaughan-Williams in this volume). It also ignores the necessary *logic* of autoimmunity, meaning a state's success can only ever also be *failure*. Democratic rights are suspended in order to preserve them. The double bind of the successful, *healthy*, state is that it necessarily attacks *its self*, its 'early warning system', making itself *diseased* – whether by terrorists attacking it due to its very openness, or by its own closure through suspension of democratic rights. Successful states, those capable of protecting citizens' security, rights and freedoms, cannot help but always be inhabited and defined by *failure*.

To some extent, the necessity of this structural failure is acknowledged within the government's response. As Straw admitted, '[w]e *cannot provide a reassurance* that nothing like this will happen in the future.... We have been successful in many ways, but *you can never provide 100 per cent security*' (Straw 2005; emphasis added). It may seem harsh to expect the state to provide such total security. Yet this has been the standard that British foreign policy has held other states to: states must '*guarantee* basic human rights: life, security, the rule of law' (Rammell 2003; emphasis added); a state fails when unable to 'control its territory and *guarantee* the security of its citizens' (Straw 2002c; emphasis added). If no assurance can be given and *in*security is inherent, then not only is Britain a failing state, *there can be no successful state*.

However, as Derrida makes plain, the most unsettling element of autoimmunity is that it is always a matter of the *self* revealing the impossibility *of the self*. Because the self cannot help acting against its self, the self cannot be singular, but must be split and divided. Autoimmunity 'consists not only in committing suicide but in compromising *sui-* *self*-referentiality, the *self* or *sui-* of suicide itself'. Placing the *sui* in doubt threatens to 'rob suicide itself of its meaning and supposed integrity' (Derrida 2005: 45). The self is fragmented, constituted by *difference* as well as sameness, a difference that *attacks* the coherent self-sameness of the subject. The terrorists were British nationals operating domestically. No matter how much we try to *exteriorize* terrorism, it is always more or less *interior*, it 'has something "domestic," if not national, about it' (Derrida 2003: 188).

The bombings have thus disturbed the simple inside/outside, self/other, domestic/foreign boundary upon which Britain's foreign policy and exteriorization of terror is built (as a successful state, which has the capacity to responsibly protect 'its' citizens both within 'its' territorially drawn state, *and* in others' territorially drawn states). The exteriorization of terrorism and insecurity is an attempt to make 'Britain' appear less autoimmune (as the attack came from the *other* not the *self*), less unstable, less incapable, less fragmented, less *failing*. Yet, as Derrida observes, this is the most effective type of terrorism, that which 'seems external and "international," is the one that installs or recalls an interior threat, *at home*' (Derrida 2003: 188). Attempts at exteriorization will always fail because it recalls that Sidique Khan *was* British, that his 'ideology' *was* taught to him in Britain, that the attack was *a 'British' attack on 'Britain'*.

The logic of domestic terrorism, the threat of domestic chaos and insecurity, is what the British government tries to evade by exteriorizing the terror of 7 July. However, inscribing that terror within the foreign policy discourse of failing states means that the government's foreign *and* domestic policy is fatally undermined. Not only do they fail to convince that the terror was 'foreign', they also undermine the basis of British foreign policy, by revealing that Britain is a 'failing' state and that 'failure' is the norm rather than the exception.

Conclusion: responding/resisting

To understand the government's response to the London bombings, and to negotiate other responses, or responses that are other, it is crucial to place it within the wider policy discourse from which it emerged. This chapter therefore explained where the represenation of 'foreign' terror came from, how it became the dominant understanding in government policy, and what links this produced with other discursive formations. This required an excavation of the government's foreign policy and its reliance upon 'failed/failing' states. Widening the context meant that responding to the London bombings is also about responding to the British government's foreign policy; not necessarily in terms of the links between the invasions of Afghanistan/Iraq and domestic terrorism, but in a more conceptual and fundamental manner. It demands a response to the framework which allowed the invasions of Afghanistan and Iraq to be thought as *possible*, let alone natural and obligatory.

In conclusion, it is suggested that at least three responses are produced both *by*, and *to*, the exteriorization of the terrorism on 7 July. All three also enact a form of resistance, a politicization and unsettling of the government's conceptual framework. First, the most obvious response/resistance is towards the domestic security policy pursued by the government since the London bombings. Events such as the shooting of Jean Charles de Menezes, increased periods of detention without trial, and the Forest Gate raid become even more problematic when viewed from an 'autoimmune' perspective. It undercuts the basis of the government's argument: 'shoot to kill' and 90-day detentions are simply 'necessary' because while civil liberties are essential, 'one basic civil liberty which is the right to life of our citizens and freedom from terrorism' is the most important of all (Blair 2005b).

Instead, a far more nuanced response is called for, one that eschews simplicity in favour of a recognition that democratic rights and freedoms are necessarily suicidal; no discursive representation of terrorism as 'foreign' can alleviate this. Rejecting simplicity also means rejecting the simplistic abandonment of democracy on the grounds of its constitutive failure. Rather, deconstructive autoimmunity makes a double gesture: on the one hand, it embraces and affirms democracy in its paradoxical perfectibility; on the other hand, it engages in a ceaseless critique and negotiation of the imperfect contemporary institutions of democracy.

Second, a response is required to a conceptual schema of foreign policy based on failed and failing states. If failure is generalized, and the opposition between success and failure is displaced, where does this leave Britain's understanding of others and its self? This critique can be used to resist the seemingly necessary pre-emptive foreign policy which emerges from state failure. In one sense, this means resisting the way this discourse claims to 'know' the other, know its problems and the necessary solutions to those problems. While at times patronizing, as in Straw's medical analogy of Britain as 'doctor' curing the 'diseased' Africa (Straw 2002c), at other times this verges on outright racism, as when MacShane suggests we should help Africans so they don't come to Europe and 'help themselves' (MacShane 2002a). Exposure of such ethnocentrism at the heart of the Labour government's foreign policy is a necessary first step to resisting it.

In another sense, however, just as with the 'domestic' resistance, this must not constitute an outright rejection to all forms of 'humanitarianism' in foreign policy. Rather, in line with Edkins' critique of famine relief and aid operations, we should acknowledge that any such decision in foreign policy is *political*; 'It is not a technological or managerial matter that can be resolved by better theories or techniques' (Edkins 2001: 152). Humanitarian foreign policies cannot be scientific, technological 'diagnoses' of state failure, as Straw claims. In fact, where some see state failure, it is possible to see 'the development of forms of political authority that are no longer based on territorial integrity or a bureaucratic system or even on consent' (ibid.: 138). While these new forms of authority *may* be undesirable, they should not be immediately dismissed as *failure* simply because of a technologized ticking of pre-determined boxes in the British Foreign Office. Rather, the recognition of a generalized state failure calls for a questioning and critique of all foreign policy decisions, a questioning which aims to keep foreign policy *political*.

Third and finally, an 'autoimmune' critique demands that a response to the London bombings must contain a politicization and displacement of the boundary between the 'domestic' and 'foreign', the national and the international, and of course, more broadly, the self and the other. If the other is always within, if domestic and foreign can truly not be separated, a suspicious resistance and questioning is required every time it is re-imposed. The implications of such a response have yet to be exhausted, in many ways they have yet to be thought. A response to the violence that occurred on 11 September 2001 and 7 July 2005 would be an increased urgency for questioning how the boundaries between the self and other, inside and outside, are negotiated from moment to moment.

Note

1 This chapter also appears as Dan Bulley (2008), '"Foreign" terror? London bombings, resistance and the failing state', *British Journal of Politics and International Relations*, 10(3): 379–94. Thanks for comments to James Brassett, Philippa Sherrington, Bal Sokhi-Bulley, Nick Vaughan-Williams and Maja Zehfuss. Errors remain my own.

References

Ashley, R. (1987), 'The geopolitics of geopolitical space: towards a critical social theory of international politics', *Alternatives*, 12(4): 403–32.
BBC (2006a), 'Profile: Mohammad Sidique Khan,' Online. Available at http://news.bbc.co.uk/1/hi/uk/4762209.stm>; and 'Profile: Shehzad Tanweer,' Online. Available at http://news.bbc.co.uk/1/hi/uk/4762313.stm (accessed 1 February 2007).
—— (2006b), 'BBC Special Report on 7 July bombings,' Online. Available at http://news.bbc.co.uk/1/shared/spl/hi/uk/05/london_blasts/investigation/html/introduction.stm (accessed 1 February 2007).
Bennett, R. (2004), 'Inside the mind of a terrorist', *Observer*, 22 August.
Blair, T. (1999a), 'Facing the modern challenge: the Third Way in Britain and South Africa', 8 January. Unless stated, speeches by Prime Minister Tony Blair were downloaded from: www.10downingstreet.gov.uk (accessed 1 May 2006–1 February 2007).
—— (1999b), 'The doctrine of international community speech', Economic Club, Chicago, 24 April.
—— (1999c), 'The new challenges for Europe', 20 May.
—— (2000), Speech to Global Ethics Foundation, Tubingen University, Germany, 30 June.
—— (2001), Speech at the Lord Mayor's Banquet, 12 November.
—— (2003a) 'Let the United Nations mean what it says and do what it means: speech to Labour Party Spring Conference', 15 February. Online. Available at www.labour.org.uk/news/tbglasgow (accessed 3 March 2006).
—— (2003b), Doorstep press conference in Beijing, 21 July.
—— (2004a), Press conference, 15 January.
—— (2004b), 'Speech on the threat of global terrorism', Sedgefield, 13 July.
—— (2005a), Speech to the General Assembly at the 2005 UN World Summit, 15 September.
—— (2005b), Monthly Downing Street press conference, 7 November.
—— (2006a) 'Clash about civilisations', 21 March.
—— (2006b) Third foreign policy speech, Georgetown, USA, 26 May.
Butler, J. (2004), *Precarious Life: The Power of Mourning and Violence*, New York: Verso.
Campbell, D. and S. Laville (2005), 'British suicide bombers carried out London attacks, say police', *Guardian*, 13 July.
Cook, R. (1997a), 'Mission Statement', 12 May. Online. Available at: www.guardian.co.uk/indonesia/Story/0,2763,190889,00.html (accessed 11 July 2003).
—— (1997b), 'Human rights into a new century', 17 July. Speeches by FO Ministers. Online. Available at: www.fco.gov.uk (accessed 1 May 2006–1 February 2007).
Derrida, J. (1988), *Limited Inc.*, Evanston, IL: Northwestern University Press.
—— (2003), 'Autoimmunity: real and symbolic suicides – a dialogue with Jacques

Derrida', in G. Borradori, *Philosophy in a Time of Terror: Dialogues with Jürgen Habermas and Jacques Derrida*, Chicago: University of Chicago Press, pp. 85–136.
—— (2005), *Rogues: Two Essays on Reason*, Stanford, CA: Stanford University Press.
Edkins, J. (2001), *Whose Hunger? Concepts of Famine, Practices of Aid*, Minneapolis, MN: University of Minnesota Press.
Freedland, J. (2006), 'How London carried on', *Guardian*, 7 July.
Gillan, A. and Muir, H. (2006), 'Lawyer condemns "wild west" police raid', *Guardian*, 5 June.
Hamilos, P (2007), 'Mass murderers jailed for 40 years as judge delivers verdicts on Spain's 9/11', *Guardian*, 1 November.
Harding, L. and Cowan, R. (2005), 'Pakistan militants linked to London attacks', *Guardian*, 19 July.
MacShane, D. (2002a), 'The return of foreign policy', 13 February. This and the following two references are from speeches by FO Ministers. Online. Available at: www.fco.gov.uk (accessed 1 May 2006–1 February 2007).
—— (2002b), 'Diplo-military politics: the future strategic context of conflict prevention and conflict resolution', 25 April.
Rammell, B. (2003), 'Why human rights matter', 25 November.
Report of the Official Account of the Bombings in London on 7th July 2005 (2006), (London: The Stationery Office).
Straw, J. (2002a), 'Principles of a modern global community', 10 April. This and the following three references are from speeches by FO Ministers. Online. Available at: www.fco.gov.uk (accessed 1 May 2006–1 February 2007).
—— (2002b), 'Human rights ensure international security and prosperity', 18 April.
—— (2002c) 'Failed and failing states', 6 September.
—— (2004), 'Shaping a stronger United Nations', 2 September.
—— (2005a), Media interviews with *Guardian Unlimited*, BBC News and ITV News, Gleneagles, 7 July.
Townsend, M. (2006), 'Leak reveals official story of London bombings,' *Observer*, 9 April.
Walker, P. (2006), 'Q&A: the De Menezes investigation', *Guardian Unlimited*, 17 July. Online. Available at: www.guardian.co.uk/menezes/story/0,,1822504,00.html (accessed 19 July 2006).
Walker, R. B. J. (1993), *Inside/Outside: International Relations as Political Theory*, Cambridge: Cambridge University Press.
Wickham-Jones, M. (2000), 'Labour's trajectory in foreign affairs: the moral crusade of a pivotal power?', in R. Little and M. Wickham-Jones (eds), *New Labour's Foreign Policy: A New Moral Crusade?*, Manchester: Manchester University Press, pp. 3–32.

5 The shooting of Jean Charles de Menezes

New border politics?

Nick Vaughan-Williams[1]

> Well, [Jean Charles] is a kind of fallen soldier. He died because of the war on terror, didn't he?
>
> (Almeida in Bland 2005)

> It's still happening out there, there are still officers having to make those calls as we speak.... Somebody else could be shot.
>
> (Ian Blair in *NBC News* 2005)

Introduction

At 10.05 on 22 July 2005 UK anti-terrorist officers killed Jean Charles de Menezes on board a stationary underground train at Stockwell Station in South London by firing 11 rounds at close range (seven bullets entered his head, one bullet entered his shoulder and three bullets missed) (*Daily Telegraph* 2005). Five-and-a-half hours after the shooting, Metropolitan Police Commissioner Sir Ian Blair issued a statement in which he claimed that the operation had been 'directly linked' to ongoing investigations into the attempted bombings in central London the previous day (ibid.). At that time, Ian Blair announced that the person shot dead at Stockwell had been acting suspiciously and was challenged by police but refused to obey instructions (*BBC News Online* 2005a). However, in a statement the following day the Commissioner announced that a 'mistake' had been made and that there was no evidence to connect Menezes with the attempted bombings or any other 'terrorist' activity (Blair in *NBC News* 2005). Six months later, following the completion of the first part of the inquiry into the shooting by the Independent Police Complaints Commission (IPCC), Ian Blair commented:

> In a terrible way, the Met was transfixed on other things. It was transfixed on: where are these bombers? And therefore, in a dreadful way, we didn't see the significance of that. That was our *mistake*. It was. It was a bad *mistake*.
>
> (Blair in *Daily Telegraph* 2006; emphasis added)

Any attempt to reflect on what happened on 22 July 2005 cannot get very far from what we might call the 'brute fact' of Menezes death without invoking some sort of angle or frame (Derrida 2003: 89). We rely upon such frames in the quest to comprehend events: they offer grounds upon which phenomena may be rendered intelligible through devices such as analogy, metaphor and narrative (Campbell 2001; Vaughan-Williams 2005). However, any given frame is not neutral or natural but a politically loaded assessment of actuality with potentially important implications: there is always a politics of framing (Derrida 1979; 1987; 1988; 1994). Discussion of the killing in the mainstream British media has been typically framed by Sir Ian Blair's explanation that it was simply a 'mistake': an error, an aberration, or a lamentable one-off tragedy (*BBC News Online* 2007; *NBC News* 2005; *Daily Telegraph* 2006; Appleton 2005; Black 2005; Davenport 2006; Taylor 2006). According to one commentator, this framing is entirely appropriate: 'by recognising that de Menezes' death was a freak mistake, we can deal with the reality of politics today – rather than worrying about whether we could be next, or wondering what the Met is hiding from us' (Appleton 2005).

On the one hand, the discourse of the 'mistake' of the shooting of Menezes, especially when read alongside familiar accounts of the feverish manhunt for suspected bombers after the attempted attacks, perhaps offers a convenient way of making sense of the killing. On the other hand, an uncritical acceptance of the discourse of the 'mistake' reifies rather than questions the very frame*work* within which the killing of Menezes has been valorized. In other words, by merely accepting the discourse of the 'mistake' as a starting point in reflecting on Menezes' death we run the risk of colluding *with* rather than offering a critique *of* the activities of sovereign power. This raises the problem of how it might be possible to analyse what happened on 22 July 2005 without risking the same form of collusion. One possible response is to examine how the dominant discourse of the 'mistake' has legitimized and/or obscured particular political practices in the aftermath of the shooting of Menezes. Such an approach allows for analysis of the way in which the above discourse has distracted attention from broader issues connecting the killing to the global 'War on Terror'. In this context I seek to develop the argument that the shooting reflects innovations in the ways sovereign power attempts to secure the spatial and temporal borders of political community in the West.

'22/7'

Despite the emergence and subsequent entrenchment of a particular narrative about what happened to Jean Charles de Menezes on 22 July 2005 ('22/7'), there are many ambiguities and unanswered questions about the circumstances leading to and surrounding his death. To some extent, the long-awaited outcome of the findings of the IPCC investigation might cast new light on these circumstances, although there are still calls by the Menezes family and 'justice4jean' campaign for a full public inquiry. However, irrespective of these findings, it is instructive to analyse how particular framings in the immediate aftermath of the shooting have led to the privileging of some questions over others and what the political implications of this agenda-setting have been. From here it might then be possible to consider alternative framings and open up new avenues of inquiry.

From Scotia Road to Stockwell Station

There are multiple blind spots in the detail of the killing of Menezes, which, in the quest to produce a coherent narrative, sometimes go unnoticed in accounts of '22/7'. One blind spot relates to the elementary issue of precisely *who* was involved in the planning, management and carrying out of the killing. According to Nafeez Ahmed, the initial report given by the police had not mentioned anything about the surveillance operation mounted outside a block of flats located on Scotia Road in the Tulse Hill area of London on the morning of 22 July (Ahmed 2006: 97). We now know that the aim of that stakeout was to find suspects linked to the attempted bombings on the London transport network the day before – in particular Hussein Osman, whose details, including a gym membership card leading to the Tulse Hill address, had been found at the site of the attempted blast in the Shepherd's Bush area (*BBC News Online* 2007). However, information about the surveillance team remains sketchy and there have been unconfirmed suggestions about the involvement of military personnel and/or members of the Special Forces (Ahmed 2006: 118; Cusick 2005). Nevertheless, many reports obscure questions surrounding this involvement by focusing on the anti-terrorist officer who was distracted from Menezes' emergence from the flats at 09.33 because he was 'relieving himself' in nearby bushes (*BBC News Online* 2007).

In one of the few extant academic treatments of the shooting, Joseph Pugliese has argued that Menezes' departure from the flats instigated a 'regime of visuality', which led from practices of racial profiling to a situation whereby he was racially suspect and produced as guilty in advance of any crime he may or may not commit (Pugliese 2006). In this way, according to Pugliese, 'fantasy and fiction ... transmuted into factual reality' and a Brazilian person became mistaken for an Asian one:

> racial profiling ... can be viewed as a type of persistence of vision: a racially inflected regime of visuality fundamentally inscribes the physiology of perception so that what one sees is in fact determined by the hallucinatory merging of stereotypical images that are superimposed on the object of perception.
>
> (Pugliese 2006: 3)

Yet, it is interesting to note that the surveillance team member otherwise occupied in the bushes had actually identified Menezes as an 'IC1 Male' (police code for a white man) (Ahmed 2006: 97–100). Even though Menezes' racial profile did not match that of Hussein Osman or any of the other suspected bombers anti-terrorist officers followed him on his 33-minute bus journey from Tulse Hill to Stockwell Station. At no point was he stopped or challenged (Taylor 2006).

A positive identification had been made before the bus arrived in Stockwell and it is thought that Cressida Dick, the police officer in charge of the 'Gold Command' centre at Scotland Yard, authorized the use of lethal force if necessary to stop Menezes boarding an underground train (ibid.). Yet, the reasons why Menezes was simultaneously mistaken as an 'IC1 male' and Hussein Osman, and not in any way challenged by surveillance team members seeking confirmation of his identity remain unclear. After alighting the bus, Menezes crossed Clapham Road and walked 1,000 metres into Stockwell station, where, contrary to initial reports about his suspicious behaviour, he picked up a free copy of the *Metro* newspaper, walked through the ticket barriers using his Oyster card as payment and then took the escalator to the northbound northern line platform (Ahmed 2006: 97–100; Pugliese 2006: 1; *BBC News Online* 2007). He only began to run towards the platform once he had noticed that a train was arriving in the station (*BBC News Online* 2007).

Having boarded the stationary underground train, Menezes sat in a carriage facing the platform (ibid.). Undercover surveillance team members flanked him and held the carriage doors open for armed anti-terrorist officers as they ran down the escalator and into the carriage in which Menezes sat (ibid.). According to one eyewitness Menezes 'looked like a cornered fox' as the officers approached him (Whitby 2005). An officer, known as 'Hotel 3', grabbed Menezes, wrapped his arms around him and pinned his arms to his side while he was shot seven times in the head and once in the shoulder. Despite being fired at point-blank range three bullets missed his body (*BBC News Online* 2007).

One eyewitness account had suggested that Menezes was wearing a heavy winter coat with wires protruding from it (Whitby 2005). However, images of Menezes' body lying dead on the floor of the carriage clearly show that he wore a lightweight denim jacket in keeping with the mid-morning temperature (64°F) ('Weather in London' 2005). No explosives were found attached to his body and he was not carrying a rucksack or bag. Despite these infamous images there is scant footage recording Menezes movements from Scotia Road to the carriage on the train at Stockwell. According to police sources there had been 'technical difficulties' with CCTV equipment on the platform and no cameras were operating in the carriage where the shooting took place because the hard drive had been taken away for examination following the failed attacks of the previous day (Pugliese 2006: 1). Yet, unofficial reports from the Tube Line Consortium, who are in charge of running the Northern Line service, maintain that at least 75 per cent of cameras at Stockwell station and all on the train should have been working (ibid.: 1).

The juridical-political response to Menezes' death

Initially, the Metropolitan Police resisted the prospect of an IPCC inquiry into the shooting by denying investigators access to the scene of the incident for three days (Ahmed 2006: 119). The purpose of the IPCC investigation was to consider whether any individual should be charged with criminal and/or disciplinary offences for Menezes' death and after the initial delay this went ahead. On 14 March 2006 it was announced that the results of the first part of the inquiry (known as 'Stockwell One') were available but that these would not be made public until the completion of the investigation as a whole. The results of 'Stockwell One' were sent confidentially to the Crown Prosecution Service (CPS) for them to decide if charges should be brought forward and, if so, against whom and on what basis.

In July 2006 the CPS finally revealed that they were not going to carry forward charges against any individuals who had been involved in the operation that led to Menezes' death on the grounds of insufficient evidence (Crown Prosecution Service 2006). Instead, the CPS announced their intention to prosecute the Met under Sections 3 and 33 of the Health and Safety at Work Act 1974 for 'failing to provide for the health, safety and welfare of Jean Charles de Menezes' (ibid.). The second part of the IPCC investigation, known as 'Stockwell Two', focuses on the conduct of Sir Ian Blair following the discovery of Menezes' identity and is ongoing at the time of writing (December 2006). However, legal representatives of the Menezes family anticipate severe delays due to the non-compliance of some senior officers in the Metropolitan Police Service (justice4jean). Moreover, despite their repeated calls, the Menezes family have still been denied a full juridical public inquiry to determine the circumstances surrounding the shooting including the controversial 'Shoot-to-kill' policy behind it (ibid.).

The public response to Menezes' death

It is possible to identify a range of variegated responses to the death of Menezes in the UK and an exhaustive analysis of these responses is beyond the remit of this chapter. However, it is possible to sketch out some key features of these responses. On the one hand, according to Jonathan Freedland writing in the *Guardian* on the first anniversary of the 7 July London bombings, there had been some 'initial sympathy' with the Met: the discourse of the 'tragic mistake' seemed acceptable in light of the need to attempt to protect Londoners from further attacks (Freedland 2006: 9). On the other hand, Freedland notes that this sympathy did not last long, especially in light of the Met's decision to plead not guilty to the Health and Safety charges: 'the Menezes case has continued to be toxic ... imperilling Sir Ian Blair's position as Commissioner' (ibid.: 9). It might also be noted that to some extent different communities within the British public have responded with varying concerns. In the immediate aftermath of '22/7' the Muslim Council of Britain was inundated with calls from 'distressed Muslims' about the shooting at Stockwell station. One caller, for example, had simply asked: 'What if I was carrying a rucksack'? (*BBC News Online* 2005c).

To some extent the British public's increasing lack of sympathy with the Met and mounting dissatisfaction with Sir Ian Blair has translated into instances of collective action. On the Sunday after the shooting there was a public vigil organized by the Menezes family and the 'Stop the War Coalition', which was halted and eventually turned back by police as protesters approached Vauxhall Bridge (*Socialist Worker* 2005). Moreover, to mark the first anniversary of Menezes' death, a joint demonstration was organized by his family and the families of those involved in the Forest Gate raids in order to protest against the use of force and question whether justice is possible in the 'War on Terror'. However, the extent of collective action in Britain has been overshadowed by the public reaction in Brazil, where, for example, there have been a series of mass demonstrations and protests organized by the Landless Rural Workers Movement outside the British Embassy in Brasilia and Consulate in Rio (*BBC News Online* 2005b). Nevertheless, the government in Sao Paulo has adopted the dominant framing of the shooting, which was described by Brazilian Foreign Secretary Celso Amorim as a 'lamentable mistake' (*Independent* 2005).

An 'autoimmune crisis'?

One of the political implications of the prominence of the discourse of the mistake is that many of the blind spots in the shooting of Menezes identified above remain obscured. Attention is distracted from what we still do not know in pursuit of a coherent narrative that foists shapeliness on events as if they were somehow scripted. In turn, this potentially acts as a disincentive to ask critical questions because it implies that the shooting can be explained by error alone.

By reading the killing of Menezes as a one-off tragedy we also run the risk of failing to appreciate the broader political context in which it took place. The main worry with the discourse of the mistake is that it isolates Menezes' death from the ongoing global 'War on Terror' and policies and practices legitimized in the name of that 'War'. Such a move to delimit '22/7' from other aspects of contemporary world politics is profoundly political and it is one that Sir Ian Blair and (former) Prime Minster Tony Blair have both struggled to sustain.

Through challenging the dominant frame of the discourse of the mistake within which '22/7' has been located and discussed it might be possible to think more critically about what is at stake in the shooting of Menezes. In order to do this the following discussion reads the shooting against the backdrop of the emergence of the so-called 'shoot-to-kill' policy of the Metropolitan Police. Reading this policy as one of several responses of the British government to the events of 11 September 2001 I employ Jacques Derrida's notion of an 'autoimmune crisis' in order to try to advance the analysis of '22/7' beyond the parameters of the discourse of the mistake (Derrida 2003).

Kratos: 'shoot to kill to protect'

Since the attacks on the twin towers of the World Trade Centre on 11 September 2001 ('9/11') the Metropolitan Police Service has recognized the potential threat of suicide bombers in central London (Taylor 2006). Soon after 9/11, Barbara

Wilding, the then Deputy Assistant Commissioner (now Chief Constable of South Wales Police), was appointed Chair of the Met's suicide bomber working party: 'It was within about ten days of 9/11 that I was asked to review strategy and come up with a plan' (quoted ibid.). At this point Wilding explains that the Met identified what they saw as a new or different terrorist threat in the capital: 'With Irish terrorism there always tended to be a warning and an escape plan. The IRA didn't want to die. They wanted to leave their bomb and live' (quoted ibid.). According to Wilding the Met had not been prepared for copy-cat attacks in London and so her working party quickly visited Israel, Sri Lanka and Russia to find examples of how other police forces deal with the threat of suicide bombers: 'We had a huge gap and we had to fill those gaps as soon as possible' (quoted ibid.).

After 9/11 the Met's anti-terrorist branch developed its own policy response to the threat of suicide bombers based primarily upon the experiences of the Israeli police who are told to shoot to the head if there is imminent danger to life. Roy Ramm, former Metropolitan Police Specialist Operations Commander, claims that this constitutes a policy shift towards 'shoot to kill' (*BBC News Online* 2005c). Such a policy is now also widely known as 'Kratos' (κράτος), meaning strength or force: 'the power to decide, to be decisive, to prevail', as defined by Derrida (Derrida 2005: 13). According to Peter Taylor, the 'Kratos' policy was signed off operationally at the headquarters of MI5 on 22 January 2005 and 'from that point it was up and running' (Taylor 2006). An article in *The Scotsman* suggests that 'Kratos' was first mentioned by the UK government on 15 July 2005, when it was announced that 'armed police officers could be given more aggressive shoot to kill orders, telling them to fire at the heads of suicide bombers' (*The Scotsman* 2005). However, as Nafeez Ahmed has pointed out, the formulation or implementation of 'Kratos' as a specific policy has never been formally debated in the UK parliament (Ahmed 2006: 117–18).

On the one hand, it seems that the shooting of Menezes was one of the earliest instances of the use of 'Kratos' in the UK.[2] On the other hand, there are aspects of what happened in Stockwell on 22 July 2005 that do not sit well alongside a common understanding of what 'Kratos' is supposed to involve. As well as a lack of evidence that Menezes was indeed a 'suicide bomber' members of CO19 were seen restraining and pinning him to the seat of the carriage while he was shot (and not only to the head but also to the shoulder). In a statement justifying shoot-to-kill, Sir Ian Blair said on 24 July 2005 that 'there is no point shooting at someone's chest because that is where the bomb is likely to be' (*CBC News* 2005). Yet, if the fear is that contact with the chest might detonate a live device on a suspected bomber, it remains totally unclear why CO19 put themselves and other passengers in the train at Stockwell in such jeopardy by doing so in the Menezes case.

'22/7' as a symptom of a broader autoimmune crisis

According to Ian Blair's statement on 24 July 2005 the Metropolitan Police Service are 'quite comfortable that the [Kratos] policy is right' (*CBC News*

2005). Moreover, the Commissioner warned, 'it's still happening out there ... there are still officers having to make those calls as we speak ... *somebody else could be shot*' (ibid.; emphasis added). In order to locate the killing of Menezes in a broader context of the global 'War on Terror', it is instructive to question the conditions of its possibility: how is it that the activities of the police, which ostensibly seek to protect people, have ended up themselves posing an imminent threat to life?

In one of his many responses to the events of 11 September 2001, Jacques Derrida argues that a peculiar feature of the global 'War on Terror' is that democratic states 'must restrict ... certain so-called democratic freedoms and the exercise of certain rights by, for example, increasing the powers of police investigations and interrogations, without anyone ... being really able to oppose such measures' (Derrida 2005: 40). Following Derrida's argument, it is possible to identify a raft of new measures introduced by the British government after the bombings on 7 July 2005, including: detention without trial for up to 28 days (in contravention of Article 5 of the EU Convention on Human Rights); a speeding-up of the timetable for the introduction of identity cards; the cultivation of a harsher legislative climate; and heightened suspicion by public and forces of law and order. In this way, the UK, like the US and other Western democracies, has arguably come to resemble its so-called enemies in corrupting and threatening itself in order to try to protect itself against the threat of terrorism (Derrida 2005: 40).

For Derrida this paradoxical logic, whereby a democratic state adopts the very characteristics of that which it is threatened by, follows the structure of what he calls an 'autoimmune process' (Derrida 2003). By this process he is referring to 'that strange behaviour where a living being, in quasi-*suicidal* fashion, "itself" works to destroy its own protection, to immunize itself *against* its "own" immunity' (ibid.: 94). On Derrida's view, since 11 September 2001 there has been a 'vicious circle of repression' unleashed in the West, whereby, in declaring the 'War on Terror', the Western coalition has ended up 'producing, reproducing, and regenerating the very thing it seeks to disarm' (ibid.: 99). This 'vicious circle of repression' is not merely meant in the sense that such a declaration of 'War' invites a response by 'enemies'. Rather, it points to the perverse dynamics of self-destruction within Western democracies themselves: 'for what I call the autoimmune consists not only in harming or ruining oneself, indeed destroying one's own protections, and in doing so oneself, committing suicide, or threatening to do so' (Derrida 2005: 40). Taking Derrida's lead, one possible way of moving beyond the discourse of the 'mistake' in analysing the shooting of Menezes is to read '22/7' precisely as a symptom of the crisis of autoimmunity in the West more generally. According to this reading the formulation and implementation of the 'Kratos' policy in the UK can be understood as part of the broader series of repressive and anti-democratic measures introduced in the West to protect the public against imminent threats to life posed by terrorists. Yet, in London on 22 July 2005 the very mechanisms intended to protect life ended up not only threatening it but also ultimately destroying it: shoot-to-kill killed precisely what it was supposed to protect.

In his book, *The London Bombings: An Independent Inquiry*, Nafeez Ahmed argues that the shooting of Menezes reflects the failure or breakdown of aspects of the British state: 'the Menezes debacle was the last major tragedy [of July 2005] illustrating the extent to which the British national security system was behaving dysfunctionally' (Ahmed 2006: 120). However, Ahmed's argument must be distinguished from Derrida's in that the crisis of autoimmunity is not an outcome of something going wrong in a conventional sense: rather it is a symptom of an aporia at the heart of the concept of democracy that is revealed when democratic states are forced to respond to the threat of terrorism. Indeed, elaborating upon Derrida's perspective and in contradistinction to Ahmed's, it can be argued that '22/7' was far from a failure or breakdown of the system. On the contrary, as I will go on to argue in the next section, the shooting of Menezes can be said to reflect innovations in the ways in which sovereign power attempts to reproduce and secure the spatial and temporal borders of political community in the West. Accordingly, it is possible to interpret the shooting as an outcome of aspects of Western politics than the discourse of the mistake would otherwise suggest.

New border politics?

Against the reading of '22/7' as a mistake, the shooting of Menezes can be viewed as a reflection of innovative ways in which, temporally and spatially, attempts are made by sovereign power to reproduce and secure the politically qualified life of the *polis*. On the one hand, the killing was a form of temporal bordering in the sense that the activation of the 'Kratos' policy aimed to secure the borders of the state by effectively acting upon the future: it was a pre-emptive strike in order to eliminate the threat of something that might have jeopardized the security of citizen-subjects. On the other hand, the killing was also a form of spatial bordering because it both resulted from and contributed to a culture of surveillance and fear in civic spaces in London that is becoming written into the architecture of those spaces. The novel spatial-temporal bordering practices of sovereign power as demonstrated on '22/7' defy conventional understandings of what and where 'borders' are and point to the way in which alternative border imaginaries are ultimately necessary in the emerging context of the global 'War on Terror'. Such imaginaries are necessary lest we are to fail to identify and interrogate different forms of bordering practices.

'22/7' as a form of temporal bordering

Reflecting on the killing of her son, Maria Otone de Menezes commented: 'An honest policeman who was doing his job properly would have spoken to my son first, stopped him and asked him where he was going, and not just have shot and killed him without knowing who he was' (quoted in Taylor 2006). Similarly, Alex Pereira, his cousin, remarked:

Jean had lived in Sao Paulo. It is a dangerous city and he knew the rules there: if you run away when the police tell you to stop, then you are dead. He knows you don't run away and his English was perfect. There is no explanation for him ignoring a warning because there was no warning.

(*Independent* 2005)

Patricia de Menezes said: 'They judged my cousin, and sentenced him, all in the space of a moment' (ibid.). What is striking and interesting about these reactions is that the family members complain in a very basic sense about the lack of *time* given to Menezes: he was denied the time to explain or defend himself as would be expected in the normal juridical process; time was quite literally 'taken away' from him.

Indeed, all in the 'space of a moment', temporary sovereigns decided that Menezes' life was not life worth living but a life that could (and should) be dispensed with. Borrowing from Giorgio Agamben, it can be argued that Menezes was produced as 'bare life': a form of life whose status is indistinct; banned from conventional law and politics and subject to exceptional practices (Agamben 1998). The decision that Menezes' life was not life worth living can be directly linked back to the concept/policy of 'Kratos' understood as: 'the power to decide, to be decisive, to prevail' (Derrida 2005: 13). On this understanding, 'Kratos' is associated with notions of clear, confident and forceful decisioning. Paradoxically, however, for this very reason the 'Kratos' policy does not actually allow for decision-making or at least forms of decision-making that take time to deal with the dilemmas provoking the need for a decision in the first place.

Brian Massumi likens this form of decisioning to a 'lightning strike' or 'flash of sovereign power' (Massumi 2005: 5–7). Moreover, he argues that this approach is the temporal equivalent of a tautology: 'the time form of the decision that strikes like lightning is the foregone conclusion. When it arrives, it always seems to have preceded itself. Where there is a sign of it, it has always already hit' (ibid.: 6). The lightning-strike decision is a foregone conclusion because it side steps or effaces the blurriness of the present in favour of a perceived need to act on the future without delay (ibid.: 5). Illustrating his argument Massumi suggests that this approach characterizes the Presidency of George W. Bush, for whom there is no time for uncertainty: 'I have made judgements in the past. I have made judgements in the future' (quoted ibid.: 5). Citing Bush's admission that it took just 12 minutes for him to 'discuss' the invasion of Iraq with cabinet colleagues, Massumi points to the way the US administration tends to skip decision-making that takes time because:

> Deliberation ... in the current lexicon ... is perceived as a sign of less of wisdom than of weakness.... To admit to discussing, studying, consulting, analysing is to admit to having been in a state of indecision preceding the making of the decision. It is to admit to passages of doubt and unclarity in a blurry present.
>
> (Massumi 2005: 5)

For Massumi, the 'lightning strike' approach in general is one that seeks to act on the future or in other words one that responds to the threat of 'an indefinite future: what may yet come' (ibid.: 4–5). However, whereas traditionally threats were responded to through 'prevention', Massumi argues that we are witnessing the birth of a new form of response in the context of the global 'war on terror': the politics of 'pre-emption' (ibid.: 6–10). This change is marked by a shift in temporal registers from the indefinite future tense to the future perfect tense: the 'always-will-have-been-already' (ibid.: 6). In other words the politics of pre-emption does not respond to events by simply trying to 'prevent' them but actually effects or induces the event:

> Rather than acting in the present to avoid an occurrence in the future, pre-emption brings the future into the present. It makes present the future consequences of an eventuality that may or may not occur, indifferent to its actual occurrence. The event's consequences precede it, as if it had already occurred.
>
> (Massumi 2005: 7–8)

Massumi illustrates his point using the analogy of a fire. A politics of pre-emption does not simply predict but actually causes fires: 'it is like watching footage of a fire in reverse: there will have been fire, in effect, because there is now smoke' (ibid.: 8–9).

The discourse of the foregone conclusion is one that is identifiable with the killing of Menezes. On the one hand, as we have already seen, Sir Ian Blair has referred to the killing as a 'mistake'. But, on the other hand, he has also warned that we should be prepared for more killings like it: 'These are fantastically difficult times.... It's still happening out there, there are still officers having to make those calls as we speak.... *Somebody else could be shot*' (Blair in *NBC News* 2005). What seems to be at stake here is precisely an attempt to securitize the future by bringing it into the present: 'it's still happening out there'. Ian Blair is effectively dealing with the consequences of future killings under the 'Kratos' banner before they actually happen irrespective of whether they actually do. In this way the 'Kratos' policy acts as a temporal bordering process: it pre-empts threats to sovereign political community that come from the future thereby securing *time* as something that belongs to the state, not terrorists. Hence, in the UK there are now distinct echoes of Pentagon policies post-9/11, which, as Didier Bigo has illustrated with reference to the film *Minority Report* (2002), place emphasis on the capacity to pre-empt anywhere and at any*time* (Bigo 2006).

'22/7' as a form of spatial bordering

In the context of the 'War on Terror' the securitization of time and space are mutually implicated as Joseph Pugliese suggests: 'the civic spaces of the city become spaces of uncivil danger, fraught with racialised taunts, repeated security checks and harassment, and the possibility of both symbolic and physical violence' (Pugliese 2006: 6). Attempts at firming up the temporal borders of sovereign political community have been played out spatially through changes to the built environment in London, which are often designed to manage rather than prevent flows among the population of the city. Sometimes these changes are visible, such as the installation of CCTV cameras across the city in tube stations, walkways, office blocks and so on. In other ways these changes can be subtler and integrated into patterns of daily life, such as the use of Oyster cards on the transport network. Yet, perhaps more subtly still, the introduction of new GPS satellite technology has also allowed for the development and emergence of new forms of electronic bordering. For example, from 12 noon to 16.45 on 7 July 2005 the mobile phone operator O2 was ordered by the City of London Police to close their network to the public for an area totalling one square kilometre around Aldgate (London Assembly 2006: 48). This emergency zoning, as discussed in the London Assembly Report, was designed to assist the service needs of the City of London police, but it also prevented other emergency services still reliant upon the O2 network from doing their job properly (ibid.: 48). As such, this form of electronic bordering is intimately connected to questions about sovereignty, territory and power, which are all raised as problems for future discussion in the Assembly Report (ibid.: section 3.12). William Walters has coined the term 'firewalling' for this type of electronic bordering process, which reflects the need for 'new metaphors and figures to capture the character of borders today' (Walters 2006: 30).

The implementation of these new forms of visible and non-visible bordering practices in London has led, *inter alia*, to an erosion of the conventional distinction between the public and private spheres. Such an erosion and the importance of its implications is emphasized by Giorgio Agamben, who has argued that:

> Every attempt to rethink the political space of the West must begin with the clear awareness that we no longer know anything of the classical distinction between *zoē* and *bios*, between private life and political existence, between man as a simple being at home in the house and man's political existence in the city.
>
> (Agamben 1998: 187)

At earlier points in history the blurring of public and private space could be more readily identified as a localized phenomenon in exceptional, marginal and peripheral areas, such as the concentration camps of the late nineteenth and early twentieth centuries:

> Inasmuch as its inhabitants have been stripped of every political status and reduced completely to naked life, the camp is also the most absolute biopolitical space that has ever been realised – a space in which power confronts nothing other than pure biological life without any mediation.
>
> (Agamben 2000: 41)

According to Agamben, the camps were born out of the state of exception and martial law and constitute spaces that are paradoxically both outside the normal juridical order and yet somehow internal to that order (ibid.: 40). He argues that the camp is a space that is opened up when the state of exception acquires a permanent spatial arrangement (ibid.: 39). As such, people in the camps 'moved about in a zone of indistinction between the outside and the inside, the exception and the rule, the licit and the illicit' (ibid.: 40–1).

However, whereas the space of the exception was once localized in spaces such as the camps, Agamben implies that in more recent times it has become more widespread or generalized in contemporary political life: 'the camp, which is now firmly settled inside [the nation-state], is the new biopolitical *nomos* of the planet' (ibid.: 45). The upshot of living in a permanent state of exception means that potentially we can no longer rigorously distinguish our biological life as living beings from our political existence: we all have the capacity to be produced as 'bare life'. Bodies and spaces are increasingly characterized by confusion or zones of indistinction in which sovereign power is able to produce subjects as 'bare life'. It is against 'bare life' that 'politically qualified' life is defined and so the production of 'bare life' can be said to act as a mechanism through which attempts are made to shore up the borders of sovereign political community.

Applying Agamben's argument, the killing of Menezes can be read as symptomatic of innovations in forms of bordering that rely upon the blurring of public and private spaces. On the one hand, the production of 'bare life' is not a new means of securing forms of sovereign political community as Agamben shows in relation to the figure of *homo sacer* in Roman law. On the other hand, what is arguably new about current bordering practices of which the shooting of Menezes is symptomatic is the location and method of the production of 'bare life'. Menezes' death, and its valorization by the authorities in their subsequent investigations, points to a new preparedness to make 'lightning decisions' about life worth living (the politically qualified life of the *polis*) and life not worth living ('bare life') potentially anywhere. With the advent of 'Kratos' such decisions are no longer localized or fixed at particular 'border sites' in the margins of sovereign territory but increasingly more widespread or diffused throughout society: a phenomenon that might be captured by the concept of a biopolitical generalized border (Vaughan-Williams 2007). After all, Menezes was not killed in a camp or space especially designated for such exceptional practices but in a tube station in Central London. In this way Agamben's chilling conclusion that 'we are all (virtually) bare life' (Agamben 1998: 111) is perhaps regrettably less sensationalist than it might first seem and calls for alternative ways of identifying and interrogating the types of bordering processes upon which sovereign power relies: 'these are fantastically difficult times.... It's still happening out there.... *Somebody else could be shot*' (Blair in *NBC News* 2005).

Conclusion

The discourse of the 'mistake' of the shooting of Menezes not only stymies critical responses to '22/7' but also colludes in the reproduction of a particular framework of understanding within which sovereign power has retrospectively valorized his death. Critical resources are therefore required in order to question and re-think this dominant framing so that we might then be able to resist such collusion in our analyses of what happened in Stockwell. By reading the shooting as one of multiple responses of the British state to the bombings of the London transport network on 7 July 2005 and the attempted bombings two weeks later it is possible to locate Menezes' death within the broader context of the global 'War on Terror' in which the 'shoot-to-kill' policy of the Metropolitan Police Service has emerged. In this context Derrida's identification of the 'autoimmune crisis' in the West offers a potentially useful way of analysing how the very mechanisms supposedly designed to protect life ended up not only threatening it but also ultimately, in the case of Menezes, destroying it. The move here is to refuse to accept that what happened on '22/7' was simply a one-off incident that can be easily isolated from broader aspects of contemporary political practice. Rather, following Derrida, the Menezes shooting is not so much a mistake as the outcome of features of the Western political system itself. Building upon this argument '22/7' can be interpreted as a symptom of innovations in the ways sovereign power attempts to secure the temporal and spatial borders of political community in this system. While Agamben suggests that the production of 'bare life' has always been a systemic feature of Western politics we are arguably witnessing not only new methods through which this form of life is produced but also new locations in which this form of bordering takes place. On this basis, the shooting of Menezes is not only of local but global significance.

Notes

1 This chapter was initially prepared for the 'London in a Time of Terror: the Politics of Response' conference, Birkbeck College, University of London, 8 December 2006. Earlier drafts were also presented at the British International Studies Association Annual Conference, University of Cork, Ireland, 18–20 December 2006 and the International Studies Association Annual Convention, Chicago, 28 February–3 March 2007. An earlier version of this paper was published in *Alternatives: Global, Local Political*, 32(2): 177–196, and I thank Lynne Rienner Publishers for the right to reprint in this volume. Other thanks are due to Louise Amoore, Dan Bulley, Jenny Edkins, Madeleine Fagan and R. B. J. Walker for their constructive criticism, feedback and advice. Finally, I owe a huge debt to Angharad Closs Stephens for her intellectual comradeship over a number of years now: thanks for being such an inspirational colleague and friend.
2 On 30 April 2005, 11 weeks before the Menezes shooting, another man named Azelle Rodney was shot dead by police in central London. However, unlike the Menezes shooting, the Rodney case has received little attention in the press and there are few details available in the public domain. See 'He was shot six times. Why?' (*Guardian* 2006).

References

Ahmed, N. (2006), *The London Bombings: An Independent Inquiry*, London: Duckworth.
Agamben, G. (1998), *Homo Sacer: Sovereign Power and Bare Life*, Stanford, CA: Stanford University Press.
—— (2000), *Means without End: Notes on Politics*, trans. V. Binetti and C. Casarino, Minneapolis, MN: University of Minnesota Press.
Appleton, J. (2005), 'Memorial to paranoia: conspiracy theorists and opportunists gather at the shrine to Jean Charles de Menezes in Stockwell', *Spiked Online*, 24 August. Online. Available at: www.spiked-online.com/index.php?/site/printable/836/ (accessed 18 March 2008).
BBC News Online (2005a), 'Man shot dead by police on tube', 22 July. Online. Available at: http://news.bbc.co.uk/1/hi/uk/4706787.stm (accessed 18 March 2008).
—— (2005b), 'Protest in Brazil after shooting', 26 July. Online. Available at: http://news.bbc.co.uk/1/hi/uk_politics/4714691.stm (accessed 18 March 2008).
—— (2005c), 'Will police now shoot-to-kill?', 22 July. Online. Available at: http://news.bbc.co.uk/1/hi/uk/4707781.stm (accessed 18 March 2008).
—— (2007), 'London attacks in depth: the Menezes killing', Online. Available at: http://news.bbc.co.uk/1/hi/in_depth/uk/2005/london_explosions/default.stm (accessed 18 March 2008).
Bigo, D. (2006), 'Protection: security, territory, population', in J. Huysmans, A. Dobson and R. Prokhovnik (eds), *The Politics of Protection: Sites of Insecurity and Political Agency*, New York: Routledge.
Black, C. (2005), *7-7 The London Bombs – What Went Wrong?*, London: Gibson Square Books Ltd.
Bland, A. (2005), 'It's war on the memorial to de Menezes', *Guardian*, 28 November.
Campbell, D. (2001), 'Imagining the Real, struggling for meaning', *InfoInterventions*, 6 October.
CBC News (2005), '"Someone else could be shot" British Police Chief Warns', 24 July.
Crown Prosecution Service (2006), 'Charging decision on the fatal shooting of Jean Charles de Menezes', 17 July. Online. Available at: www.cps.gov.uk/news/pressreleases/146_06.html (accessed 18 March 2008).
Cusick, J. (2005), 'A cover up? And if so … why?', *Sunday Herald*, 21 August.
Daily Telegraph (2005), 'De Menezes "shot 11 times during 30 seconds"' 26 August.
—— (2006), 'Met chief admits serious mistake over Menezes', 31 January.
Davenport, J. (2006), 'Met Chief admits Menezes mistakes', *Evening Standard*, 30 January.
Derrida, J. (1979), 'The Parergon', *October*, 9(3): 3–40.
—— (1987), *Positions*, trans. A. Bass, Chicago and London: University of Chicago Press.
—— (1988), *Limited Inc.*, Evanston, IL: Northwestern University Press.
—— (1994), 'The deconstruction of actuality: an interiew with Jacques Derrida', *Radical Philosophy*, 68: 28–30.
—— (2003), 'Autoimmunity: real and symbolic suicides – a dialogue with Jacques Derrida', in G. Borradori (ed.), *Philosophy in a Time of Terror: Dialogues with Jürgen Habermas and Jacques Derrida*, Chicago and London: University of Chicago Press.
—— (2005), *Rogues: Two Essays on Reason*, trans. P. Brault and M. Naas, Stanford, CA: Stanford University Press.
Freedland, J. (2006), 'How London carried on', G2, *Guardian*, 7 July: 9.

Guardian (2006), 'He was shot six times. Why?', 7 December.
Independent (2005), 'Jean Charles de Menezes: in the wrong place. at the wrong time', 25 July.
justice4jean, the Jean Charles de Menezes Family Campaign. Online. Available at: www.justice4jean.com (accessed March 2008).
London Assembly (2006), *Report of the 7 July Review Committee*, London: Greater London Authority.
Massumi, B. (2005), 'The future birth of the affective fact', proceedings of the 'Genealogies of Biopolitics' conference, Online. Available at: http://radicalempiricism.org (accessed 10 September 2006).
NBC News (2005), 'UK police defend shoot-to-kill after mistake', *NBC News* 24 July.
Pugliese, J. (2006), 'Asymmetries of terror: visual regimes of racial profiling and the shooting of Jean Charles de Menezes in the context of the war in Iraq', *borderlands ejournal*, 5(1).
Scotsman (2005), 'Police may receive shoot to kill orders', 15 July.
Socialist Worker (2005), 'Shoot to kill is state murder', 30 July.
Taylor, P. (2006), 'Special report: the death of Jean Charles de Menezes', *Guardian*, 8 March.
Vaughan-Williams, N. (2005), 'International relations and the "problem of history"', *Millennium: Journal of International Studies*, 34(1): 115–36.
——— (2007), 'The generalised border: re-conceptualising the limits of sovereign power', paper presented at the Annual ISA Convention, 28 February–3 March 2007, Chicago, IL.
Walters, W. (2006), 'Rethinking borders beyond the state', *Contemporary European Politics*, 4, Special Issue: 'Re-thinking European Spaces: Territory, Borders, Governance'.
Whitby, M. (2005), 'I saw tube man shot – eyewitness', *BBC News Online* 22 July. Online. Available at: http://news.bbc.co.uk/1/hi/uk/4706913.stm (accessed 18 March 2008.
'Weather in London, UK, on 22 July 2005', www.weatherunderground.com.

6 Terror time in Toronto

A response to the response to the arrests of the Toronto 17

Patricia Molloy[1]

Introduction

On the evening of Friday, 2 June 2006 and into the next morning, some 400 heavily armed members of a joint 'counter-terrorism' task force (consisting of the Royal Canadian Mounted Police, the Canadian Security and Intelligence Service and the Ontario Provincial Police, as well as the Metropolitan Toronto, York, Durham and Peel regional police forces) conducted a series of raids across the Greater Toronto Area (GTA) arresting 17 young men, most in their twenties and five of them youths, charged under Canada's Anti-Terrorist Act with plotting bomb attacks on several sites in Southern Ontario. Considered one of the largest 'terrorist sweeps' in North America since 11 September 2001, the arrests of what the media came to dub 'the Toronto 17'[2] put 'Toronto the Good' in the international spotlight for days while the provincial courthouse, in the Toronto suburb of Brampton, where the suspects were arraigned was transformed into a veritable fortress, under siege by local and international news media as much as law enforcement officers (which included sharpshooters on nearby rooftops and tactical units armed with submachine guns).

That all the men and boys arrested were Muslim and are Canadian citizens – with most having been born and raised in Canada – did not go unnoticed by the media, public, police or politicians. As in Britain following the London terror bombings, allegations of 'home-grown terrorism' resounded throughout both police and media discourse and in an address to military personnel the day after the arrests, Prime Minister Stephen Harper expressed his 'happiness' with the police action, congratulating himself for boosting spending on national security, adding that 'Canada is not immune to the threat of terrorism' and is under attack because of its democratic values (Harper in Jones 2006). While police officials warned the public against any acts of retaliation or backlash directed at the GTA's sizeable Muslim population, a mosque in the suburb of Etobicoke was nonetheless vandalized the night following the arrests.

A week later, the Munk Centre for International Studies at the University of Toronto held a panel discussion entitled 'Terrorism in Toronto: What Does it Mean for Canadian Multiculturalism?', its wording adjusted slightly from 'What does the threat of home-grown terrorism mean for multiculturalism in Canada', which originally appeared on the events listings of the Centre's website. Nonetheless, the framing of the panel presents two problematics that I address in this chapter. First (aside, perhaps, from the attack on the mosque), there has been no act of 'terrorism' in Toronto, thus no terrorist event to speak of. Rather, it is the manner of speaking and writing of the arrests which mark the event. Second, the title of the panel clearly frames the issue as a crisis of and for multi-culturalism. Although the panellists concluded that Canada's immigration and multiculturalism policies are *not* to 'blame' for the (supposed) rise of 'home-grown terrorism', none raised the possibility that Canada's official state policies and practices may have perhaps failed the 17 men and boys who were arrested. In response to the paucity of the Munk Centre response, a second panel discussion entitled 'National Security, Arbitrary Arrests and the Criminalization of Dissent in Canada' was held at Ryerson University, organized by a coalition of community activists, academics (including academics of colour who were not invited to speak at the Munk Centre), human rights lawyers, trade unionists and students.

In addition to examining these responses, it is necessary to consider the timing of the arrests themselves as a politics of response. Although they followed a two-year investigation and could have been made at any time, the arrests occurred the week after the much publicized funeral for the first female Canadian soldier killed in Afghanistan, and shortly before both the Anti-Terrorism Act was up for review in Parliament and the report on the Maher Arar affair was scheduled to be released. The arrests thus occurred at a time of vulnerability for Prime Minister Stephen Harper's minority Conservative government.

17 is the new 24

For anyone who caught the early news reports of the arrests or the police press conference the next morning (less than 12 hours after the story broke), the message was clear: Canada can no longer assume that terrorism happens 'elsewhere', beyond the sanctity of our (multicultural) borders or that 'we' are safe from the 'Islamic extremism' which purportedly threatens the West at large. As the American daily, the *Christian Science Monitor*, put it in its headline: 'Canada faces "jihad generation" ', which smacks not only of Islamophobia but a moral panic over wayward Muslim youth in particular (Cook Dube 2006).[3]

For Toronto specifically, being home to its very own 'Al Qaeda inspired' terrorist cell was exactly what the city didn't need to shake its already tarnished image arising from the previous year's 'summer of the gun' and 'Boxing Day shootout' which garnered much international media attention (and increased racial profiling of Black youth). That the 'Al Qaeda inspired' terrorist cell, as the official police statement read, had no actual *links* to Al-Qaeda was not admitted by police until the question period following the press conference.

Moreover, while the initial news reports of the arrests indicated that the group had purchased three tonnes of ammonium nitrate, three times more than was used in the 1995 Oklahoma City bombing of a US federal building, the police statement the next day was worded that the group had taken 'steps to acquire' the fertilizer frequently used in making bombs. It took another 48 hours for the information to come to light that the Royal Canadian Mounted Police had in fact intervened and switched the fertilizer to a less harmful variety before any actual delivery had been made, raising questions about a police sting or possibly even a case of entrapment. At the press conference, however, an array of 'evidence' laid out on a table and presented for the (many) television cameras included a 'sample bag' of real ammonium nitrate. Other examples of indisputable evidence of a vast terrorist plot included batteries and cellphones (supposedly to be used as detonators), boots and a (single) handgun.

If, for even the casual viewer the evidence presented may have seemed, well, lame, for many a Torontonian, news of a mass roundup of young Muslim males hearkened back to August 2003 when the RCMP, with support from the Department of Citizenship and Immigration Canada, arrested 23 Pakistani and one East Indian man on suspicion of terrorist activities under 'Project Thread', so named because of the men's connection by a common thread: they were all Muslim, all but one were from Pakistan, and all were enrolled in the same business college in Toronto ('Project Threadbare' online). In addition, a few had enrolled in a flight school. If that weren't enough to prove beyond a reasonable doubt that all 24 men were sure-fire terrorists, there was the RCMP's startling discovery during the raids that many of them shared small apartments furnished with only mattresses on the floor and an abundance of computers. In other words, they were students. As it turned out, the men were victims of a scam: the school they had enrolled in and paid tuition fees to prior to coming to Canada didn't exist. All allegations of terrorism were dropped within two weeks and all the men were eventually deported (after spending two to five months in a maximum security prison) on the grounds of immigration violations, but without their names having been officially cleared or an apology issued (ibid.).

The spectacular bungling that was Project Thread (or Project Threadbare, as it was renamed by a Toronto activist arts coalition) and other Royal Canadian Mounted Police/Canadian Security and Intelligence Service joint task-force embarrassments (most notably the 25-year investigation of the Air India bombing over the course of which the RCMP accidentally erased all of its wiretap tapes) were in fact pointed out by the *Toronto Star* in its spread of the Toronto 17 arrests in the 3 June print edition, stating that these latest arrests are 'critical for Canada's international reputation'.[4] The arrests were also critical for the *Star*'s own reputation given that it was the *Star* that initially broke – and continued to fuel – the Project Thread story (*NOW Magazine* 2006: 17). Nonetheless, it was the *Star* that first scooped the Toronto 17 story, a day ahead of the *Globe and Mail*, the *National Post* and the *Toronto Sun*. With a huge headline of 'Terror cops swoop GTA' and, underneath that, 'The Star takes you inside the spy game that led to last night's dramatic arrests across the GTA', the paper's coverage of the arrests, as lauded in the *New York Times*, encompassed some 3,000 words and several pictures over a three-page spread (including the front page) (Austen 2006). So impressed was the *Star* with the *Times*'s scoop of *its* own scoop, that it subsequently ran a full-page ad reprinting the *Times* story.[5]

Once the other Toronto dailies caught up with the *Star*, the coverage of the arrests shed no new light, with each applauding the police action, confirming the now almost official discourse that our tolerant and benevolent nation called Canada is under siege by ungrateful 'home grown' extremists under the influence of evil extremists 'abroad', while at the same time condemning the virtual destruction of the Etobicoke mosque. How anyone could have been surprised by the attack on the mosque, however, is in itself surprising given a) the media hysteria surrounding the arrests of 'the friendly zealots next door' (the *Globe*), and b) the general hysteria surrounding Arabs and Muslims in Canada following the (real) terrorist attacks of 11 September in the US, which saw a 66 per cent increase in hate crimes in Canada in 2001 (with the largest increase against Muslims)[6] and reports of race-based harassment in the Canadian workforce increase from 7 to 9 per cent (Ng 2006).

I will return to the latter issue and myths of Canadian benevolence later in the paper. In the meantime, it bears emphasizing that the possibility that the 'friendly zealots' might not be getting a fair shake by either the media or the police was in fact raised in the same mainstream newspaper that broke the story in the first place. Indeed, in the 5 June edition of the *Toronto Star*, Linda Diebel wrote that the sort of spectacle and spin-doctoring both at the Brampton courthouse and initial press conference is a concept more associated with politicians than police chiefs. The massive degree of police security, with televised images of the shackled suspects in leg irons, the carefully selected 'evidence' and long line of police chiefs from across the GTA standing behind the RCMP Assistant Commissioner at the press conference, is its own form of police tampering with public perception, 'as much about creating an image for the public as about charging the individuals' (Diebel 2006). Diebel suggests that the 'theatrical atmosphere' surrounding the arrests seemed more like an awards show, or, better yet, an episode of *24*. Citing University of Toronto professor Michael Edmunds, she writes:

> Unconsciously, receptive audiences for police actions are created by such shows as the Fox hit 24, starring Kiefer Sutherland as counter-terrorist agent Jack Bauer. Viewers sympathize with Bauer, no matter what he has to do, because they want him to get the bad guys and protect the free world.
> (Edmunds in Diebel 2006)

Catching (if not inventing) terrorists, it seems, would also do much to improve the increasingly fragile state of Canada/US relations. To be sure, much ado was made in the local media of how the arrests were featured prominently in the international news media (*Globe and Mail* 2006). As Edmunds wryly notes, making the front page of the *New York Times* in particular shows the Canadian public that '[n]ow we know what the police did was good.... It's vindication when our brothers and sisters in the United States see it, too' (Edmunds in

Diebel 2006). US Secretary of State Condoleeza Rice concurred, stating on CNN that

> We have excellent counterterrorism cooperation with Canada and we're very glad to see this operation being a success.... We don't know of any indication that there is a US part to this, but by all means, we have the best possible cooperation.
>
> (Rice in Shane 2006)

Presumably unbeknown to Rice, the day after the Toronto arrests the FBI said that there *had* been contact between two of the Canadian suspects with two men in Georgia who had also recently been arrested but that 'there is no current outstanding threat to any targets on US soil emanating from this case' (Shane 2006). Whether the threats to Canadian soil had perhaps emanated from the US, I will leave to the conspiracy theorists. Besides, we have the words of Stephen Harper to console us that '[t]hese individuals were allegedly intent on committing acts of terrorism against their own country and their own people' (Harper in Austen and Johnson 2006).

For those needing more than Harper's alarmist rhetoric or the sensationalism of the Toronto and national news media, there's always 'the most trusted source in fake news' to turn to, namely Jon Stewart of Comedy Central's *Daily Show* (which airs in Canada on CTV). Stewart's political satire is a sort of litmus test of newsworthiness and, well aware of the size of his Canadian audience, accords a considerable amount of CanCon (Canadian content). In a segment titled 'Maple Leaf Rage' on his 5 June show, Stewart expressed bewilderment as to how 'the terrorists' could hate Canada.

> You hate Canada? That's like saying 'I hate toast'.... I can understand being angry at *us*. We're arrogant, leading the whole war on terror, but Canada? For God's sake, Canada opposed the war in Iraq. You're mad 'cause you want them to withdraw troops from Afghanistan? That is sooo two jihads ago.

There are two elements from this segment that need to be addressed. First is the perception of Canada as innocuously 'bland as toast' and less bellicose than our neighbours to the south. Second, and related, is Canada's involvement in the 'two jihads ago' war in Afghanistan which, in February of 2006, 75 per cent of Canadians still thought was a peacekeeping mission. In doing so, it is necessary to turn to the 12 June panel discussion.

The (g)loss of innocence: the University of Toronto and the poverty of response

The panel discussion at the Munk Centre drew (according to the *National Post*) approximately 80 people, not including those (such as myself) who were herded into a smaller room in the basement to watch the proceedings on live video. The event also attracted a substantial number of media (more than I would have thought, considering that the panel was held as the first preliminary bail hearing for the 17 was underway in Brampton). Moderated by Lou Pauly (who introduced the proceedings by quoting Jon Stewart), the panel included three University of Toronto faculty (all white, and all affiliated with the Munk Centre), two representatives from 'the Muslim community', and the unabashedly right-wing *Globe and Mail* columnist, Margaret Wente.

As I've already stated, the title of the event, despite the fact that no act of terrorism was committed, was 'Terrorism in Toronto: What Does it Mean for Canadian Multiculturalism?' reflecting the broader discourse of multiculturalism as a 'tolerance for diversity', which, according to popular opinion throughout the week, clearly isn't working to prevent 'Muslim extremism' from reaching 'us'. This was implicit in the words of Wente, the first speaker, however explicit she was about remaining optimistic about multiculturalism as 'the Canadian social experiment'. Oblivious to the aforementioned and highly reported attack on the Etobicoke mosque, Wente claimed at the outset of her address that there has been no backlash against the Muslim community as a result of the arrests, arguing that the issue is 'not about foreign policy, racism, or alienation' but about extremism, via the internet and 'young Muslim men'. Moreover, for Wente 'it's not "us" – it's not coming from "us"', though failing to clarify who this 'us' is.

Though space doesn't permit a full treatment of all the speakers' responses, two general themes emerged throughout the course of the morning. First is that multiculturalism in Canada is working well and fine and that 'our' Muslims are no more or no less integrated in 'Canadian society' (whatever that means) than other minority groups. Rather, the problem for many speakers is the alienation of Muslim youth. Arguing contra Wente, Randell Hansen, who holds a Canada Research Chair in Immigration and Governance, claimed that the problem is indeed one of alienation and youthful rebellion, both Muslim and non-Muslim. Although foreign policy is relevant, it's not about Islam per se. Rather, 'the terror structure' exists already, historically, in subcultural movements such as punk, goth and 'extreme environmental movements' and even, for French youth in the 1960s, the Front de libération du Québec (FLQ). But for Alia Hogben of the Canadian Council of Muslim Women, foreign policy is more important than Hansen is willing to admit. Said Hogben, 'we can't ignore the effects of world politics and wars against Muslim countries on the youth'. Canadian Muslim youth are seeking an identity in the world community of Muslims which, she added, is aided by elders 'with a limited view of what it means to be a "good Muslim"', thus falling into a familiar rhetoric of 'good Muslims' and 'bad Muslims', a discourse through which it is up to the 'good Muslims' to police and contain the 'bad Muslims' who threaten the otherwise peaceable 'community' (of Muslims, Toronto, and 'Canada'.) So successful is multiculturalism in 'integrating' Canadian Muslims that pollster Michael Adams recently reported that 'nearly nine in 10 [Muslim Canadians] say that ordinary law-abiding

Muslims have a duty to report any extremism they may be aware of in their own communities' (Adams 2007).

With multiculturalism now (presumably) off the hook and the problem of (still non-existent) 'terrorism' in Toronto squarely on the shoulders of rebellious youth corrupted by 'bad Muslims' (not to mention punk rock and the FLQ), where does the Canadian state factor in? Multiculturalism in Canada is, after all, an official state policy; schools are state-funded and administered; and, last I heard, law enforcement, national security and 'intelligence' gathering, and of course, war, are state practices. Although, Alia Hogben did suggest wars against Muslim countries as a possible factor in alienating Canadian Muslim youth, she didn't implicate Canada's own combat mission in Afghanistan or Canada's support of Israeli policy in the Occupied Territories. Not one speaker acknowledged a history of racism in Canadian immigration and refugee policy; systemic racism in Canadian schools, military and police forces; the rise in Islamophobia and increase in hate crimes towards Canadian Muslims and Arabs following 11 September 2001; or the ongoing and perpetual colonialist practices of marginalization, demonization and violence towards First Nations peoples. Any acknowledgement of these current and historical practices would disrupt the deeply embedded myths of benevolence which construct both the Canadian imaginary and, it would seem, the Munk Centre itself (Kassamali and Ahmad 2006).[7] Rather, when the issue of the current struggle over a Native land claim/ occupation in Caledonia (near Toronto) was raised by an audience member, he was quickly dismissed and told that this was not the 'appropriate forum' for this discussion. When another audience member, Rinaldo Walcott, also on the University of Toronto faculty (and Canada Research Chair *not* affiliated with the Munk Centre) rose to question the framing of multiculturalism by panel organizers and participants (Wente in particular) without attendance to its historical grounding in White racism and colonialism, he too was dismissed.[8]

Of the entire panel, only one speaker, Melissa Williams of the University of Toronto's Centre for Ethics (affiliated with the Munk Centre), suggested that we're perhaps asking the wrong questions (regarding multiculturalism) and that we have to question the timing and design of the arrests, the sensationalist staging of the press conference, as well as the role of the media: all of which, she argued, and I would agree, exhibit 'a politics of passion over reason'. Although Williams did offer that there is no causal relationship between multicultural policy and Muslim extremism, she, as with the rest of the speakers, failed to ask if the multiculturalism policy by which Canada defines and moreover prides itself did little to prevent the racist manner in which the arrests were conceived, conducted and mediated, and which frames (limited) notions of 'Canadian identity' itself.

Multiculturalism and other myths of Canadian benevolence

While exacerbated by the arrests of the Toronto 17 and a post-11 September climate in general, multiculturalism in Canada has been under attack by both the right and left for quite some time. For conservatives, 'special consideration' of minority groups threatens an already fragile Canadian unity and 'way of life', whereas those on the left see multiculturalism as a literal whitewash of systemic racism. Indeed, the paradox of multiculturalism is that it 'celebrates diversity' while simultaneously managing and containing it.

Canada's official policy of multiculturalism, brought into law by the Canadian Multiculturalism Act in 1988, was first introduced in 1971 by Pierre Trudeau's Liberal government two years after the Official Languages Act mandated English and French as Canada's official languages. The principles of the 1971 policy include the preservation of human rights, development of Canadian identity and reinforcement of Canadian unity, and the encouragement of 'diversification within a bilingual framework'. Couched in a liberal discourse of equal and collective rights, the original policy states that

> Canadian multiculturalism is fundamental to our belief that all citizens are equal. Multiculturalism ensures that all citizens keep their identities, can take pride in their ancestry and have a sense of belonging. Acceptance gives Canadians a feeling of security and self-confidence, making them more open to, and accepting of, diverse cultures.

The policy also confirmed 'the rights of Aboriginal peoples and the status of Canada's two official languages' (Government of Canada 2008).

For critics on both the right and left, legislating unity through diversity could only fail. For sociologist Richard Day, multiculturalism is a dominant culture's attempt to categorize its citizens in relation to itself in an effort to achieve national unity. However, 'this state-sponsored attempt to design a unified nation has paradoxically led to an increase in both the number of minority identities and in the amount of effort required to "manage" them' (Day 2002: 3). More specifically, for Day, multiculturalism can be understood in Hegelian terms in signifying a dominant culture's attempt to assimilate its Others in order to define its own mastery and achieve identity. 'This is precisely what continues to happen in English Canada, which famously lacks a positive identity, and has been enslaved by its own history of mastery and failed identifications' (ibid.: 225–6).

In stronger terms, multiculturalism articulates a barely disguised White supremacy. As Rinaldo Walcott argues, modern 'satellite' nation-states such as Canada, America, New Zealand and Australia, are founded on a fictional notion of a '"natural" sameness', which is ruptured with the arrival of each successive migration of formerly colonized peoples. For Walcott, 'it is these Others who have most clearly challenged the fictions of nation-state sameness as a racialized code that produces Canada as a "white nation"' (Walcott 2003: 116). The very structure of the nation-state cannot but produce inside/outside binaries which articulate and distinguish 'here' from 'there' and 'us' from 'them'. In this way, says Walcott, drawing on Homi Bhabha, the nation is Janus-faced: offering a two-sided and conflictual articulation of citizenship as evidenced in Canada's official policy of multiculturalism. He writes: 'The policy textually inscribes those who are not French or English as Canadians, yet at the same time it works to textually render a continued understanding of those people as from elsewhere and thus as tangential to the nation-state' (ibid.: 117–18). In effect, 'the colonizing English and French are left textually intact as "real" Canadians while legislation is needed to imagine other folks as Canadian' (ibid.: 117–18).

While, as Walcott emphasizes, there is nothing specific in Canada's official policy to define multicultural as non-white, it is implicit in commonsense understandings which guide discussions of immigration and education. The popular notion of multiculturalism as referring to non-whites is 'rife with the recurring myth of Canada as a benevolent, caring and tolerant country that adapts to "strangers" so that strangers don't have to adapt to it' (ibid.: 119). The myth of Canadian benevolence and tolerance towards 'our' multicultural Others was, as I have discussed, reinforced in the days following the arrests of the Toronto 17. A common thread occurring throughout the media and political discourse was that 'we' gave these men and boys every opportunity and advantage and look how 'they' repay 'us'? But how benevolent is tolerance itself? Ghassan Hage, for example, argues in *White Nation* that multiculturalism's discourse of 'tolerance' for ethnic and cultural difference is grounded in a relationship of power which effaces any notions of racism.

Writing about Australia, Hage explains that since its emergence as a state policy in the early 1970s, 'multiculturalism has been portrayed as marking a radical break with its previously racist Australian past characterizsed by the White Australia Policy, which barred non-Whites from entering the country, and by the more recent policies of assimilation and integration' (Hage 2000: 82–3). In its reconfigured state, Australian multicultural policy ushered in a 'cultural egalitarian' era in which migrants were *encouraged*, not just allowed, to preserve the cultural traditions of their home countries (ibid.: 82–3). This cultural egalitarianism was predicated on a new emphasis on tolerance. To be sure, according to one of the architects of the new policy, its aims were 'to turn the classrooms of the nation into crucibles of tolerance' (Grassby 1984: 64; quoted in Hage 2000: 83). While this may sound well and good, the problem of 'tolerance' is that it can only coexist with intolerance; can only be understood in relation to one's capacity to be *intolerant*. When speaking of multicultural tolerance specifically, those who are called upon to tolerate 'others' are the very ones who feel entitled to engage in acts of intolerance as it remains firmly within their power. Put simply, in multicultural society those who tolerate can only belong to the White dominant culture. As Hage explains, and is worth quoting in full,

> When the request 'Tolerate!' is made, only those who recognize in themselves the capacity not to tolerate are likely to raise their heads. Why would anyone bother asking someone who has no power to be intolerant to be tolerant? And why would those who are not in a position of power feel that the concern for tolerance is of any concern to them? Indeed, while many people issue calls for tolerance in Australia, those who actually make direct state-

ments concerning how tolerant they are always and inevitably are White Australians. The very idea that a newly arrived migrant is tolerant of White Australians is clearly ridiculous.

(Hage 2000: 87–8)

As with Walcott, for Hage, then, multicultural tolerance is a spatial practice of nationalist power in which the tolerated Others are part of 'our nation' but only when we 'accept' them. Whereas outright acts of racist violence are a practice of exclusion, for Hage, tolerance is a nationalist practice of inclusion with both 'practices confirming an image of the White Australian as a manager of national space' (ibid.: 90–1).

I return here to pollster Michael Adams' recent assertion of the success of Canadian pluralism and multiculturalism insofar as it reiterates many of the themes which circulated at the Munk Centre in June 2006 in a problematic defence of multiculturalism and denial of its failings as outlined above. Indeed, an excerpt of Adams' new book, *Unlikely Utopia: The Surprising Triumph of Canadian Pluralism*, published in the *Toronto Star* in November 2007, is prefaced with a headline subtitle that the book 'argues immigrants are neither failing or being failed. We need to start looking past alarmist headlines' (Adams 2007). One such headlining event featured in the excerpt (which we should presumedly look past) is the decree issued by the town council of Herouxville, Quebec, in February 2007, of ground rules for newcomers called its 'code of life' (including a prohibition on headscarves and veils of any sort). Writes Adams:

> The Herouxville decree was ridiculed in some quarters as the expression of a small town's hysteria about issues of which it had little experience. Quebec Premier Jean Charest called the document an 'isolated case'. But others – both politicians and journalists – took the episode as important evidence that Canadians (particularly Quebeckers) were growing increasingly anxious about the cultural integration of newcomers and minority groups.
> Since then, two ideas have appeared consistently in the national media. The first is that Canadians are losing their vaunted openness to newcomers. The society that once wore multiculturalism as a badge of honour now sees riots in the suburbs of Paris, 'homegrown terrorists' in the United Kingdom, and ethnic clashes on the beaches of Sydney and senses it has bitten off more than it can chew.... The second idea is that newcomers are not having such a great time becoming Canadian.... A consensus is emerging that Canada is growing less enthusiastic about newcomers and newcomers are not so thrilled about Canada either.

(Adams 2007)

While Adams does acknowledge that the proportion of Canadians believing that 'too many immigrants don't adopt Canadian values' has risen sharply from 58 per cent in 2005 to 65 per cent in 2006, he attributes this as a natural outcome of anxiety about Canada having 'the single most ambitious immigration program in the world', rather than 'becoming a hotbed of xenophobia overnight' (ibid.). As the pollster sees it, 'Canadian attitudes ... remain overwhelmingly positive'. He continues:

> Canada has the highest immigration rate in the world, but when asked if this country accepts too many immigrants, most of us say no. Canadians are by far the most likely of any G8 country to say immigrants are good for the country, and that immigrants help the economy grow rather than 'taking jobs away from other Canadians'.
>
> (Adams 2007)

According to Statistics Canada, however, the results of the 2006 Canadian census, released 4 December 2007, shows that while immigration is at its highest rate in 75 years with one in five Canadians being foreign-born (19.8 per cent), an increase from 13.6 per cent in 2001; this ranks us as having the *second*-highest immigrant population of any Western country, the highest being Australia. Moreover, as reported on the CTV news two days prior to the release of the census figures, according to another pollster, Bruce Anderson of Decima Research, 'public opinion polls suggest anywhere between one-third and half of the population feels immigration levels are too high'. Yet, in a similar discourse of denial to that of Adams, Anderson argues that 'despite those numbers ... there's a strong desire amongst Canadians to avoid the kind of "controversial social debate" that occurs in the United States around such issues' (CTV News). In Adams own findings, '[i]n naming things that make them proud to be Canadian, more Canadians say multiculturalism than hockey or bilingualism' (Adams 2007).

What the preceding suggests is that Canadians' attachment to the *idea* of multiculturalism as a distinctly Canadian value overrides any collective responsibility for racist practices and realities as 'such issues' do not happen 'here' but elsewhere, namely the United States. What emerges is another set of binarisms wherein 'they' have a history of slavery, but 'we' have multiculturalism. As inferred by Adams, Canada has an understandable 'anxiety' about 'too many immigrants' which is somehow, astonishingly, different from xenophobia. So deeply entrenched is the myth of a benevolent multiculturalism in the (White) Canadian imagination in setting 'us' apart from 'them', that, according to one Ontario teenager, 'it's illegal to be racist' in Canada (Hayes 2004: 72). Far from suffering from a terminal inferiority complex, as the popular stereotype would have it, 'Canada' exhibits greater symptoms of a *superiority* complex which assumes not just a mythic, but a phallic dimension.

In making this distinction, I refer again to Ghassan Hage who more recently has written about how contemporary warring societies, having much in common with colonial settler societies, legitimize undemocratic and unethical practices (like torture, lying and manipulation) which they would not otherwise consider in 'normal situations'. Drawing on Giorgio Agamben, Hage writes that a state of exception allows a citizen to legitimize to themselves, and to each other, being undemocratic and unethical, while maintaining the belief in their ethical selves by continuously moving between the two states: in moment A I am a nice democratic ethical person, in moment B I am a warrior who has to kill but soon after I can return to moment A and be myself. Like the soldier, the citizen conscript has to say: 'it's true that I am killing the enemy but I am not a killer. Now that I am out of my warring state of exception I can go back to being a good non-killer'.

(Hage 2006: 46)

When a state of exception becomes permanent, however, the citizen stops fluctuating between the two moments and splits themself into two. In other words, 'the citizen can actually manage to continuously support unethical practices while still maintaining their ultimate, essential ethical selves' (ibid.: 46).

In this way, warring societies gradually vacate their democracies to the extent that they become phallic democracies: in competition and on display. Phallic democracies 'are democracies for others as opposed to the democracies for ourselves' (ibid.: 46). They are for show, rather than to live in. Once you even claim to have a democracy, you enter the competitive arena and the phallic logic creeps in. Writes Hage: 'My democracy is *bigger* than your democracy. In fact, not only [can] my democracy be bigger than your democracy, my democracy can be the only thing there is. You probably have no democracy *at all*!'. We see this logic with the Israelis versus the Palestinians and white South Africans versus black South Africans. *We* have democracy but *you* don't (ibid.: 46).

We also see this phallic logic at work in the 'war on terror' as Western nations proclaim their superiority in having democracy which Arab and Muslim states clearly lack. As I've suggested, we can extend this logic to a phallic multiculturalism wherein settler societies such as the United States, Australia, Britain and Canada project their superiority regarding the 'tolerance' we exhibit towards 'our multicultural others'. Where it gets even more phallic is Canada's popular (mis)conception of being the most multicultural (and most tolerant) country in the world. Not only is our multiculturalism bigger and better than yours, but we were the first to even *have* multiculturalism. As proudly stated on the Canadian Heritage website: 'In 1971, Canada was the first country in the world to adopt multiculturalism as an official policy' (Government of Canada n.d.). As for Toronto itself, everyone knows that we are the most multicultural city in the world as declared by the UN. Except that we're not. As revealed by Albert Nerenberg in his 2007 documentary, *Let's All Hate Toronto* (saving me considerable research), the UN has never made such a statement and Toronto's claim to have the highest immigrant population in the world, more than New York or London, is a myth that most Torontonians (even, I admit, myself) are not aware of.[9] Returning to Hage, the problem with phallic projections of democracy, and we can add multiculturalism, is that they 'come hand in hand with the undermining and gutting of *lived* democracy' and multiculturalism (Hage 2006: 47).

Exceptional state, or state of exception?

The fate of the Toronto 17 is still uncertain. With charges against one of the youths dropped in February 2007 and subsequently stayed against another three, the preliminary hearing for the remaining 14 suspects began on 4 June 2007 but was suddenly halted on 24 September when the Crown, via the federal justice minister, announced it was proceeding directly to trial in what is called a preferred indictment (Tyler 2007). While preferred indictments are relatively rare, usually invoked for the most serious cases (including notorious sex killer, Paul Bernardo in 1995), a year prior the justice minister moved to a direct indictment against Momin Khawaja of Ottawa on charges (the first to be laid under the new Anti-Terrorism Act) in connection with an alleged bomb plot in Britain, thus, for criminal law professor David Paciocco, a pattern may be emerging (ibid.). As the defence lawyer for one of the suspects sees it, 'We can't discount the political implications of this prosecution – showing the world that we're tough on terror' (Motee in Teotonio 2007). Indeed, what marks the direct indictment of the Toronto terror suspects as particularly unusual is that in most cases in which the Crown rules against a preliminary hearing, it does so at the outset, not, as in this case, half-way through the proceedings and in the middle of a Crown prime witness's testimony. For *Toronto Star* columnist, Thomas Walkom, this raises the question of whether something may have been about to be revealed that the government didn't want anyone to hear, including the reliability of its own informants (Walkom 2007).

While under the Canadian Criminal Code people charged with serious offences have the right to a preliminary hearing by which defence counsel may hear and test evidence against their clients, this same right is not guaranteed by the Charter of Rights and Freedoms (thus revoking it is not considered unconstitutional) (Tyler 2007). This begs the question of what sort of rights the Toronto 17 actually have. As I stated at the outset of this chapter, the suspects were charged under Canada's Anti-Terrorist Act (ATA) which was introduced by the then Liberal government a mere 34 days after 11 September 2001, as Bill C-36; an amendment to the Criminal Code, the Official Secrets Act, the Canada Evidence Act and the Proceeds of Crime (money laundering) Act. Included in the Bill were provisions to make it easier for law enforcement and national security agencies to use electronic surveillance; to amend the Canada Evidence Act to prevent information deemed to be of 'national interest' from disclosure before the courts; to give law enforcement powers to make preventative arrests and detain suspects for up to 72 hours without charge; as well as require individuals to testify at 'investigative hearings'. The Bill would also give the Solicitor General the power to create a 'List of Terrorists' without notification to individuals or groups on the list (Fortier 2006). Although the justice minister's claim that the Bill would strike the right balance between civil liberties and national security, human rights critics have pointed out that the only recognition on the side of rights was 'an amendment to the Criminal Code to add "online hate" and "mischief against places of religious worship/religions property" and to amend the Canadian Human Rights Act to prohibit "spreading repeated hate messages" by communications technology' (ibid.).

Critics also warned that the definition of terrorism under the Bill was broader and more vaguely defined even than that of the United States. Whereas in the US, terrorism is 'premeditated, politically motivated violence perpetrated against non-combatant targets by subnational groups or clandestine agents' (ibid.), and doesn't include any reference to religion, Canadian terrorism is an act or omission that is committed 'in whole or in part for a political, religious or ideological purpose, objective or cause' that intentionally causes death or serious bodily harm, endangers a person's life, causes serious risk or safety of the public, or 'causes serious interference with or serious disruption of an essential service, facility or system, whether public or private, other than as an act of lawful advocacy, protest or dissent or stoppage of work...' (Government of Canada 2008). Needless to say, under this definition, 'terrorist activity' also extends to illegal strikes and civil disobedience as well as peaceful forms of protest which, by their very nature, are 'ideologically motivated'. For Amnesty International's Alex Neve, 'the line between "lawful" and "unlawful" is too fine and often too arbitrary to say that one is acceptable, and perhaps even commendable, and the other is "terrorism"' (Neve in Fortier 2006).[10] Put differently, the line of distinction between lawful and unlawful which collapses under anti-terrorist legislation signals a suspension of law itself wherein we see a transformation from a state of emergency or siege (which applies laws of war in a time of crisis) to what Agamben describes as a state of exception, 'a threshold of indeterminacy between democracy and absolutism' which becomes permanent. As discussed above in relation to a democracy which legitimizes non-democratic practices, a state of exception gives legal form to what cannot otherwise be legal (Agamben 2005: 1–5; Chapter 1 this volume; Chapter 5 this volume).

This has special significance not just for Canada's 'home-grown terrorists' whose rights to hear evidence against them were (legally) suspended but also for six non-Canadian citizens currently detained without charge and on secret evidence under Canada's 'security certificate' system. I will return to this below. First however, it is necessary to note that following a number of amendments, including to the definition of terrorism, Bill C-36 was formally passed into law as the Anti-Terrorism Act in November 2001, receiving Royal Assent that December. Under the new definition, the word 'lawful' was struck from the definition of advocacy, protest or dissent to ensure that protest activity, whether lawful or unlawful, would not be considered a terrorist act unless it was intended to cause death, bodily harm or endangerment of life or public safety. In addition, an interpretive 'for greater certainty' clause was added wherein 'the expression of a political, religious or ideological thought, belief or opinion does not come within ... the definition of "terrorist activity" ... unless it constitutes an act or omission that satisfies the criteria' (Government of Canada n.d.; Fortier 2006). Nonetheless, the very inclusion of religion in the definition of terrorism led an Ontario Superior Court judge to quash that portion of the ATA in the trial of the aforementioned Momin Khajawa on the grounds that it infringes on freedom of religion as guaranteed in the Charter of Rights (Dobrota 2006: A1).

Other amendments to the ATA included a three-year Parliamentary review and a five-year 'sunset clause' for two of its most contentious provisions: preventative arrests and investigative hearings which allow for arrest without charge and compelled testimony, both of which, according to the Canadian Arab Federation 'are stark departures from Canada's legal values' (Action Alert 2007). Or are they? While the motion to extend these two ATA provisions was (narrowly) defeated in the House of Commons by 159 to 124 on 27 February 2007 (O'Neill and Mayeda 2007), the big news that week was the Supreme Court's unanimous (nine to zero) decision striking down as unconstitutional Canada's security certificate system which grants the government sweeping powers to use secret evidence to imprison non-citizens without charge indefinitely, and then deport them with few being the wiser. Although brought into law in 1978 under the Immigration and Refugee Act, and used against approximately two dozen foreign nationals from various countries prior to 2001,[11] outside of activist circles few Canadians seemed to be even aware of the policy or that it is currently being used to 'detain' six Muslim men (some of whom are refugee claimants) of North African and Middle-Eastern countries for a combined 273 months ('Homes Not Bombs'). While some remain in a federal prison dubbed Guantanamo North, others have been released on bail and are currently under house arrest and electronic surveillance (Makin 2007; Shephard and Barnes 2007: A1; Struck 2007: A10; Austen 2007).

Perhaps not surprisingly, neither the ATA nor the use of security certificates was up for discussion at the Munk Centre's event in June 2006. They did, however, dominate the subsequent panel discussion at Ryerson University, as did systemic racism and Islamophobia experienced in Toronto schools, workforce and everyday life. For Rocco Galati, a defence lawyer for some of the terror suspects; race, immigration and multiculturalism isn't the main issue. Rather, the arrests were 'a political show trial to test Canadians' resistance to the installation of a police state' (author's own conference notes). While this may indeed be so, at the same time this police state called Canada is highly racialized. Drawing on Agamben, panellist Sherene Razack from the University of Toronto emphasized that the arrests of the 17 were concurrent with the use of security certificates, renewal of the ATA, and Stephen Harper's upping of support for Canada's presence in Afghanistan; all of which authorize the suspension of law (particularly as it regards, or doesn't regard, Muslim bodies). 'Race thinking', said Razack, 'coincides with bureaucracy in states of exception' which began in the colonies when 'European law didn't apply to "barbarians"' (author's own conference notes).

Finally, then, a year and a half after the arrests, Canada's terror suspects, whether formally charged under the ATA or more ambiguously under security certificates, were all still living in state of legal(ized) limbo, or what Agamben calls a juridical void (Agamben 2005: 41–2). For the latter in particular, the Supreme Court decision is not the victory it might at first seem. Indeed, the

Terror time in Toronto   127

striking down of a law which suspends law is itself a suspension as the Court gave Parliament one year to draft new legislation. For some in the media, however, Canada is restoring its status as an exceptional state. A *New York Times* editorial reads:

> The United States was not the only country to respond to the horror of the Sept. 11 terrorist attacks with policies that went much too far in curtailing basic rights and civil liberties in the name of public safety. Now we see that a nation can regain its senses after calm reflection and begin to rein back such excesses, but that heartening news comes from Canada and not the United States.
>
> (*New York Times* 2007)

Or, as the *Star*'s Thomas Walkom put it, 'Canada is on its way to becoming a civilized country again' (Walkom 2007: A1). While acknowledging that the security certificate policy was not fully invalidated, the Court's decision 'does go some way to clearing up a law that has become a searing embarrassment for Canada' (ibid.: A1). Would that Canada's (mythic) reputation as a benevolent nation was all that was at stake.

Notes

1 The author gratefully acknowledges that financial support for this research was received from a grant partly funded by WLU operating funds and partly by the SSHRC Institutional Grant awarded to WLU. Heartfelt gratitude is extended as well to the editors of this volume and participants at the 'London in a Time of Terror' conference; as well as Lisa Taylor, Eve Haque and Jasmin Zine for comments, suggestions and encouragement in writing the final draft.
2 An 18th suspect was arrested later in the summer and four have since had charges dropped. However, since this paper examines the media narratives and academic responses which the initial arrests produced, I retain the term the Toronto 17.
3 Special thanks to my students in CS305 (Cultural Studies) at Wilfrid Laurier for noting the youth moral panic angle.
4 The paragraph recalling prior hasty arrests and unsubstantiated cases was also in the early morning online edition of the *Star*, but curiously absent in subsequent online editions throughout the day of Saturday 3 June.
5 How carefully the *Star*'s editor in chief, Giles Gershon, read the *NY Times* article is questionable, for Gershon is quoted in the *NYT* as expressing his doubts about the promotion of *Star* crime reporter Michelle Shephard to national security issues as '[t]here have been a number of cases she has covered that didn't amount to anything at all'. As the left-leaning *NOW Magazine* points out, 'Defence lawyers should have a field day with that one' (*NOW Magazine* 2006: 17).
6 Of the 121 hate crimes linked directly to 11 September in Canada in 2001, 45 were against Muslims, 20 against Jews and 38 against other groups (Zine 2003).
7 For an extensive treatment on the role of myths of benevolence in propping up the tradition of Canadian peacekeeping see Razack (2004). Also see Jiwani (2006).
8 For pure entertainment value, see Wente (2006).
9 Not only is Toronto not the most multicultural city in the world, it's not even the most multicultural city in Canada. As revealed in the 2006 census, while almost half of the

population of Toronto is foreign-born, Richmond, BC, has the highest foreign-born population at 57 per cent.
10 In a brief submitted to the House of Commons, Amnesty International Canada presented five examples of human rights defenders and activists who would have been considered terrorists by their respective governments under the proposed legislation, including past recipients of international human rights awards. See: www.nooneisillegal.org.
11 For a list of eight cases currently pending and 20 others held, and deported, under security certificates since 1991, see: http://en.wikipedia.org/wiki/Security_certificate.

References

Adams, M. (2007), 'Surprise, Canadian pluralism is working', the *Toronto Star*, 10 November. Online. Available at: www.thestar.com (accessed 11 November 2007).
Action Alert, (2007), press release, 9 February. Online. Available at: www.caf.ca. (accessed 13 February 2007).
Agamben, G. (2005), *State of Exception*, Chicago and London: University of Chicago Press.
Austen, I. (2006), 'In bomb plot news coverage, a Toronto newspaper shines', *New York Times*, 5 June.
—— (2007), 'Canadian court limits detention in terror cases', *New York Times*, 24 February 24. Online. Available at: www.nytimes.com (accessed 26 February 2007).
—— and Johnston, D. (2006), '17 held in plot to bomb sites in Ontario', *New York Times*, 4 June. Online. Available at: www.nytimes.com (accessed 4 June 2006).
Cook Dube, R. (2006), 'Canada faces "jihad generation"', *Christian Science Monitor*, 6 June. Online. Available at: www.csmonitor.com (accessed 17 October 2006).
CTV News. Online. Available at: www.ctv.ca/servlet/ArticleNews/story/CTVNews/20071202/immigrant_census_071202/20071202.
Day, R. J. F. (2002), *Multiculturalism and the History of Canadian Diversity*, Toronto: University of Toronto Press.
Diebel, L. (2006), 'Police put on a "good spectacle"', the *Toronto Star*, 5 June. Online. Available at: www.thestar.com (accessed 5 June 2006).
Dobrota, A. (2006), 'Portion of law on terror struck down', *Globe and Mail*, 25 October: A1.
Fortier, C. S. (2006), 'Off-balance? Security, anti-terrorism and rights in Canada after 11 September', 15 June. Online. Available at: http://toronto.nooneisillegal.org (accessed 26 June 2006).
Globe and Mail (2006), 'Arrests make headlines around the world', 4 June.
Government of Canada (2008). Online. Available at: www.pch.gc.ca/progs/multi/inclusive_e.dfm?nav=2 (accessed 5 January 2008).
—— (n.d.). Online. Available at: www.parl.gc.ca/LEGISINFO/index.asp?Language=e&chamber=n&startlist=a&endlist=z&session=9&type=0&scope=i&query=2981&list=toc-1.
Grassby, A. (1984), *The Tyranny of Prejudice*, Melbourne: A. E. Press.
Hage, G. (2000), *White Nation: Fantasies of White Supremacy in a Multicultural Society*, New York and London: Routledge.
—— (2006), 'Warring Societies (and Intellectuals)', *Transforming Cultures eJournal*, 1(1) (March).
Hayes, D. (2004), 'Fear of (and fascination with) a black planet: the relocation of rap by white non-urban youth', *Topia: Canadian Journal of Cultural Studies* (Fall), 72.

Homes Not Bombs. Online. Available at: www.homesnotbombs.ca (accessed 3 January 2008).

Jiwani, Y. (2006), *Discourses of Denial: Mediations of Race, Gender and Violence*, Vancouver and Toronto: University of British Columbia Press.

Jones, K. (2006), 'Canadian government, media use alleged terrorist plot to push right-wing agenda', *World Socialist Website*, 7 June. Online. Available at: www.wsws.org/articles/2006/jun2006/cana-07j_prn.shtml (accessed 20 June 2006).

Kassamali, S. and Ahmad, U. (2006), ' Multiculturalism, the "Toronto 17", and the national imaginary', *The Peak: Simon Frazer University's Student Newspaper*, 123(7), 19 June.

Makin, K. (2007), 'Court puts security certificates in limbo', *Globe and Mail*, 24 February.

New York Times (2007), 'Canada's move to restore rights', Editorial, 27 February. Online. Available at: www.nytimes.com (accessed 27 February 2007).

Ng, W. (2006), (Canadian Labour Congress) Ryerson University panel discussion, 23 June.

NOW Magazine (2006), 'Reality check: terror in the details', 25(41), 8–14 June: 14.

O'Neill, J. and Mayeda, A. (2007), 'MPs reject extending anti-terror provision', *Ottawa Citizen*, 27 February. Online. Available at: www.canwest.com (accessed 27 February 2007).

Patrick, K. (2006), 'Panelists agree multiculturalism not linked to terror', *National Post*, 13 June.

'Project Threadbare'. Online. Available at: www.threadbare.tyo.ca (accessed 25 November 2006).

Razack, S. (2004), *Dark Nights and White Threats: The Somalia Affair, Peacekeeping, and the New Imperialism*, Toronto: University of Toronto Press.

Shane, S. (2006), 'Canadian border proves difficult to secure', *New York Times*, 5 June. Online. Available at: www.nytimes.com (accessed 5 June 2006).

Shephard, M. and Barnes, T. (2007), 'Men denied fair hearing, court rules', *Toronto Star*, 24 February, 24: A1, A10.

Struck, D. (2007), 'Jailing without trial rejected in Canada', *Washington Post*, 24 February: A10.

Teotonio, I. (2007), 'Homegrown terror case goes to trial', *Toronto Star*, 24 September.

Tyler, T. (2007), 'Lawyers can't stop decision to go straight to trial', *Toronto Star*, 25 September. Online. Availble HTTP: <thestar.com (accessed 29 September 2007).

Walkom, T. (2007), 'Terror trial proceedings troubling', *Toronto Star*, 25 September.

Walcott, R. (2003), *Black Like Who?: Writing Black Canada*, Toronto: Insomniac Press.

Wente, M. (2006), 'Another day in the life of a burka-bashing white oppressor', *Globe and Mail*, 15 June: A19.

Zine, J. (2003), 'Dealing with September 12: the challenge of anti-Islamophobia education', *Orbit*, 33(3).

7 Response before the event
On forgetting the war on terror

Louise Amoore

> On the streets of London, there is no such thing as a war on terror.
> (Macdonald 2007)

> We use this data to *focus on* behavior, not race and ethnicity. In fact, what it allows us to do is move beyond crude profiling based on prejudice, and look at conduct and communication and actual behavior as a way of determining who we need to take a closer look at.
> (Chertoff 2007a: 6)

Introduction: 'there is no war on terror'

In January 2007, the British Director of Public Prosecutions, Ken Macdonald, declared the 'war on terror' to be a 'dangerous concept', making the case that 'the fight against terrorism on the streets of Britain is not a war but the prevention of crime' (Macdonald 2007: 2). Other British authorities rapidly followed this example, warning of the provocative political implications of the concept and favouring instead a turn to counter terror as the prevention of crime. In a speech to the US Center on International Cooperation, International Development Secretary Hilary Benn argued that 'in the UK we do not use the phrase "war on terror", because we can't win by military means alone' (Benn 2007: 1). One year on, the UK Home Office had produced a 'phrase book' for civil servants, calling for them to reject the phrase 'war on terror' and adopt a language of 'assisting vulnerable communities in building resilience against violent extremism and criminal murder' (*Guardian* 2008).

What is at stake, then, in responding to a post-7 July London by forgetting the war on terror? For those who would forget the concept, there appear to be a number of issues at stake. One is that for them the 'fight against terrorism on the streets of Britain', so readily identified by Macdonald, is not strictly to be considered a 'war', nor even a militarization of public space. Another is that the way of governing security in a post-7 July context has shifted to the deployment of crime and criminal acts. Thus, for Macdonald, 'the men who killed the victims were not soldiers, but fantasists, narcissists, murderers and criminals and need to be responded to in that way' (Macdonald 2007: 3). Perhaps above all, though, the cultivation of a 'post-war-on-terror' language is thought to diffuse the direct targeting of young Muslim men, rendering this an evidence-based fight against crime and not a racially profiled war on terror. Thus, for the Home Office officials newly equipped with their phrase book, it apparently becomes possible to 'talk to Muslim communities about the nature of the terrorist threat without implying they are to blame' (*Guardian* 2008: 2).

There can be little doubt that the idea of forgetting the 'war on terror' is extraordinarily seductive. Indeed, in the immediate weeks following 11 September, Jacques Derrida considered that 'the violence that has now been unleashed is not the result of "war"', the expression 'war on terrorism being one of the most confused' (Derrida 2003: 101). The task of philosophy, he suggested, was to deconstruct the distinction between war and terror and to 'analyze the interests such an abuse of rhetoric actually serve' (ibid.: 101). And yet, is it sufficient to deconstruct the distinction between war and terror? Must we not also attend to their very conjunction, to the work that they do when they are pulled into an irrevocable pairing? And might it be the case that the work done by the conjunction of 'war' and 'terror' is precisely extended under cover of a feigned dissolution of the concept? Could it be that to forget in this context is to respond in a way that creates space for the elaboration of the violent practices carried out in the name of the war on terror? If we authorize the claim 'this is not a war on terror', then do we also make it possible to say 'this is not profiling, racism or prejudice'?

Consider, for example, four months on from the British authorities' collective forgetting of war on terror, the statement of US Secretary for Homeland Security Michael Chertoff, addressing an audience at Johns Hopkins University after the conviction of the British 'fertilizer bombers'. Making the case for a pre-emptive fight against terror, Chertoff argued that the mining of airline passenger data represents a 'move beyond crude profiling based on prejudice, to look at conduct and communication and actual behaviour' (Chertoff 2007a). Of course, in many ways practices such as this are indeed war-like, at least in so far as they conduct 'a continuation of war by other means', the appeal to technology and expertise rendering the violent force of war somewhat ordinary and invisible (Foucault 1976/2003: 16). 'The role of political power', writes Foucault, 'is perpetually to use a sort of silent war to reinscribe the relationship of force, and to reinscribe it in institutions, economic inequalities, language, and even the bodies of individuals' (Foucault 1976/2003: 16–17). Understood in this way, to forget the war-like qualities of the practices of the war on terror is potentially also to conceal the reinscription of violence. In fact, Michael Chertoff's claim that we can forget prejudice and racism in the techno-science of algorithmic profiling does indeed conceal a stark choice. To reject what would become the routinized practices of the war on terror (risk scoring of all air passengers, to 'single out those potentially dangerous people'), he said, would be to accept instead the withdrawal of the visa waiver from all British citizens 'of Pakistani origin' (Chertoff 2007b).

In this chapter I suggest that an ethical response – one that takes responsibility to be the heart of what it means to respond – may not proceed by forgetting the war on terror. Instead it must engage in remembering, reiterating, revealing the very violences that are perpetuated in the name of the war on terror. It must consider the modes of sovereign authority that are authorized by the process of forgetting – the peculiar assemblage of state security, technology and expertise that wages a different kind of war, one that focuses on identifying norm and anomaly, visualizing suspicion and threat ahead of time, seeking to pre-empt the unknown future. Understood in this way, the appearance of the cessation of war in favour of crime actually deepens the logics of a war on terror, following as it does a genealogy of 'war on drugs' and 'war on crime' (Simon 2008). In problematizing the act of forgetting the war on terror, though, I do not wish to diminish the political potential that the idea of forgetting may itself contain. I will outline a possible alternative ethics of forgetting, one that forgets what we have come to see as 'normal', settled out and secured, and attends instead to that which is always forgotten and slips away from our attention. Put simply, many of the contemporary violences of the war on terror depend upon the routinized norms of daily life and, crucially, on the identification of deviation or transgression of norm. An ethics of forgetting capable of responding to this would need to dwell on what we have forgotten how to see – the surprising, the affective and the unexpected that exposes the calculation itself and the violences within.

Projected futures: responding before the event

Among the careful plastic-windowed advertising posters on the London Underground – 'register for Oystercard and get 10% off in London's museums and galleries'; enter an art competition and design a future Tube station; download coupons to your mobile phone – the Metropolitan Police Anti-terrorist hotline posters call us to attention: 'if you suspect it, report it'; 'look out for unusual or suspicious activity'; 'use all your senses'; 'you are that someone'. In so many ways already part of the prosaic and unnoticed sensory backdrop to the daily commute, the specific call for attention at the homefront of the war on terror asks us to single out, from the cacophony of background noise in public spaces, that which demands a closer *look*, that which is out of the *ordinary*.

In many ways, there is nothing at all novel or significant in the appeal to 'ordinary ways of life' – that which is an all but forgotten backdrop in the milieu of daily life – as a means of responding to the uncertainty of terrorist acts. Recall in the aftermath of 11 September how the routines of daily life were called up as a source of resilience. 'We were told to shop', says Susan Willis, 'shop to show we are patriotic Americans. Shop to show our resilience over death and destruction' (Willis 2003: 122). The London bombings on 7 July met with similar celebrations of the 'vibrant and resilient city, getting back to normal, going back to work, getting back on the Tube' (Blair 2005). And yet, how is it that ways of life come to be known and recognized as such? How is a 'normal' way of life settled out, and how does it identify deviations from norm? What does the call to attentiveness to 'conduct' or 'behaviour' ask us to pay attention to? How do we know what it is that we should pay attention to? What has to be discarded or forgotten in order for us to be attentive to the 'unusual'?

As the contemporary global economy has sought to incorporate practices of attention, perception and affective judgement ever mode closely into circuits of production and consumption – promoting touch-button 'interactivity', placing the screen in the palm of the hand, engaging playfully with the consumer – so, at the same time the state's security practices have sought to mobilize culture broadly defined – ways of life, looking out for the out of the ordinary, sifting the patterns of life left in transit or consumer transactions, providing hotlines for people's reported unease or suspicion. Thus, London Metropolitan police's 'if you suspect it' campaigns offer the transaction receipt as one fragment of a picture of a person that could be built; the mobile phone images and video clips from the 2005 London bombings are translated from 'careless cinema' into the data-driven analysis of actionable intelligence (Sinclair 2005); the flotsam residue of our travel bookings on global reservations databases are extradited to the US authorities.[1] Across these apparently disparate domains there is a resonance in ever more finite targeting of behaviours, conduct, the actions and inferred intentions of people. Someone as yet unknown is apparently identified and made visible, literally 'brought to attention', singled out and immobilized while all around him moves on. Like the screened visualizations of migrants and travellers that allow the 'border guard to become the last and not the first line of defence', or the London Underground pedestrian surveillance systems that 'mean you don't have to watch the screen all the time', how we see, what we remember, to what we give our attention, takes on renewed significance (Department of Homeland Security 2004; *New Scientist* 2003).

As art historian Jonathan Crary has argued, the significance of attention and our attentiveness to the world is not confined to visual culture, but rather to entire ways of governing life, culture and the modern social world. Regimes of attentiveness, then, are not 'primarily concerned with looking ... but rather with the construction of conditions that individuate, immobilize, and separate subjects, even within a world in which mobility and circulation are ubiquitous' (Crary 1999: 74). In this sense, the question of to what we pay attention, what or who we remember or forget is part of a broader set of practices that work to divide, differentiate and isolate people, one from an/other. As I have argued elsewhere, the interface of the screen – whether windscreen, mobile phone or PDA screen, computer screen, or security 'pre-screening' – has become an important site where sovereign decisions (who belongs to the nation, who is dangerous to 'us', what the 'other' looks like) are made (Amoore 2007). 'The screen', writes Kaja Silverman, 'is the site at which social and historical difference enters the field of vision' (Silverman 1996: 135). It is not only that the screen becomes the mode of visual communication of difference, though of course this is important. Instead, the screen itself enters into the constitution and performance of difference. So, when the British government rejects the US move to deny visas to Britons of Pakistani 'origin', but accepts instead 'screening at their end, sharing intelligence with the Americans' and 'deporting Britons who failed screening once they arrived at an airport in the US' (*New York Times* 2006a), they defer a decision based on racial categories into a screened calculation based on ever more finite classifications of difference. The computer screen, understood this way, as Anne Friedberg has shown, 'is both a "page" and a "window", at once opaque and transparent'. The flat surface of the screen, the 'page' that represents the calculation in this instance, is given depth by the layers and leaves of data, the multiple other screens and screenings that may appear transparent to the viewer but remain opaque to the person who is displayed there. The surface of the screen has, then 'a deep virtual reach to archives and databases, indexed and accessible with barely the stroke of a finger' (Friedberg 2006: 19).

The screened forms of attention that are dominating contemporary homeland security practice function through a process of 'screening out'. In essence, they function precisely by authorizing the forgetting of that which is the norm, filtering out large quantities of data, multiple sources of stimuli, and classifying that which will appear on the surface. It is, of course, only pixelated fragments that enter the visualization, vast quantities of data simultaneously falls out of the calculation, becomes 'background noise' and is screened out. In many ways this focusing of attention via the annulment of other sensory data is integral to the histories of practices of perception:

> Whether it is how we behave in front of the luminous screen of a computer or how we experience a performance in an opera house, how we accomplish certain productive or creative tasks or how we more passively perform routine activities like driving a car or watching television, we are in a dimension of contemporary experience that requires that we effectively cancel out or exclude from consciousness much of our immediate environment.
>
> (Crary 1999: 1)

For Crary, the way that we have come to focus our attention on particular items, tasks or people cannot be understood without also acknowledging the processes that cancel out, forget or exclude other stimuli. When we attend to one set of sensory data, in order to make it count we necessarily discount other sources. When the call is to look for that which is abnormal, out of the ordinary, or when the data on an individual is sorted according to patterns of normality and deviation, most of the detail behind the data is cancelled out. Conduct and behaviour that could, if attended to or seen differently, be an integral part of the 'norm', becomes part of the conduct and behaviour designated deviant from norm and rendered suspicious. Thus, what might be expected to be 'normal' patterns of travel or financial transactions for a British citizen with family in Pakistan – travel to visit relatives, wire transfers of monetary gifts, telephone calls – will, within the screened attentiveness to passenger data, be designated suspicious.

The practice of focusing attention on that which appears as anomalous – and the necessary annulling of other ways of seeing that entails – is a form of targeting that is prominent in the war by other means that is indeed being fought on our city streets. To target in this sense is to position in the sights, to identify in movement someone or something threatening to the normal ways of life that continue immediately around it. As Samuel Weber describes it, this is a seizing of a 'target of opportunity', an intervention that identifies unknown and mobile enemies in advance:

> However different the war on terror was going to be from traditional wars, with their relatively well-defined enemies, it would still involve one of the basic mechanisms of traditional hunting and combat, in however modified and modernized a form: namely 'targeting'. The enemy would have to be *identified* and *localized*, *named* and *depicted*, in order to be made into an accessible target.... None of this was, per se, entirely new. What *was*, however, was the mobility, indeterminate structure, and unpredictability of the spatio-temporal *medium* in which such targets had to be sited.... In theatres of conflict that had become highly mobile and changeable, 'targets' and 'opportunity' were linked as never before.
>
> (Weber 2005: 3–4; emphasis in original)

The *identification, localization, naming* and *depiction* of mobile targets is, in this war by other means, conducted in and through daily life, in advance of any possible future strike or intervention. The targeting of unknown people is, put simply, becoming a matter of both positioning in the sights (targeting and identifying) and visualizing through a projected line of sight (pre-empting, making actionable). In this mode of targeting, even the most overloaded sensory domains are drawn into apparent management: the busy and noisy border crossing is stilled on the border guard's screened list of 'selectees' to single out for further attention; the crowded subway ticket hall quietly selects anomalous smartcard data and intercepts at the barrier; the radio frequency identification technology (RFID) data from a football fan's swipecard transmits an automatic signal to the local police. From the pre-emptive identification of a person is derived the possibility to act on that person. 'Ideally, I would like to know', said Michael Chertoff, 'did Mohamed Atta get his ticket paid on the same credit card. That would be a huge thing. And I really would like to know that in advance, because that would allow us to identify an unknown terrorist' (*New York Times* 2006b).

Put simply, then, the response to the events of 11 September and 7 July in particular has, in effect, been to authorize multiple responses *in advance of* uncertain events. Most often derived from the residue of daily life left in the reported suspicions of citizens, and in the patterns of travel, financial and consumer transactions (Amoore and de Goede 2005; 2008), the practices appear to make possible the conversion of ex post facto evidence in the war on terror into a judgement made *before the event*. The significant point here is that diverse data from daily life, like specified 'pixels' in a digital image, are drawn together in association, producing a recognisable whole. It is not strictly, then, a picture or a snapshot of a person that is taken – an image from a specific and limited temporal standpoint – rather, it is a projected line of sight that seeks to capture the 'unknown unknowns'.[2] As Friedrich Kittler has argued compellingly, projections are produced from fragments of visual data, from individually isolated characteristics that are then selected, differentiated and reintegrated into a visual whole (Kittler 1997). Of course, gaps persist between the lines that join the pixilated dots. These gaps, though, are filled with mobile and projected images that produce a seamless whole. Describing the illusion of a moving picture that is produced in the cinematic process of projecting still frames, Anne Friedberg suggests 'for motion to be reconstituted, its virtual rendition relies on a missing element, a perceptual process that depends on the darkness between the frames' (Friedberg 2006: 92; see also Friedberg 2002). To state my argument simply here, the vigilant visuality of suspicion requires some gaps and invisibilities, it positively relies upon cultivated practices of forgetting.

In pre-emptive homeland security practices such as those I have discussed here, responsibility appears only in the guise of responsible and vigilant citizenship. An appeal is made to the body of knowledge of daily life that creates a prosaic expertise in making security judgements. As a result, the response before the event can never be a responsible response, for it can never decide in the absence of algorithmic formulations of risk and threat. From the algorithmic 'decision trees' that appear on the screens of the anti-terror hotline operator, to the pre-screened visualizations of the border guard, in fact no decisions are taken at all, they are only deferred into a pre-programmed calculation. A decision cannot, as Jacques Derrida understands it, be determined by the acquisition of knowledge, for then it is not a decision but 'simply the application of a body of knowledge of, at the very least, a rule or norm' (Derrida 1994: 37). An apparent decision taken on the basis of what is 'seen' evidentially, via the calculations of experts, or in the screened results of algorithmic visualization, is not a decision at all. 'The decision, if there is to be one', writes Derrida, 'must advance towards a future which is not known, which cannot be anticipated' (Derrida 1994: 37). To respond by seeking to anticipate an uncertain future is, at least for Derrida, to respond without responsibility. A responsibility worthy of the name would need to 'answer to the other, before the other' (Derrida 1995: 26) in a way that is 'beyond knowledge', for if it cannot then 'there is no decision, no responsibility, no event' (Derrida 2003: 118).

To put the argument simply at this point, the Home Office civil servants' 'forgetting' of the war on terror is a tolerance of the other made possible only by the deferral of decisions into techno-scientific calculations. While governmental programmes such as passenger pre-screening or anti-terror hotlines may appear to visualize a picture of a person that is culturally nuanced – every minute and prosaic 'behaviour', every aspect of a way of life potentially becoming a part of the classification – they actually efface difference in their drive for identification. They may appear to be peculiarly dependent on culture or 'ways of life', and yet they make a representation of culture that attends too (and makes us attentive to) some aspects of sameness and difference, while always failing to respond in a way that confronts the agonistic difference at the heart of political life (Connolly 1991: 170–1). The claims that this war by other means is not akin to war itself – that, indeed, it displaces targeting, racial profiling and other prejudicial judgements, simply cannot be upheld. It is always through the visualization of the identity of the 'other' that the sanctity of 'we the nation', 'we the people' is sustained. As Connolly puts it, the 'self reassurance of identity' is made 'through the construction of otherness' and this otherness is readily adopted as the 'definition of difference' (ibid.: 9). The algorithmic mode of attentiveness becomes the 'multicultural'[3] society's technology of choice precisely because it gives the appearance of living alongside difference, of deciding without prejudice – 'we are interested in behaviour not background'; 'this is not racial profiling'; 'we prefer screening to visa restrictions'; 'no more border guards taking decisions based on appearance' – when in fact it categorizes, isolates and annexes in ways that conceal the violence inside the glossy wrapper of techno-science.

There is an intensely important political question at stake in how to respond to the dominance of security practices carried out in the name of the war on terror. We are faced with a technique of governing that makes humane, responsible or ethical ways of responding extraordinarily difficult. Consider, for example, Waverly Cousin, former police officer and one of the 43,000 'screeners' employed by the US Transportation Security Administration to deploy the 'screening passengers by observation technique' (SPOT) at airports, ports and border crossings. 'The observation of human behaviour is probably the hardest thing to defeat', explains Waverley, 'you just don't know what I am going to see' (*New York Times* 2006a). We do not know what he is going to see because the 'SPOT' calculation, while it engages all of the time in pre-emptively targeting what Dana Cuff calls an 'object of interest' (Cuff 2003), is itself always forgotten, invisible and never an object of interest. Because every ordinary everyday act itself becomes a means of settling out the norm and identifying the other that is anomalous, a responsible decision that 'advances where it cannot see', is particularly elusive. What becomes important politically, I want to suggest in my concluding section, is the capacity precisely to forget the 'body of knowledge' – to forget norm and suspicion, and to remember the surprising, the unanticipated, that which we thought we could never see.

Remembering what was forgotten: responsibility before the event

'Man's struggle against power', writes Milan Kundera in his novel *The Book of Laughter and Forgetting*, 'is the struggle of memory against forgetting' (Kundera 1979: 18). For Kundera, the problem of forgetting is both intensely personal and prosaic – 'forgetting is a form of death forever present within life' (Kundera 1980: 1) – and necessarily also political – 'forgetting is the great problem of politics'. The problem of what we forget and what we attend to is a perennial problem of life and, for Kundera, it is mirrored by a politics of what he calls 'organized forgetting' that seeks to govern what is held in the collective memory of nation or populace. In his many works set against the backdrop of the experiences of life under a Stalinist regime, Kundera exposes the co-presence of practices of forgetting within memory itself, and yet for him it is the struggles of personal memory that have the political potential to resist organized forgetting.

What I want to explore in this section is the question of whether certain practices of forgetting, precisely because they are forever present within life itself, can be politically productive. That is to say, could it be that the 'forgetting of the self' that Kundera and others identify with totalitarian politics, may also always already contain the possibility of a decentred subject and a seeing of the world anew? If, as I have argued, it is the case that regimes of attentiveness in security practice rely upon a knowledge of what is normal/anomalous; safe/dangerous; ordinary/suspicious, then this itself is a form of organized forgetting that allows the targeting and screening out to take place. Could it be, though, that a possibility for an ethics of forgetting may reside precisely in a forgetting of ourselves in relation to the other, a forgetting that troubles the 'architectures of enmity' that delineate self from other, citizen from stranger (Shapiro 1997)? To forget oneself in this way would, as Judith Butler has put it 'tear us from ourselves', literally to be taken outside of oneself and 'become implicated in lives that are not our own' (Butler 2004: 24–5). Such a form of forgetting implies a state of mind and consciousness that by-passes reasoned calculation and confronts the absolute unknowability of the future.

In the tradition of social theories of visual culture, the co-presence of states of reverie, daydreaming and enchantment within regimes of looking, paying attention, separating and dividing are well acknowledged. As Jonathan Crary has argued, though industrialization and the market economy saw 'perception function in a way that insures a subject is productive, manageable, and predictable, able to be socially integrated and adaptive', simultaneously the management of attention reached limits characterized by more 'creative states of deep absorption and daydreaming' (Crary 1999: 4–5). So, while the conduct of commerce and trade required particular attentive habits, it stimulated also the more creative and subjective ways of seeing that flourished in the arts (ibid.: 52). An 'absorbed attentiveness', writes Crary, is not only a 'necessary part of the individual's functioning within a modern world of economic facts and quantities', but is always also essential for the 'creative exceeding of the limits of individuality' (ibid.: 53). Because relations of power inextricably contain the possibility of resistance, there could never be a fully efficient attentive subject whose attention to the world is entirely amenable to management. Indeed, as Crary has it, 'the more one investigated, the more attention was shown to contain within itself the condition for its own undoing' (ibid.: 45–6).

It is not only in concepts from the arts, but also in the *practices of artistic intervention* that we find a potentially valuable ethics and responsibility in how we pay attention to or forget ourselves and other people. The embedding of technologies into everyday objects; the visualization of unknown futures; the screened projection of mobile bodies; the economies of the mundane and the surprising in public space: these are not novel ideas to many contemporary artists. Indeed, far from focusing on trivial and transient events, innovative artistic practice engages in a deeply historical process of reflection on perspective, human subjectivity, and cognition. Put simply, the 'resonances' that so many of our contemporary philosophers, social theorists and political economists are observing across science, technology, politics and culture, have long been at the heart of leading edge artistic interventions. I will focus here on three areas where I consider artist interventions to open up clear space for questions of ethical forgetting and political responsibility in the face of technical depoliticization.

Modes of attentiveness in contemporary homeland security practice, as I have argued, are particularly dependent on logics that designate anomaly on the basis of a screening of the norm. The cultural practices of the visual arts precisely invert the logic of 'looking out for the out of the ordinary' – that which transgresses the norm – in order to identify danger, suggesting instead that the act of being surprised by the extraordinary can make us see the norm anew. Even in quite mainstream installations of temporary artworks in public spaces, there is an emphasis on deploying surprise as a means of seeing daily life differently, *remembering what was forgotten*. In the spaces of the London Underground, for example, Platform for Art has confronted, to a degree, the post-7 July fear of the unexpected, inviting international artists to install their work on the Piccadilly line stations, platforms and trains. In the *Thin Cities* project, the artist's installations were produced in 'unexpected places on the Tube network', offering new ways of seeing the daily commute, 'revealing new perspectives on London' and 'promoting greater understanding' (Platform for Art 2006).

In this sense, artistic interventions have capacity to call the norm into question, reminding us of what we do not pay attention to, creating what Tom Mitchell says 'looks like a picture of something we could never see' (Mitchell 2005: 260). This is, argues Crary, 'experimental activity' that 'involves the creation of unanticipated spaces and environments in which our visual and intellectual habits are challenged and disrupted' (Crary 2003: 7). In contrast to an attentiveness that tries to anticipate on the basis of the fragments that are seen, then, some installation artwork in public space offers us new ways of attending to the very images we had already screened out as normal. American artist Rozalinda Borcila's *Geography Lessons*, for example, seeks to 'intervene in apparently controlled spaces' that are 'policed through technologies of visualization and information management' (Borcila 2006). Making 'counter-surveillance' videos of airport security and urban transport systems (and deported from the Netherlands when she video-recorded Schipol airport's security), Borcila projects her multiple screen films, rendering extraordinary what have become the forgotten rituals of searching, removing shoes, interrogating, detaining.

The question of responsibility in attentive practices of security arises only in terms of the responsibility for vigilance, for paying attention and not becoming distracted. As I have argued, following Derrida, there is an absence of responsibility in the sense that these forms of attentiveness seek to anticipate, to foresee an unknown future on the basis of an algorithmic calculation. If Derrida is correct, then a responsible decision would have to 'advance where it cannot see', confronting the difficulty and undecidability of all decisions, and recognising that calculation cannot substitute for a judgement that may have to be made in the absence of pre-programmed information (Derrida 1992; see also Derrida 2003). Artistic interventions, I want to suggest, embody the potential to confront the political difficulty of decision and to intervene in ways that are 'unanticipatory', advancing where they cannot see.

What is particularly interesting about artistic practices that engage with some of the emergent technologies of security, is that they do not seek out a *resolution* to the political difficulties posed. Instead, they create a plural space for the articulation of difference, 'integrating technological tools into plural zones of creative activity' and providing ways of imaging the problem outside of narratives of security or consumption (Crary 2003: 9). By way of example, consider New York artist Meghan Trainor, whose current work integrates RFID tags – ubiquitous in the visualization of consumers and security 'threats' – into public installations and performances. The installation 'lets viewers encounter RFID tags in an application outside of its common commercial or surveillance context', explains Trainor, 'allowing for different reactions to its current and expanding ubiquity in our lives' (Trainor 2004). Indeed, for Trainor and her collaborator Michelle Anderson it is the role of art to 'make you forget what you thought you had learned about the world'.[4]

Rather than seek to resolve the paradoxes and contradictions of these technological forms of attentiveness, then, the artworks function 'as catalyst' to the exposure of paradox and contradiction (De Oliveira 2003). They remind us that within apparently disciplined and securitized regimes of attention and forgetting there are also interstitial spaces of distraction, enchantment or reverie that may work against prejudicial and individualized practices. 'To be enchanted', writes Jane Bennett, 'is to be struck and shaken by the extraordinary that lives amid the familiar and the everyday' (Bennett 2001: 4). Bennett argues that 'joy can propel ethics' in the sense that the magic of the future and the promise of life not yet lived is kept open (ibid.: 156). Where calculative and pre-emptive orientations to the future annul the possibility of the unanticipated and surprising, to momentarily forget oneself and be enchanted by life is to accept the unknowability of the future, even where it may contain dangers and fears.

Finally, the artistic interventions that seek to recover what is forgotten in our lives has, as its raison d'être, a form of critique that runs 'against the grain' of dominant knowledge about how we pay attention to the world. In Edward Said's last book before his death, he documents the 'late' work of visionary artists and musicians as not that which has 'harmony and resolution', but that which embodies 'intransigence, difficulty, and unresolved contradiction' (Said 2006: 14). In contrast to a line of sight that sees clearly and rationally, then, art against the grain is that which transgresses prevailing modes of thought in order to see the world differently. Thomas Keenan conjures a comparable alternative critical cut against the grain when he speaks of politics 'on the bias', where there is 'a withdrawal of the rules or the knowledge on which we might rely to take our decisions for us' (Keenan 1997: 166). Here we find an ethics of forgetting that does indeed proceed where it cannot look ahead or foresee: to forget the rules, logics and calculations on which we have relied to make judgements and to confront fully the difficulties and impossibilities of political life.

Notes

1 Reservations databases Amadeus, Galileo and Sabre, used by the major airlines and hotel and other travel groups, are now the conduit for the routine submission of passenger data to the US authorities before a flight departs for the US.
2 In a speech to NATO in 2002, Donald Rumsfeld pondered the importance of taking decisions on the basis of an absence of evidence, of taking into account the 'unknown unknowns':

> The message is that there are no 'knowns'. There are things we know that we know. There are known unknowns. That is to say there are things we know that we don't know. But there are also unknown unknowns. There are things we don't know we don't know [....] There is another way to phrase that and that is the absence of evidence is not evidence of absence.
>
> (Rumsfeld 2002)

Hence, the sense that attention is to be paid to that which is not seen, has not been seen, but can nonetheless be 'projected'.
3 As Slavoj Žižek has it:

> multiculturalism is a disavowed, inverted, self-referential form of racism, a 'racism with a distance' – it respects the Other's identity, conceiving of the Other as a self-enclosed 'authentic' community towards which he, the multiculturalist, maintains a distance rendered possible by his privileged universal position.
>
> (2006: 171)

Thus, the decision based on a risk calculation is precisely a self-referential form of racism, a racism that disavows itself by stripping out its own role in identifying the Other that is threatening and dangerous.
4 Interview with Meghan Trainor and Michelle Anderson, New York City, 1 November 2007.

References

Amoore, L. (2007), 'Vigilant Visualities: The Watchful Politics of the War on Terror', *Security Dialogue* 38(2): 139–56.
Amoore, L. and de Goede, M. (2005), 'Governance, Risk and Dataveillance in the War on Terror', *Crime, Law and Social Change* 43(2): 149–73.
—— (2008), 'Introduction: Governing by Risk in the War on Terror', in L. Amoore and M. de Goede (eds), *Risk and the War on Terror*, London: Routledge.
Benn, H. (2007), 'The Global War on Terror', speech delivered to New York University's Centre for International Cooperation, 16 April.

Bennett, J. (2001), *The Enchantment of Modern Life: Attachments, Crossings, Ethics*, Princeton, NJ: Princeton University Press.
Blair, T. (2005), *Statement to Parliament on the London Bombings*, 11 July. Online. Available at: www.number-10.gov.uk/output/Page7903.asp (accessed March 2008).
Borcila, R. (2006), 'Geography Lessons', Online. Available at: www.borcila.tk/geographie/index.html (accessed April 2007).
Butler, J. (2004), *Precarious Life*, London: Verso.
Chertoff, M. (2007a), 'Remarks by Secretary Michael Chertoff to the Johns Hopkins University Paul H. Nitze School of Advanced International Studies', 3 May. Online. Available at: www.dhs.gov/xnews/speeches/sp_1178288606838.shtm (accessed May 2007).
—— (2007b), 'US Seeks Closing of Visa Loophole for Britons', *New York Times*, 2 May.
Connolly, W. (1991), *Identity/Difference: Democratic Negotiations of Political Paradox*, Minneapolis, MN: University of Minnesota Press.
Crary, J. (1999), *Suspensions of Perception: Attention, Spectacle, and Modern Culture*, Cambridge MA: MIT Press.
—— (2003), 'Foreword', in N. De Oliveira, N. Oxley and M. Perry (eds), *Installation Art in the New Millennium: The Empire of the Senses*, London: Thames and Hudson.
Cuff, D. (2003), 'Immanent Domain: Pervasive Computing and the Public Realm', *Journal of Architectural Education*: 43–4.
De Oliveira, N. (ed.) (2003), *Installation Art in the New Millennium: The Empire of the Senses*, London: Thames and Hudson.
Department of Homeland Security (2004), 'Homeland Security from the Citizens' Perspective', Washington, DC: Council for Excellence in Government.
Derrida, J. (1992), 'Force of Law: The "Mystical Foundations of Authority"', in D. Cornell, M. Rosenfeld and D. G. Carlson (eds), *Deconstruction and the Possibility of Justice*, London and New York: Routledge.
—— (1994), 'Nietzsche and the Machine' (in conversation with Richard Beardsworth), *Journal of Nietzsche Studies* 7: 7–65.
—— (1995), *The Gift of Death*, Chicago: Chicago University Press.
—— (2003), 'Autoimmunity: real and symbolic suicides', in Giovanni Borradori *Philosophy in a Time of Terror: Dialogues with Jürgen Habermas and Jacques Derrida*, Chicago: Chicago University Press.
Foucault, M. (1976/2003), *Society Must Be Defended: Lectures at the College de France, 1975–76*, London: Penguin.
Friedberg, A. (2002), 'Urban Mobility and Cinematic Visuality', *Journal of Visual Culture* 1(2): 183–204.
—— (2006), *The Virtual Window: From Alberti to Microsoft*, Cambridge, MA: MIT Press.
Guardian (2008), 'Whitehall Draws Up New Rules on Language of War on Terror', 4 February.
Keenan, T. (1997), *Fables of Responsibility: Aberrations and Predicaments in Ethics and Politics*, Stanford, CA: Stanford University Press.
Kittler, F. (1997), *Literature, Media, Information Systems: Essays*, Amsterdam: Arts Limited.
Kundera, M. (1979), *The Book of Laughter and Forgetting*, New York: Alfred Knopf.
—— (1980), 'Philip Roth Interviews Milan Kundera', 30 November. Available at: www.kundera.de (accessed February 2008).

Macdonald, K. (2007), 'There Is No War on Terror in the UK, says DPP', by Lucy Bannerman, *Times*, 24 January. Online. Available at: http://business.timesonline.co.uk/tol/business/law/article1295756.ece (accessed January 2008).

Mitchell, W. J. T. (2005), 'There Are No Visual Media', *Journal of Visual Culture* 4(2): 257–66.

New Scientist (2003), 'Smart Software Linked to CCTV Can Spot Dubious Behaviour', 11 July.

New York Times (2006a), 'Faces Too, Are Searched at US Airports', 17 August: 8.

—— (2006b), 'Officials Seek Broader Access to Airline Data', 23 August: 3.

Platform for Art (2006), *Thin Cities: 100 Years of the Piccadilly Line*, London: Platform for Art.

Rumsfeld, D. (2002), 'Press Conference by US Secretary of Defence Donald Rumsfeld', NATO, Brussels, 6–7 June. Online. Available at: www.nato.int/docu/speech/2002/s020606g.htm (accessed April 2007).

Said, E. (2006), *On Late Style: Music and Literature Against the Grain*, London: Pantheon.

Shapiro, M. (1997), *Violent Cartographies: Mapping Cultures of War*, Minneapolis, MN: University of Minnesota Press.

Silverman, K. (1996), *The Threshold of the Visible World*, New York: Routledge.

Simon, J. (2008), 'Choosing Our Wars, Transforming Governance: Crime, Cancer, Terror', in L. Amoore and M. de Goede (eds), *Risk and the War on Terror*, London: Routledge.

Sinclair, I. (2005), 'The Theatre of the City', *Guardian*, 14 July.

Trainor, M. (2004), exhibition notes accompanying RFID Project, part of the 2004 Winter Show of the Interactive Telecommunications Program at the Tisch School of Art, New York University: http://itp.nyu.edu/show/winter2004/_projectdetail.php?project_id=29. (The full exhibition page is unavailable.)

Weber, S (2005), *Targets of Opportunity: On the Militarization of Thinking*. New York: Fordham University Press.

Willis, S. (2003), 'Old Glory', in F. Lentricchia and S. Hauerwas (eds), *Dissent from the Homeland*, Durham, NC: Duke University Press.

Žižek, S. (2006), *The Universal Exception*, London: Continuum.

Part III
Possibilities of response?

8 Cosmopolitanism vs terrorism?
Discourses of ethical possibility before and after 7/7

James Brassett

Introduction[1]

> July 2005 in the UK started with a *strongly positive feel*. On 6 July London won the competition to host the 2012 Olympic Games. A few days earlier the Live 8 concerts had sent an unprecedented powerful message to world leaders about poverty in Africa. On 7 July, G8 leaders were meeting in Gleneagles.
> (*Report of the Official Account of the Bombings in London on July 2005* 2006; emphasis added)

The 'strongly positive feel', that accompanied the Make Poverty History (MPH) campaign to lobby the G8, was clearly interrupted by the events of 7 July 2005. But was this interruption just an unfortunate circumstance? Or can more be read into it? In a recent article, Andrew Linklater remarks that campaigns like MPH provide a clear sign that *cosmopolitanism* 'has become central to the political imagination' in the twenty-first century (Linklater 2007: 19). On 7 July, in the wake of a series of bomb attacks in London, Tony Blair left Gleneagles to be present in London. He held a brief press conference, stating that '[j]ust as it is reasonably clear that this is a terrorist attack, or a series of terrorist attacks, it is also reasonably clear that it is *designed and aimed to coincide with the opening of the G8*' (Blair 2005; emphasis added).

Using 7 July 2005 and, indeed, 11 September 2001 as pivotal moments, this chapter interrogates an evolving relationship between cosmopolitanism and terrorism, via the question of response. How does cosmopolitanism respond to terrorism? What limits does this response contain? How might we go beyond such limits?[2] Far from being mere circumstance, it is argued, the events of 7 July 2005 provide a fulcrum for a discussion of the possibility and *limits* of global ethics, in contested political circumstances.

The discussion and argument proceed below in three sections. The first analyses the responses of specific cosmopolitan authors to the events of 11 September 2001. A brief survey suggests that, for cosmopolitans, international law, democratic international institutions and the alleviation of global poverty form the best response, or strategy, in the context of divisive mainstream discourses. The second then moves to an analysis of the Make Poverty History campaign, as a practical embodiment of cosmopolitan ideas, which can illustrate the possibilities and *limits* of cosmopolitan thinking in political context.

When the London bombings happened, the primary response made by Blair and echoed by campaigners, was that the terrorist attacks were an attack on the G8 reformers, *indeed an attack on cosmopolitanism*. There was an immediate and general lament that the bombers should do it 'today of all days', when MPH and the G8 were actually trying to address the issue of global poverty. But, it is argued, such moralising had the ironic effect of setting up a dichotomy between cosmopolitanism and terrorism. Straightforward oppositions between 'barbaric terrorists', and 'civilised cosmopolitans' served to construct cosmopolitanism as a *coherent and united*, global community. Available tactics were reduced to 'more of the same' – more aid, more global democracy – and assertions of 'moral equivalence' between Bush and 'Terror', such that 'you are either with cosmopolitans or you are with the War on Terror.'

Finally, the third section suggests some ways of thinking beyond such a dichotomy, in order to retain the potential for critical openness in cosmopolitan ethics. With reference to the MPH campaign the argument suggests how we might (re)think the dominant global imaginaries of cosmopolitanism, of a 'we' and a 'they', of powerful and helpless.

Cosmopolitanism in a time of terror: ethical responses to 11 September 2001

The violent acts of 11 September and the war against Al-Qaeda and the Taliban are unique in raising profound questions about how modern societies should deal with many diverse forms of suffering. Modern societies face the challenge of ensuring that efforts to protect innocent civilians from terrorist attacks do not damage the moral ideal of freeing all human beings from unnecessary suffering (Linklater 2002: 303).

In sharp distinction to the essentialising rhetoric that typified the mainstream responses to 11 September 2001 – e.g. 'with us or against us'; capture Bin Laden 'dead or alive' 'the axis of evil', etc. – the cosmopolitan response to 11 September 2001 has been marked by an emphasis on understanding, learning, and a set of efforts aimed at avoiding the future production of terrorism: 'In moments of crisis, it is not sufficient to oppose. It is also necessary to make concrete proposals to weaken terrorism. Which is what the cosmopolitan perspective puts forward' (Archibugi 2001: 5).

In a bullish paper, written soon after 11 September 2001, Daniele Archibugi set out what he termed the 'simple ethical principle' that underpins a cosmopolitan response to terrorism: 'it is necessary to give equal value to human life, irrespective of whether an individual belongs to "our" or to "another" political and social community' (ibid.: 5). In times of war when such principles are forgotten, he argued that the deployment of certain basic agendas could help to 'equalize the value of our lives with the value of the lives of others'. These are to moderate 'methods of conflict', to support 'democratic participation', to impose 'financial controls' on terrorist capital, to move from a 'law of arms to the arms of law', to support 'peace in Palestine', and to bolster the 'United Nations' (ibid.: 5).

The hope is, for Archibugi, that by recognizing the *value* of the individual lives of all, including terrorists, or at least the areas and communities where terrorists might be constructed, then the production of future 'enemies/threats' will be lessened. Democratic participation, it is supposed, will involve disaffected peoples in debates about world politics in a way that a global war on terror could not possibly hope to achieve. Closing down terrorist financing will stem the activities of terrorist networks and the extension of cosmopolitan law via institutions like the International Criminal Court would take the tinge of American unilateralism out of the west's response to 11 September 2001.

This faith in the power of cosmopolitan law chimes with the response of Jürgen Habermas to the post-11 September 2001 insecurity discourse. Speaking just a few months after 11 September 2001, he goes beyond the axiomatic assertion that law is the answer to contemplate the political strategies that may be required. He identifies the 'clever, albeit fragile, coalition against terrorism brought together by the US government' that 'might, in the most favorable case, be able to advance the transition from classical international law to a cosmopolitan order' (Habermas 2003: 27). However, he continues by lamenting the fact that the European powers have failed to support any such possibilities, preferring to distance themselves from, rather than engage with, the US. Finally, as with many contemporary cosmopolitan arguments, the specter of globalisation is never far away from analysis. Habermas argues that

> [w]ithout the political taming of an unbounded capitalism, the devastating stratification of the world will remain intractable. The disparities in the dynamic of world economic development would have to at least be balanced out regarding their most destructive consequences – the deprivation and misery of complete regions and continents comes to mind. This does not merely concern the discrimination toward, the humiliation or, or the offense to other cultures. The so-called 'clash of civilizations' is often the veil masking the vital material interests of the West...
>
> (Habermas 2003: 36)

Habermas was far from alone in this understanding of the ills of globalisation. His concern for the 'the discrimination toward, the humiliation of, or the offense to other cultures' was ever present in the Leftist discourses, where a mix of poverty and Palestine was often invoked to explain the emergence of terrorism. An appropriate cosmopolitan response is therefore, arguably, to redistribute wealth on a global scale. Indeed, Archibugi argues that

> Europe has to rediscover the pride of guiding the world through a period as difficult as the present one; not only by hunting down the terrorists but also

by promoting economic development plans in the Third World with programs analogous to the Marshall Plan, in half a century's time the whole world – our American brothers first and foremost – would surely be grateful to us.

(Archibugi 2001: 8)

The limits of response

This brief summary of cosmopolitan responses to the terrorist attacks in New York serves to highlight two important tenets of the response.

1   Cosmopolitans are concerned to mark out an alternative response to that of the mainstream, US, media response.
2   Cosmopolitans are deeply concerned with how to prevent the production of future terrorist atrocities. This can be done via a combination of cosmopolitan law, participatory democracy and global justice (usually read as the redistribution of wealth to poor countries).

In essence, there is a credible attempt to first understand the causes of terrorism, the 'discrimination', 'humiliation' and 'unnecessary suffering' that inhibits opportunities for freedom and causes resentment in the world, and second, to suggest mechanisms to counteract them. For these reasons, there is a confident suggestion that cosmopolitanism is itself an important resource to draw from. As David Held quipped, 'Globalization without cosmopolitanism could fail' (Held n.d.: 9).

However, for writers in a long tradition of thought that may be termed poststructural, it is the ethics *of* ethics that must be first placed in question. Poststructural writers are sceptical of the way in which ethical responses are often guided by the use of abstract principles that may become cemented in a political programme.[3] On this view, cosmopolitan responses to 11 September 2001, while laudable, may risk closing the political moment where we might question the subjectivities and rationalities that make suffering possible. As Rob Walker argues, for these reasons 'cosmopolitanism must be read as a constitutive aspect of the problems that many of those attracted to cosmopolitanism seek to address' (Walker 2003: 268).

In *Precarious Life* Judith Butler suggests that the potential for an ethical response to 11 September 2001, to terrorism and to suffering is curtailed by the monopolisation of the legitimate meaning of 11 September 2001 in public discourse (Butler 2004). The very possibility of questioning the mainstream narrative of the attacks is cut off by logics like 'with us or against us'. Even the profusion of critical and conspiracy-theory type responses that typified the post-11 September period confirmed the centrality and self-obsession of the US with its place at the centre of the world. Deeper understandings, mourning for the loss of life, mourning for the other and the possibility of even recognizing the suffering of others are often curtailed. Butler therefore places a 'politics of mourning' at the forefront of her analysis. While popular debates have made hay about the theoretical oppositions between post-structural and approaches to ethics like cosmopolitanism, at the level of substance there is much to be gained from engagement. Such arguments can be seen as congruent with, *and even a prerequisite to*, thinking the possibilities for global ethics. For instance, no disavowal of the cosmopolitan response is made. Rather, elements and logics that might inhibit a proper working through of cosmopolitan ambitions are brought into question and, on one interpretation, enlarging 'our understanding of what the cosmopolitan project still must grapple with' (McRobbie 2006: 70).

While Butler is perhaps less explicit about the way her arguments speak to broader cosmopolitan debates on global ethics, Jacques Derrida was direct in his engagement. In cosmopolitan fashion, he states that 'in the first place' and 'as imperfect as they may be ... international institutions should be respected in their deliberations...' if only as a temper on the 'serious failings of "Western" states' in their commitment to international agreements (Derrida 2003: 114). However, he argues that, when seeking to embed cosmopolitan norms via institutions and law: 'Reflection (of what I would call a "deconstructive" type) should ... without diminishing or destroying these axioms and principles, question and refound them, endlessly refine and universalize them' (ibid.: 114). He continued:

> I'm not unaware of the apparently utopic character of the horizon I'm sketching out here, that of an international institution of law and an international court of justice with their own autonomous force. Though I do not hold law to be the last word on ethics, politics or anything else, though this unity of force and law ... is not only *utopic* but *aporetic* (since it implies that beyond the sovereignty of the nation-state, indeed beyond democratic sovereignty – whose ontotheological foundations must be deconstructed – we would nonetheless be reconstituting a new figure, though not necessarily state-related, of universal sovereignty, of absolute law with an effective autonomous force at its disposal), I continue to believe that it is faith in the possibility of this impossible and, in truth undecidable thing from the point of view of knowledge, science and conscience that must govern our decisions.
>
> (Derrida 2003: 115)

While post-structural authors critique the straightforward response of cosmopolitans to terrorism then, they do leave open the possibility for engagement. For Butler, consideration of 'our' 'own' vulnerability might be a 'point of identification', a route to recognising the vulnerability to suffering of others. For Derrida, 'faith in the possibility of this impossible' programme of cosmopolitan law is the difficult, aporetic, impulse that must guide responses. However, having mapped a range of ethical responses to 11 September 2001, it becomes clear that the debate works at a level of abstraction which might question its practical worth. The next section will therefore shift focus to the Make Poverty

History campaign, as an embedded cosmopolitan practice that entered into a strong circumstantial and discursive relation with 7 July 2005.

Terror in a time of cosmopolitanism: 7 July as the 'other' of Gleneagles

If many of the ethical discourses before 7 July 2005 can be read as cosmopolitan responses to terrorism, the confluence of events surrounding the G8 and the Make Poverty History campaign mark out the events in London as the incidence of 'Terror in a Time of Cosmopolitanism'. This section first suggests that the confluence of the Make Poverty History campaign with British support for the UN's Millennium Development goals is an embedded example of the kind of cosmopolitan reforms to which the first section alluded. It then addresses some of the discursive manoeuvres which underpinned cosmopolitan responses to 7 July 2005. Briefly stated, campaigners from within global civil society, leftist sympathisers in the media and reformist politicians all chimed with the lament that the 7 July 2005 bombers would disrupt the very processes aimed at making a better world for 'them'.

What is at stake, in this assessment, is the capacity of cosmopolitan ethical discourses to translate into a meaningful alternative to those of the mainstream. In a powerful critique of the national response, Angharad Closs Stephens argues that '[p]eople were asked to choose: either they were with the British people, and the British government representing "our way of life", or they were with the people who acted through terrorism' (Closs Stephens 2007). The argument below suggests that this dichotomy was (re-)enacted at the global level via the depiction of cosmopolitanism as a united and defiant community. When read through this lens, the cosmopolitan response to 7 July 2005 collapses into '*either* you believe that a combination of cosmopolitan law, participatory democracy and global justice is the only way to prevent the production of terrorism, *or*, you accept and perpetuate the terms of the global war on terror'. You are either with 'our' cosmopolitan values or against them. In this sense the critical edge of cosmopolitanism – as a credible alternative to the mainstream discourse of response – is severely blunted.

Make poverty history

> If Britain can't turn its values into action against extreme, stupid poverty ... if this rich country with the reins in its hands, can't lead other countries along this path to equality, then the critics tomorrow will be right.... Listen, this is a real moment coming up, this could be real history, this could be something that your children, your children's children, that our whole generation, will be remembered for at the beginning of the century.
>
> (Bono in Gumbel 2005)

In line with Archibugi's call for a global 'Marshall Plan', cosmopolitan justice became hugely popular (and indeed populist) in the post-11 September 2001 period. In short, discourses of ethical possibility before 7 July 2005 were very positive. Much of the popularity of cosmopolitan idea(l)s rested in campaigns related to the achievement of the UN's Millennium Development Goals (MDGs). The United Nations Millenium Declaration, signed in September 2000, commits the states to: 1) eradicate extreme poverty and hunger; 2) achieve universal primary education; 3) promote gender equality and empower women; 4) reduce child mortality; 5) improve maternal health; 6) combat HIV/Aids, malaria and other diseases; 7) ensure environmental sustainability; and 8) develop a global partnership for development (UN 2000). Numerous strategies have been outlined for how to achieve such laudable ambitions by various dates, but Make Poverty History was a central initiative.

Make Poverty History (MPH) describes itself as the 'biggest ever anti-poverty movement' that comprises hundreds of NGOs, faith groups, charities and other groups sympathetic to the achievement of the MDGs (*Make Poverty History* n.d.). Its key proposals for acheiveing the MDGS included: 1) trade justice (and a direct call on the UK Government to change EU trade policies and Europe's push to have some of the poorest nations on the planet sign up to grossly unfair trade deals); 2) debt cancellation; and 3) more and better aid (*Make Poverty History* n.d.; Gumbel 2005).

The importantce of MPH for this discussion is twofold. First, its key aims clearly ally with the cosmopolitan ambition to build cosmopolitan law, participatory democracy and global justice. The campaign's three-pronged agenda for trade justice, debt cancellation and improved aid, described by Lenny Henry in a campaign film as a 'magic cocktail' for reform, is ostensibly a temper to global neo-liberalism that was, crucially, acceptable, or at least speak-able, in multilateral circles (*Make Poverty History* n.d.). Easy critiques that the campaign was mere rhetoric, or too similar to Blair and Brown, were common to the more radical left and within global civil society. But, again, these arguments ignore the way in which such campaigns develop cosmopolitanism as an embedded way of thinking and acting in the world (Smith 2007: 72–89). Second, in a related point, the Make Poverty History campaign was *very effective* at achieving global publicity. Couched in broadly understandable terms, the campaign was welcomed by G8 leaders and by the UK leadership in particular. It reached a massive global audience with an avowedly updated and more sophisticated message on development than the charity discourses of Live Aid: 'We're not asking for your money, we're asking for your voice' (US One Campaign Film n.d.).

Read in campaign strategic terms then, MPH had a clear cosmopolitan platform, a direct route into the multilateral decision-making room of the G8 and a massive popular constituency sympathetic to, and increasingly aware of, the global governance of development. However, the London bombings changed the environment. As Ann Pettifor suggests:

> The Leeds bombers provided world leaders with momentary relief from their responsibilities, shocked economic justice campaigners – in particular

the many millions that thanks to Make Poverty History had joined for the first time – and pushed major issues off the media's agenda.

(Pettifor 2006)

7 July: a cosmopolitan response?

The shock that accompanies terrorist attacks was compounded in the British media by the swift reversal of mood. The 'strongly positive feel' in Britain (*Report of the Official Account* 2006: 2) gave way to a general recognition that the long expected terrorist attack on the UK had arrived. Likewise, the discourses of ethical possibility which have been building positively prior to 7 July 2005 quickly faded from being a central point of focus for the media to a laconic 'might have been'. Tony Blair was quick to speak:

> It is particularly barbaric that this has happened on a day when people are meeting to try to help the problems of poverty in Africa, and the long term problems of climate change and the environment. Just as it is reasonably clear that this is a terrorist attack, or a series of terrorist attacks, it is also reasonably clear that it is designed and aimed to coincide with the opening of the G8.
>
> (Blair 2005)

Blair's manoeuvre quickly 'others' the bombers by constructing the terrorists as 'barbaric'. It laments the fact that such barbarism should attack civilization on the day when it is trying 'to help the problems of poverty in Africa'. This enforces a dichotomy between cosmopolitanism and terrorism by suggesting that the attacks were 'clearly aimed to coincide with the opening of the G8'. While this narrative suggesting that the bombings were an attack on the G8 was quickly superseded in the media by the narrative that the bombings were an attack on British values, it continued to play among activists within global civil society. In a trenchant critique, Ann Pettifor echoed and extended the dichotomy:

> With one murderous act, the Leeds bombers, aided and abetted by their leaders in al-Qaida, helped strengthen the forces that have attacked peaceful and innocent Muslim communities; undermined civil liberties in the United Kingdom and the United States; and pushed and maintained imperial forces in Iraq, Afghanistan and Palestine.
>
> (Pettifor 2006)

The critical tone suggests that the bombers have strengthened the War on Terror logic of the UK–US axis. The violence is therefore self-defeating, as it will perpetuate the cycle of violence towards 'innocent Muslim communities' and, moreover, that civilisation will probably stop being so civilised via a curtailment of civil liberties. Pettifor extends the dichotomy between 7 July 2005 and Make

Poverty History, between terrorism and cosmopolitanism, by re-affirming the point that the attacks actually harm Muslims:

> At the same time their violent attack on innocent people immediately weakened the millions mobilised around Make Poverty History, and fighting to defend the interests and environments of the world's poor, including vast Muslim communities in countries like Nigeria, Indonesia and Bangladesh.
>
> (ibid. 2006)

This move is interesting because it not only affirms the dichotomy, but it also creates a clear hierarchy. While it is clear that the London bombings distracted attention from the campaign, something understandably disappointing to any campaigner, there is a vitriolic tone in the construction: 'you stopped us helping you'. The implication is that despite anger at losing the campaign, cosmopolitans can content themselves in the knowledge that that they have done all they can to help 'vast Muslim communities'. Thus a clear conditionality emerges in this representation of cosmopolitanism vs terrorism. Whereas the cosmopolitan responses identified in the second section were intent on reducing the scope for the production of future terrorism, there is an emergent explanation: you are either with the cosmopolitans or against them, i.e. against yourselves. Indeed, Pettifor suggests that Bush and Blair were probably 'relieved' that the bombers acted to take poverty off the global political agenda (Pettifor 2006). Of course, these dichotomies – barbarism–civilisation, terrorism–cosmopolitanism – were contested by sympathetic commentators. Polly Toynbee took the idea as an opportunity to re-affirm the aims of the Make Poverty History campaign:

> How barbaric, Tony Blair rightly said, that the terrorists should strike just as the G8 at least strives to do better on Africa and climate change. Yes indeed. But then barbarism is in the eye of the beholder and every act of war is justified in the warped minds of its perpetrators. Barbaric might also be 30,000 children a day dying in Africa while a mere 25,000 US cotton farmers keep their trade-denying subsidies. Or Bangladesh soon to be washed away in global-warming floods. Or arms sold to those who will force them upon child soldiers, or any number of worldwide atrocities.
>
> (Toynbee 2005)

While ostensibly challenging the dichotomy however, this argument plays to an old leftist problematic, often selectively invoked, of moral equivalence. Instead of undermining the dichotomy between cosmopolitanism and terrorism/barbarism, the moral equivalence argument re-affirms it from a different angle. The cosmopolitan impulse is affirmed as opposition to both terrorism *and* the forces that support global poverty. Simply stated, *'you are with us or you are with logic of the War on Terror.'*

A cosmopolitan resistance to cosmopolitanism?

In such moralising responses to 7 July 2005, the cosmopolitan programme began to display its limits, running in dichotomous circles around the very 'thing', which we might expect cosmopolitans to articulate an alternative response, to. In essence, cosmopolitanism was able to provide little more, by way of a response, than the mainstream discourses themselves. The implications of this argument are twofold.

First, we need to interrogate how cosmopolitan arguments succumb to a programme: what elements of the Make Poverty History campaign entrench a technology of ethics, such that global ethics itself becomes de-politicised and frozen to instrumental and institutional bargaining? Second, we need to build on this by thinking about how cosmopolitans could respond to terror differently. This, no doubt, is a tougher question that requires an ongoing engagement with the political actors involved. Ultimately, what might cosmopolitans draw from the Make Poverty History campaign and the responses to 7 July 2005?

Cosmopolitanism as technology

> [W]hen a responsibility is exercised in the order of the possible, it simply follows a direction and elaborates a program. It makes of action the applied consequence, the simple application of a knowledge or know-how. *It makes of ethics and politics a technology*.
>
> (Derrida 1992: 42)

The more programmatic elements of Make Poverty History were arguably entrenched in a rationality of global development ethics. In *Whose Hunger?* Jenny Edkins argues that '[m]odernity's desire or hunger for philosophical certainty, the sovereign subject, and the bounded society translates into processes that depoliticize and technologize' (Edkins 2000: 156). In particular, famine, poverty and other issues surrounding the meta-narrative of development are portrayed as 'social emergencies', 'crises', as large societal question marks to be 'answered'. All that is supposedly required is the political will of the powerful. But, Edkins argues,

> far from being a problem that could be solved if only the technical procedures were improved, famine is a product of power relations. It is not a question of finding better early warning systems, more participatory development projects or faster methods of delivering relief. Nor is it a question of seeking deeper, more structural causes of famines, nor its complexities. Famine is a product of violence. Even where war is not implicated directly, the state enforces laws of property that can lead to some people's starvation. Aid processes and interventions to which technical concepts of famine give rise are practices that reproduce particular political and international power relations.
>
> (Edkins 2000: 156)

Such ambiguities are clearly evident in the central pillars of the Make Poverty History campaign. First, MPH aligned with the campaign for 'trade justice', calling for an end to agricultural subsidies. However, MPH has since criticised the stand-off which has emerged over the issue of how far developing markets should open their own markets in exchange for cutting subsidies (*Make Poverty History* n.d.). But what is meant by trade justice? Or rather, can modified trade relations really be understood to embody grand ethical terms like justice at all (Watson 2006: 435–51)? For instance, it could be argued, that emerging discourses of global trade justice have produced a set of limits. The ethical line which is emerging from those trade negotiators and NGOs who posit the normative benefits of reducing agricultural subsidies (*Make Poverty History* n.d.), and even those 'South-ist' campaigners who argue for the legal protection of local production and supply chains (Rangnekar 2004), can be seen as constructing a limit to the way in which we can think about global trade justice. Neither approach questions the logic of mass food production, nor do they address other hierarchies of power like human domination of the environment, gender and or class hierarchies. Thus, the construction of a large, singular campaign that apparently expresses the limit of global trade justice may actually be set detrimentally low.

Equally with the second plank in the campaign platform, debt cancellation, there are significant questions over the distinctiveness of the proposal. The principle of a debt write-off actually does very little to question either the logic of debt or the idea of a universal capitalist route to 'development'. Quite the reverse is the case, in fact, when one considers that most debt write-offs are underpinned by the need to secure future debt repayments for private sector actors, as well as a set of conditionalties regarding the neo-liberal reforms of 'beneficiary' states.[4]

Finally, the principle of 'more and better aid' in the MPH campaign was underpinned by a number of proposals that may construct a set of limits for thinking global ethics. In particular, the emphasis on Tobin Tax (Stamp Out Poverty Briefing 2005) in the campaign can be heavily criticised. While the Tobin Tax is seen by many as an embodiment of global justice, through its capacity to calm financial markets, and provide vast revenues for redistribution, a number of ambiguities can be identified.

First, the Tobin Tax is a moderate, small tax, imposed on currency transactions. Therefore, while it seeks to calm financial speculation, it ironically feeds off of such activity: it therefore reifies a certain level of global capital mobility. And second, building from this point, the Tobin Tax provides a cash-based approach to global justice, where large amounts of money are collected in the 'North' and handed to the 'South', thus implying a problematic financial universalism. On this view, the Tobin Tax acts to construct the financial system as a singular, unitary whole, which 'we' must react to, failing to explore alternatives that may arise in partially, or non-developed financial systems (Derrida 2003: 115).

Moments of resistance

In this sense, the cosmopolitan programme elaborated by the Make Poverty History campaign served to entrench the idea of cosmopolitanism as a straightforward technology. This entrenchment meant that the step towards other-ing terrorism after the London bombings was a straightforward manoeuvre drawn from the repertoire of a perceived 'united community' of global cosmopolitans. The capacity to think differently, to open the spaces to the kinds of 'limits' and 'ambiguities' of responses to, indeed, *the very know-ability of*, terrorism was radically curtailed.

What follows is a cursory and limited attempt to address the possibility for thinking differently. Again the strength of the critique of cosmopolitanism outlined may imply a move to forget the possibility of cosmopolitanism or of a cosmopolitan response. However, with Derrida, 'it is faith in the possibility of this impossible and, in truth undecidable thing ... that must govern our decisions' (Derrida 2003: 115). Again, perhaps in line with this, Robert Fine suggests that,

> Cosmopolitanism is not a fixed idea – which is why it may be preferable to substitute the term cosmopolitan outlook for cosmopolitan*ism* – but rather an ongoing and incomplete research project marked by a refusal to wash over the extremes of human behaviour or be engulfed by them.
>
> (Fine 2006: 51)

It is this possibility, a refusal to be engulfed by terrorism, a refusal to be engulfed by extreme poverty, which could be productively explored and developed through such questions as: *How do we resist?* Edkins argues that,

> If humanitarianism is technologized, intervention is no longer a question of responsibility and political decisioning but the application of a new system of international law to a case. Any challenge would have to come from a charismatic figure like Bob Geldof who can constitute (briefly) an opposing regime of truth.
>
> (Edkins 2000: 159)

On one level this argument is slightly peculiar. Geldof in both his Live Aid and Live 8 manifestations is a man bound up with a fairly straightforward answer to poverty, i.e. *throw money at it*. However, this ignores the political moment that such figures create. Geldof's interventions clearly bring an emotional tone to the subject. Moreover, he clearly articulates the problem(s) in a way that translates to larger and more variegated audiences than existing structures of development can reach.

If we think more particularly about Live 8, it can be argued that a key contribution of the campaigns and concerts was to introduce a larger audience to the idea that there is in fact something called the G8, whose decision-making processes have a credible impact on the lives of millions. From the point of view of global ethics, this expansion of the scope of the global political sphere is surely a condition of thinking possible alternatives. The conversation that emerges from within this sphere may obviously proceed in limited and problematic directions. But from a cosmopolitan outlook its expansion and engagement is to be commended. Beyond such interventions though there needs to be more imaginative engagement. For instance, in the wake of the London bombings about the best response that could be articulated was a 'more of the same' remedy. As Toynbee argued:

> George Bush is the one person who could and should have felt beholden to give a good response to this disaster, in support of his ally. But with typical inadequacy it was beyond his imaginative grasp to be extra magnanimous either to Blair or to the world in his offers on climate change, aid and trade. What a fine contrast it would have made to the bombers if this had redoubled the west's determination to do the right thing. It would not be giving in to terrorism, but denying it the oxygen of justification.
>
> (Toynbee 2005)

On the one hand, such interventions risk fetishising the idea that terrorism is caused by poverty. This was never the argument of cosmopolitan theorists considered in the first section. On the other hand, it reproduces the mantra that cosmopolitan global justice is about exporting a universal conception of development and values.

Problems involved with a universal ontology of global ethics include the reification of a problem (poverty) and a respondent (*we cosmopolitans*) risking a concomitant marginalisation of alternative possible futures. For instance, Marieke de Goede argues that this is a problem with many discussions of the reform of globalisation and global finance, more specifically. As she attests, the 'assumption that re-regulation of financial markets on a global scale and through state co-operation is the *only* viable response to liberalized finance is flawed, for three reasons' (de Goede 2005: 147). First, such regulation has the effect of depoliticising financial economic practices by marking out a realm of 'normal finance' beyond politics. Second, attempts to regulate global finance typically seek to avoid crisis thus constructing non-crisis periods as 'normal'. Third, there is a 'degree of defeatism' in such a large blueprint for global reform. The act of resisting a monolith like 'globalisation' or 'global governance' reifies that very idea and reduces possibilities for 'effective' resistance.

In this sense, agendas for the 'reform of global capitalism' must, in some way, internalise the logics of global capitalism, and equally, it might be argued, democratisation of the institutions of global governance usually involves the re-articulation of norms of sovereignty. Instead, a more critical ontology of 'the global' is perhaps required.[5] If cosmopolitanism was to adopt a spatially sophisticated and multidimensional social ontology of globalisation, new possibilities for engagement and interaction might be thought (Scholte 2005). Importantly, this multilevel understanding does not rehearse the universal fallacy – how do we respond to global poverty? Instead, it permits multiple questions concerned with the project to build alternative and more ethical futures. For example, a significant point of resistance to MPH arose over precisely this issue. Numerous Southern campaigners organised to question the notion of 'the global' at the heart of the campaign, suggesting that it masked an exclusively Northern constituency. As John Gaventa and Marj Mayo recount:

> While on the one hand the northern citizens expressed their solidarity for the poverty of citizens in other parts of the world, through attempting to influence the powerful leaders of the G8 through mass mobilisation, a number of southern civil society groups increasingly expressed their concerns about representation, as symbolized in the slogan, 'not about us without us'.
> (Gaventa with Mayo 2006)

The call for greater cross linkages and involvement of local groups in the affairs of global development is one way, moderate and long-term, in which cosmopolitanism may learn about its limits in, and through, practice.

Finally, we might return to the 'politics of mourning' suggested by Judith Butler. If cosmopolitanism, read through the Make Poverty History campaign, has a 'resource' for responding to terrorism, then it is the abject awareness of, and concern with, death. Unfortunately, however, the representations of death in the campaign were machine like. The death statistic, '30,000 people a day', became like a mantra. One of the key images of the US Live 8 concert was that of the actor Will Smith, clicking his fingers every second to mark the death of another person living in poverty. Again, while we might feel that the basic promotion of awareness on such issues is a necessary first step to building a truly global ethics, there is a sense in which the singularity of each death is effaced. Just as cosmopolitanism began to self-identify as a coherent we-community, so there was a risk that a 'they', the wretched statistics, was also emerging. This is unfortunate primarily because it empties the signified of political agency, the political agency that might be required to engage with cosmopolitan ethics. Instead then, a politics of mourning should be conducted in more intimate terms. As Judith Butler suggests:

> To grieve, and to make grief itself into a resource for politics, is not to be resigned to inaction, but it may be understood as the slow process by which we develop a point of identification with suffering itself.
> […]
> this can be a point of departure for a new understanding if the narcissistic preoccupation of melancholia can be moved into a consideration of the vulnerability of others. Then we might critically evaluate and oppose the conditions under which certain human lives are more vulnerable than others, and thus certain human lives are more grievable than others.
> (Butler 2004: 30)

This is not a panacea for the ills of globalisation, or even for the more totalising elements of cosmopolitanism. But, it does represent one credible resistance that breathes life into the broad cosmopolitan desire to de-limit the scope of ethical concern. It also speaks directly to the more specific intentions of the cosmopolitans looked at in the first section: to first understand the causes of terrorism, the 'discrimination', 'humiliation' and 'unnecessary suffering' that inhibits opportunities for freedom and causes resentment in the world.

Notes

1 For helpful comments on previous articulations of this argument the author thanks Dan Bulley, Angharad Closs Stephens, Jenny Edkins, Jack Holland, Chris Holmes, the IPE Working Group at Warwick University, Robert Fine, Matt McDonald, Nick Vaughan-Williams, Lena Rethel and William Smith.
2 Within the confines of this chapter, it is cosmopolitanism and cosmopolitan responses to 'terrorism' that are at issue. This does not ignore the equally problematic question of what is 'terrorism'. Indeed, it may even speak to that question via analysis of the constitutive frame provided by the cosmopolitan response. However, the main target remains the ethical conversation as it developed before and after 7 July 2005.
3 For instance, at his most categorical, Nietzsche suggests that

> we stand in need of a critique of moral values, the value of these values itself should first of all be called into question. This requires a knowledge of the conditions and circumstances of their growth, development and displacement (morality as consequence, symptom mask [...] illness, misunderstanding: *but also morality as cause, cure, stimulant, inhibition, poison.*
>
> (Nietzsche 1994: 8; emphasis added)

4 I am grateful to Lena Rehtel for discussion and advice on this subject. See also Rehtel (2007).
5 See for instance, Shah (2006).

References

Archibugi, D. (2001), 'Terrorism and Cosmopolitanism', SSRC Working Paper: 5. Online. Available at: www.ssrc.org/sept11/essays/archibugi_text_only.htm (accessed March 2007).
Blair, T. (2005), 'PM's Statement on the London explosions', Gleneagles, 7 July. Online. Available at: www.pm.gov.uk/output/Page7853.asp (accessed March 2007).
Brassett, J. (2006), 'Deliberative and Pragmatic Approaches to the Tobin Tax Campaign' GARNET Working Paper 07/06. <<<to delete at proofs? NO REF IN TEXT>>>
Butler, J. (2004), *Precarious Life: the Powers of Mourning and Violence*, London and New York: Verso.
Closs Stephens, A. '"7 Million Londoners, 1 London": National and Urban Ideas of National Community in the Aftermath of the 7th July Bombings in London', paper presented at the ISA Conference, Chicago, 2007.
de Goede, M. (2005), *Virtue, Fortune and Faith: A Genealogy of Finance*, London: University of Minnesota Press.
Derrida, J. (1992), *The Other Heading. Reflections on Today's Europe*, Bloomington, IN: Indiana University Press.

—— (2003), 'Autoimmunity: Real and Symbolic Suicides: a Dialogue with Jacques Derrida', in G. Borradori (ed.), *Philosophy in a Time of Terror: Dialogues with Jürgen Habermas and Jacques Derrida*, Chicago and London: University of Chicago Press.

Edkins, J. (2000), *Whose Hunger? Concepts of Famine, Practices of Aid*, London: University of Minnesota Press.

Fine, R. (2006), 'Cosmopolitanism and Violence: Difficulties of Judgement', *British Journal of Sociology* 57(1).

Gaventa, J. with Mayo, M. (2006), 'Not About Us Without Us': Linking Local and Global Citizen Advocacy'. A research proposal. Working Group on citizenship and Engagement in a Globalised World, January.

Gumbel, N. (2005), *Make Poverty History*, London: Alpha International.

Habermas, J. (2003), 'Fundamentalism and Terror – A Dialogue with Jürgen Habermas', in G. Borradori (ed.), *Philosophy in a Time of Terror: Dialogues with Jürgen Habermas and Jacques Derrida*, Chicago and London: University of Chicago Press.

Held, D. (n.d.), 'Globalization after 9/11'. Online. Available at: www.polity.co.uk/GLOBAL/pdf/After%209.pdf (accessed March 2007).

Linklater, A. (2002), 'Unnecessary Suffering', in K. Booth and T. Dunne (eds), *Worlds in Collision: Terror and the Future of Global Order*, Basingstoke: Palgrave Macmillan.

—— (2007), 'Distant Suffering and Cosmopolitan Obligations', *International Politics* 44(1): 19.

McRobbie, A. (2006), 'Vulnerability, Violence and (Cosmopolitan) Ethics: Butler's *Precarious Life*', *British Journal of Sociology* 57(1).

Make Poverty History (n.d.), Online. Available at: www.makepovertyhistory.org (accessed March 2007).

Nietzsche, F. (1994), *On the Genealogy of Morals*, Cambridge: Cambridge University Press.

Pettifor, A. (2006), 'Gleneagles, 7/7 and Africa', via Open Democracy.net, www.opendemocracy.net/globalization-terrorism/g8_3708.jsp.

Rangnekar, D. (2004), *Demanding Stronger Protection for Geographical Indications: The Relationship between Local Knowledge, Information and Reputation*, UNU-INTECH Discussion Paper, Maastricht No. 2004-11.

Rehtel, L. (2007), 'Developing Islamic Capital Markets: Reifying the Status Quo of Global Finance', paper presented at the CSGR Conference, 'Pathways to Legitimacy? The Future of Global and Regional Governance', 17–19 September 2007.

Report of the Official Account of the Bombings in London on 7th July 2005 (2006), London: The Stationery Office.

Scholte, J. A. (2005), *Globalization: a Critical Introduction*, Basingstoke: Palgrave Macmillan.

Shah, N. (2006), 'Cosmopolitanizing and Decosmopolitanizing Globalization: Metaphorical Re-description and Transformations of Political Community', *Globalizations* 3(3): 393–411.

Smith, W. (2007), 'Anticipating a Cosmopolitan Future: The Case of Humanitarian Intervention', *International Politics* 44(1): 72–89.

Stamp Out Poverty Briefing (2005), 'How a stamp duty on sterling currency transactions can help pay for the Millennium Development Goals'. Online. Available at: www.stampoutpoverty.org/?lid=9816.

Toynbee, P. (2005), 'Let the Olympics Be a Memorial', *Guardian*, 8 July.

UN (2000), *UN Millennium Development Goals*. Online. Available at: www.un.org/millenniumgoals/ (accessed March 2007).

US One Campaign Film (n.d.), Online. Available at: www.makepovertyhistory.org/video.
Walker, R. B. J. (2003), 'Polis, Cosmopolis, Politics', *Alternatives, Global, Local, Political* 28(2): 284–5.
Watson, M. (2006), 'Towards a Polanyian Perspective on Fair Trade: Market-bound Economic Agents and the Act of Ethical Consumption', *Global Society* 20(4): 435–51.

9 Finding meaning in meaningless times
Emotional responses to terror threats in London

Chris Rumford

Introduction

While it is undoubtedly true that the dangerousness of contemporary society is exaggerated, it is almost certainly the case that we have become unusually sensitive to fear and risk, that anxiety and trepidation permeate our everyday consciousness. There are two dimensions of the growing discourse on fear and risk that are particularly significant. One is that the main threat comes from the unpredictability of the future. What is portrayed as particularly dangerous is the risk represented by the future – uncertain, unknowable, not amenable to calculation – and the impossibility of being able to assess fully the risk such unpredictability poses. During his time as Prime Minister, Tony Blair was keen to assert that the world had changed post-11 September, and such a world requires a new style of politics: 'a new world order needs a new set of rules'. One result is that the threat (and reality) of terrorism in the UK has been mobilized to emphasize the dangerousness of the post-11 September world; a world which 'no longer makes sense' according to the logic of conventional politics.

The other dimension is that what is most threatening about our world is the global nature of the threat. For example, the realization that jihadist terror networks are 'more global' than the US and its allies who seek to neutralize them (Devji 2005) has caused no little consternation and has provoked the need for new types of protection: a global 'war on terror'. This can also be seen in the way that responses to the London bombings of July 2005 are characterized by a tendency to construct global linkages in order to explain the events of 7 July; homegrown terrorists are linked (by association) to global terror networks; domestic insecurities are linked to foreign threats. The two dimensions are brought together in the political responses to terrorism voiced by Tony Blair who, as David Runciman points out, 'uses the language of risk to raise the spectre of the total unmanageability of the new world order' (Runciman 2006: 11).

The argument developed in this chapter is that responses to terrorist attacks (the events of 11 September and 7 July are given consideration here) by the UK and US governments have a strong emotional charge. This is not to suggest that George W. Bush's call for a 'war on terror' was merely a knee-jerk reaction or nothing more than a desire for revenge for the 11 September attacks. What is suggested is that many political responses display a strong emotional dimension which has displaced, to a certain extent, a rational appraisal of political realities. For example, the political choices made by Blair and Bush have been justified on the basis that they were 'gut reactions' to exceptionally difficult situations (after all, weapons of mass destruction were believed to exist in Iraq despite evidence to the contrary). Tony Blair and his ministers have justified the conduct of British soldiers in Iraq on the basis of the British sense of 'fairness' on the battlefield rather than reminding the military of their obligations to uphold global values of human rights and agreements governing the treatment of prisoners. In both the UK and the US, suspects have been held on the basis of their supposed 'dangerousness', rather than according to any evidence of criminality.

What this points to is the necessity of developing an understanding of politics which is alive to the emotional dimensions of policy rationales and political framings. It is not only terrorists who are acting without (or beyond) rationality; the decisions and intentions of political leaders, policy entrepreneurs, and commentators can also be non-rational and emotional. We need to understand the 'politics of emotion' when understanding the actions of both Tony Blair and George Bush *and* the terrorists they have engaged in the 'war on terror'. This should not be taken to mean that emotions and rationality are polar opposites. By asserting the need to understand the emotional dimensions of contemporary politics I am not suggesting that emotions somehow replace rationality: the two are in fact indivisible. The emphasis on emotions here then is more of a corrective; emotions are normally down played when attempting to understand the rationality of political responses (Clarke *et al.* 2006).

The chapter proceeds as follows. In the first section we look at ways in which the world appears not to 'make sense' any more, by examining some of the arguments that have emerged around our governments' attempts to control terrorist suspects without prosecuting them, through use of 'control orders' and by invoking the extra-legal (and emotional) category of 'dangerousness'. In the following section, we examine explanations for 7 July offered in terms of 'cultural trauma' derived from the work of Alexander *et al.*, which it is argued are too rational to capture the range of responses to the traumatic events in London in July 2005, seeking as they do to turn emotional responses into rationalizations of learning and social healing. A better option, which is outlined in the following section, is represented by Stjepan Mestrovic's idea of 'postemotional politics'. This is appropriate in a context where the problem of terrorism, according to the UK's Labour government, requires not a conventional rational political response but a response based on 'gut feeling'. The strengths of the 'postemotional society' approach will be outlined through a discussion of the 'victim' status of the UK in relation to terrorism. This will be further explored through an examination of the postemotional dimensions of a speech given by John Reid, during his time as Minister for Defence in Tony Blair's government. The theme of 'victimhood' is further explored in a discussion of the globalization of minorities suggested by the work of Arjun Appadurai. The chapter concludes with a discussion of emotionally-driven attempts to find meaning in meaningless times, and how explorations of this theme in contemporary works of literature could offer some important pointers for future academic research.

The politics of dangerousness

The idea of dangerousness has become very important in the post-11 September and post-7 July world (Butler 2004). In this section we will examine two examples of dangerousness. One is the 'control orders' introduced by the Blair government to restrict the freedoms of suspected terrorists (without initiating criminal proceedings), the other is a comparable example from the US. We will start with the latter, which is the case of the suspected bombers detained in Chicago recently (six men suspected of plotting to blow up the Sears Tower). Described as 'home-grown terrorists' the men were suspected of Al-Qaeda sympathies; according to the charges brought against them they had 'sworn allegiance to al-Qaeda but had no contacts with it' (*BBC News* 2006a). After being charged they were refused bail on the ground that, in the opinion of the judge, they posed a danger to society (*BBC News* 2006b). What is so unusual about suspected terrorists charged and held in detention? It is not so much the decision to detain them but the rationale used which deserves our attention.

Although they were thought to pose a threat to society by the judge, government officials quoted by the BBC said, 'they posed no real threat because they had no actual al-Qaeda contacts, no weapons and no means of carrying out the attacks' (*BBC News* 2006b). Another BBC news story reported that officials said the men 'posed no danger' (*BBC News* 2006a). The BBC was alert to the fact that US officials were making contradictory statements. One BBC journalist remarked that official statements both confirmed that the alleged plot was not far advanced and the terrorists were 'aspirational rather than operational', at the same time as the US Attorney General saw it as evidence that there exists a heightened possibility of home grown terror plots (Coomarasamy 2006). Mr Gonzales said that 'the lack of direct link to al-Qaeda did not make the group any less dangerous.... Left unchecked these home-grown terrorists may prove as dangerous as groups like al-Qaeda' (*BBC News* 2006a).

Clearly, those that pose no clear danger can still be thought dangerous. The 'war on terror' asserts its own temporality, stretching into the distant future. Likewise dangerousness is a latent property which may only reveal itself in the future. Judith Butler, in her book *Precarious Life*, makes the point that one line of defence used by the US for detaining 'enemy combatants' at Guantanamo Bay indefinitely and without the prospect of a trial is that they are 'dangerous people' (Butler 2004: 74–7). Butler demonstrates how in the eyes of the US authorities someone detained in Guantanamo Bay could be still deemed dangerous even if a trial found him not guilty of a particular charge. She argues that the determination of dangerousness is extra-legal, 'a certain level of dangerousness takes a human outside the bounds of law ... makes that human into the state's possession, infinitely detainable. What counts as "dangerous" is what is deemed dangerous by the state' (ibid.: 76).

There are UK parallels in the response to 'dangerousness'. The much-debated 'control orders', introduced by the Blair Government in March 2005 in cases where there is insufficient evidence to prosecute suspected terrorists, are motivated by the same need to address dangerousness. Control orders replaced emergency laws introduced after 11 September, which permitted the indefinite detention of suspects, but were adjudged illegal by the House of Lords in December 2004. The newer control orders are designed to limit the mobility of suspects who to this end are tagged, confined to their homes, and restricted in their communication. Although they are applied to those deemed dangerous, the danger that they actually represent has been the subject of much debate. For example, Shami Chakrabarti, director of Liberty, was quoted by the BBC as saying 'if someone is truly a dangerous terror suspect, why would you leave them at large?' (*BBC News* 2006c).

Moreover, the control orders have themselves been deemed dangerous (to individual liberties), and Britain has been criticized by the Council of Europe for introducing this measure. The need for control orders is in fact central to a continuing debate on the contemporary nature of rights and freedoms. Human rights are no longer sacrosanct. The Labour government portrays them as outmoded, being framed in Europe in an era in which the memory of 'state fascism' was still fresh (see Tempest 2006). Alvaro Gil-Robles, voicing the views of the Council of Europe, has warned that across Europe (but nowhere more so than in the UK) there has been a tendency 'to consider human rights and excessively restricting the effective administration of justice and the protection of the public interest' rather than the 'very foundation of democratic societies' (quoted in Gillan 2005). In the contemporary context in which a Home Office minister can suggest the introduction of 'a stronger version of control orders which would depart from the European Convention on Human Rights' the status of 'dangerous terror suspect' in both the UK and the US is clearly of central importance. Identifying dangerousness trumps the need to prove guilt.

'Cultural trauma' explanations

One dominant framework for understanding major disasters and events such as the 7 July bombings is that of 'cultural trauma' as developed by Jeffrey Alexander, Neil Smelser and their colleagues in the US (Alexander *et al.* 2004). The 'cultural trauma' approach is a productive way of understanding collective responses to traumatic events such as 11 September and as such holds much promise for understanding responses to 7 July.

According to Alexander 'cultural trauma occurs when members of a collectivity feel they have been subjected to a horrendous event that leaves indelible marks upon their group consciousness, marking their memories forever and changing their future identity in fundamental and irrevocable ways' (Alexander 2004: 1). Importantly, this sociological approach emphasizes that trauma does not exist in nature but is constructed by society. The approach adopted by Alexander *et al.* thus differs from 'common sense' understandings of trauma in that they do not assume that the trauma is a 'given', an intrinsic property of events themselves (ibid.: 2). They reject this 'naturalistic fallacy': 'events are not inherently traumatic. Trauma is a socially mediated attribution' (ibid.: 8). In other words, massive societal disruptions do not necessarily become traumatic: economic crisis or mass unemployment may be traumatic for individuals but will be not become collective traumas unless 'social crises ... become cultural crises' (ibid.: 10). For this, what is needed are 'carrier groups' in society – 'collective agents of the trauma process' (ibid.: 11) – who construct events as trauma. Specifically, the carrier groups organize the collective response; giving meaning to the group's injury, establishing the victim, attributing responsibility, and establishing the consequences (ibid: 22). Part of this process involves the reconstruction of identity by means of revising the collective memory and the institutionalization of commemoration. Significantly, for the theme of this chapter, the process of trauma construction outlined by Alexander works to calm and manage emotional responses by putting them in some explanatory perspective or coherent narrative. In Alexander's words, 'once the collective identity has been so reconstructed, there will eventually emerge a period of "calming down" ... and emotion become[s] less inflamed' (ibid.: 22).

In relation to the events of 11 September, Alexander *et al.* place it squarely within the realm of cultural trauma: collective shock and disbelief at the unexpected nature of the attacks, a sense of national violation, widespread collective mourning, a strong sense of the indelibility of the trauma, a sense of national brooding, collective endowment of the events with a sacred character, deliberate attempts at commemorialization, altered sense of national identity and mission (victimhood) (Smelser 2004: 265–7).

This attempt to capture the traumatic nature of 11 September (and the 'cultural trauma' approach more generally) is deficient in one crucial regard; it lacks an emotional dimension. More particularly, the emotional dimensions of the response to 11 September are downplayed in the 'cultural trauma' account, and where emotions are considered to be a significant dimension of the response they are treated in an unsystematic and rather confused way. For example, in his account of 11 September as cultural trauma Smelser accords a contradictory role to emotions. The initial reaction of Americans to the 11 September attacks was both 'emotional numbing' and revealed 'a level of emotionality perhaps unprecedented' (ibid.: 266). Emotional responses can certainly be contradictory but the form they take in this case needs explaining. In relation to patriotism, which of course was heightened in the aftermath of the attacks, Smelser does not interrogate its emotional significance and is rather accepting of the 'old-fashioned ... flag-waving patriotism ... a feeling of pride in the American way of life ... a feeling that we, as Americans were one again' (ibid.: 270), even though earlier he acknowledges that this 'oneness' tended to exclude Muslim Americans. As Abrams, Albright and Panofsky point out, any sense of 'unity' was constantly undermined by the continuing sense of threat and danger; who could be trusted (Abrams *et al.* 2004: 197)? Who should be feared? 'These problems necessarily called into question the nature of the community and its boundaries, awakening an "enemy in our midst" type of suspicion' (ibid.).

The cultural trauma approach is important because it draws attention to the constructed nature of traumatic events and how they become established in society as such. There are also some significant weaknesses which, once revealed, can add to our attempts to understand responses to 11 September and 7 July. First, we might note in passing that Smelser in particular downplays the contested nature of responses to 11 September, portraying them as consensual and 'displaying a notable lack of contestation' (Smelser 2004: 280). This account is challenged by Abrams, Albright and Panofsky who point out the contestation that emerged around ideas of patriotism, community and commemoration (Abrams *et al.* 2004). Second, and perhaps more importantly, for Alexander *et al.* the cultural construction of trauma is a way of rationalizing, managing and absorbing massive shocks to the social system. Through the collective acknowledgment of cultural trauma society is able to mobilize its healing mechanisms, draw strength, and 'move on'. What begins as a massive collective shock which provokes a series of inchoate responses, will, through the process of constructing cultural trauma, become a rational way of managing feelings of distress, anger, responsibility, guilt and processing them as a useful and constructive episode of social learning. Thus, through social trauma emotion is translated into rationality and the 'world turned upside down' is righted once more. In this way 'social groups interact with emotion to create new and binding understandings of social responsibility' (Alexander *et al.* 2004, publisher's jacket blurb). In other words, cultural trauma is a mechanism for apprehending and understanding the inexplicable and for formulating a rational response.

Beyond trauma: postemotional society

The above section has explored the applicability of explanations for 7 July rooted in the sociology of cultural trauma and concluded that these downplay the emotional dimension of politics. A way forward, it is suggested, is to engage with the work of the American sociologist Stjepan Mestrovic and his work on 'postemotional society'. Mestrovic shows us how emotions are an integral part of rationality and action in the contemporary world: emotions and rational behaviour are not polar opposites. Mestrovic advances an understanding of the role of emotions in political life in ways which do not reduce emotions to secondary importance or perceive them as needing to be mastered or harnessed by rational human actors.

'Postemotional society harks back to the distant past in order to create synthetic moral indignation and other emotional responses in the present' (Mestrovic 1997). For Mestrovic postemotionalism indicates not only that emotions are manipulated and mechanized in contemporary public life – 'intellectualized, mechanical, mass-produced emotions – but importantly dead emotions are recycled (ibid.: 26, 2). The mass production of emotions and their manipulation comes together in 'the oppressive ethic of niceness' (ibid.: 44). The postemotional individual is other-directed (a term Mestrovic borrows from Riesman) rather than the inner-directed figure associated with modernity (driven by goals, a sense of purpose, and an internal moral compass). The other-directed type wants to be all things to all people, nice to everyone, concerned with what others think of him/her, and attempts to be emotionality in tune with others. Tony Blair is the first postemotional Prime Minister (although John Major deserves a mention), as Bill Clinton was the first postemotional President (ibid.: 47).

In the context of the 7 July bombings, the difference between an emotional response and a postemotional one is that the former would involve immediate outrage and anger; criticisms of the government perhaps and the performance of the security services. The postemotional response draws upon 'dead' emotions, recycling ideas of the Blitz spirit for example, and results not in outrage but in indignation (as shown in the attitude displayed by some towards human rights legislation for not permitting infinite detention of suspects, for example). Emotions have been socially transformed into objects for consumption: 'anger becomes indignation ... envy an objectless craving for something better. Hate is transformed into a subtle malice that is hidden in all sorts of intellectualizations. Heartfelt joy is now the bland happiness represented by the "Happy Meal"' (Mestrovic 1997: 62).

One central aspect of postemotionalism is the rhetoric of victimhood. Mestrovic makes the case that anger and outrage have been replaced by 'dead' emotions retrieved from history (as is the case with recent episodes of ethnic violence in the former Yugoslavia). Victimhood has become a celebrated state – and a licence (Staples in Mestrovic 1997: 9). Not surprisingly perhaps, initial responses to both 11 September and 7 July emphasized victimhood. With the benefit of a longer-term perspective, perhaps, the victimhood status of the US was overstated, and is rather dismissed by Ulrich Beck: 'Fifteen suicidal terrorists armed with carpet knives sufficed to compel the global hegemon to see itself as victim' (Beck 2006: 153). In any case, victim status served the US well in the early days of the 'war on terror'. As Smelser points out, the victimization of the US served as a considerable asset 'in mobilizing the support and cooperation of other countries' (Smelser 2004: 272). I want to focus on one aspect of the UK's 'victim status' and offer a reading based on Mestrovic's 'postemotional society' thesis. The example I have chosen to focus on is the then Defence Minister John Reid's defence of the actions of UK soldiers in Iraq (made in the light of growing evidence of abuse of Iraqi citizens in and around Basra).

In a speech at King's College, London on 20 February 2006 Reid stated that he is not attempting to defend the indefensible. The army must be responsible for maintaining high standards. However, he is concerned with what he sees as a lack of 'balance and fairness towards our troops' who today have to fight on a 'changed and hugely uneven battlefield' (Reid 2006). We, the public, do not always understand military life: 'the public have a continually looser grasp of what it means to be a soldier' (ibid.). What we do not comprehend, Reid asserts, is that the enemy are unconstrained by any law and unfettered by any sense of morality: 'we intrinsically value life, they do not'. 'Indeed, the enemy is unrecognisable from the past.... It is the completely unconstrained terrorist' (ibid.).

According to Reid, the freedoms of the Western media can result in public opinion being turned against our own troops. Al-Qaeda are adept at releasing video footage of 'isolated unlawful acts by those ranged against them' (Reid 2006) and exploiting the resulting sway of public opinion. (We must note in passing that what starts as a speech defending the actions of British soldiers in Iraq quickly mobilizes the (non-Iraqi) threat of Al-Qaeda in order to frame the difficulties that those troops face.) Because of media openness and the access of the terrorists to that media our troops are under greater scrutiny than ever before. 'British troops are forced to operate on what I call "an uneven playing field of scrutiny" ... there is now asymmetric – uneven – scrutiny of warfare' (ibid.). The crux of the matter is that 'it is this uneven battlefield of one-sided scrutiny which has done so much to encourage the perception among our troops that they are increasingly constrained while the enemy is freer than ever to perpetrate the most inhumane practices and crimes' (ibid.).

Reid's message that we need to be 'slower to condemn, quicker to understand' the forces is packaged emotionally, and indeed postemotionally. The speech makes its case for not dwelling disproportionately on isolated acts of wrongdoing by British soldiers by appealing to historically-relevant experiences of war, and more particularly to emotional constructions such as good versus evil, sacrifice versus freedoms, and 'fairness' versus human rights. The good/evil dichotomy is based on more than a reminder that the enemy are 'beyond the pale' and possess no moral legitimacy, although this is a key motif: 'we' fight for what is right and oppose what is wrong, the adversary 'revels in mass murder' and 'sets out to cause the greatest pain it can to innocent people' (Reid 2006). Reid draws upon the enemy imagery of Hitler and the Nazis to point up the magnitude of the evil which Al-Qaeda is capable, unfettered as it is by any sense of morality: 'it is the rule of law and the virtue of freedom of expression versus barbarism' (ibid.).

Another key theme in Reid's speech is that of 'sacrifice versus freedoms', which again is rooted in the postemotional resonance of resistance to Nazism. 'Without the wartime generation that made sacrifices to defeat Hitler, we wouldn't have the means to fight this more modern evil' (Reid 2006). The freedoms referred to here are press freedoms, and the sacrifices are those associated with a curtailment of press freedom 'in the national interest'. Reid's argument is that Al-Qaeda will exploit media images for their own ends; 'it is the media's responsibility to ensure that in reporting the facts ... it does not fall victim to this campaign' (ibid.). The enemy seeks to undermine our public morale by using 'our democratic freedom of speech to destroy our will to fight for our democratic values' (ibid.). It is a battle of ideas which, like earlier ideological struggles against communism and Nazism, can be won. Reid portrays the struggle against the modern enemy in postemotional terms drawing heavily on the fixed emotional reference points associated with WWII and the struggle against communism. In his attempts to mobilize society in the fight against terrorism ('the struggle has to be at every level, in every way and by every single person in this country' (*BBC News* 2006d)) he is drawn to equate the terrorist threat to the UK with the earlier threat of Nazism; 'Britain is living in the most threatening time since the second world war' (Tempest 2006). In doing so he overplays his hand. Terrorism is an ugly thing but, as many commentators have pointed out, it 'is not a threat to human society to rank with a world war' (Jenkins 2006).

Another key theme in his speech is 'fairness' versus human rights and this links strongly with the previously discussed themes of good versus evil and sacrifice versus freedom. As we noted earlier, Reid argues that British troops are operating on an 'uneven playing field of scrutiny': 'we' not only have to play to the rules, but we have to be seen to be doing so. This has resulted in a 'perception among our troops that they are increasingly constrained while the enemy is freer than ever to perpetrate the most inhumane practices and crimes' (Reid 2006). Reid reiterates that British troops go to great lengths to stay within the law, treat people fairly ('even the enemy'). Fairness is built in to military operations, the problem however is human rights legislation which, 'has improved lives in so many areas' but 'has also sometimes become the convenient banner under which some who are fundamentally opposed to our Armed Forces, or to the government of the day, or to a particular military conflict, have chosen to march' (ibid.). This is a problem, states Reid, because in the soldiers' perception 'human rights lawyers and ... the International Criminal Court are waiting in the wings to step in and act against them' (ibid.). They need to know that they operate under British law not European and International law. Reid opposes 'fairness', an intrinsic decency rooted in the professionalism of an army which 'seeks to inject morality – right and wrong – into the harsh reality of warfare' (ibid.) to the idea of Human Rights, which is portrayed as well-meaning but in reality benefiting the enemy. In a striking postemotional passage in which Reid reflects on the sacrifices of the Second World War generation and the courage of modern troops he states, 'both these groups must sometimes feel that if Lord Haw-Haw was still around today, someone would be telling us that human rights demand that he be given a weekly column in the newspapers'. Reid quotes with approval Michael Ignatieff's view that 'the decisive restraint on inhuman practice on the battlefield lies within the warrior himself' (Ignatieff 2001). In other words, human rights legislation is no substitute for an innate sense of fairness and the knowledge that we are fighting for what is right. Human rights can only be established by treaties, legislation and international agreements. What is right and what is fair, on the other hand, is instinctive and the result of 'gut feeling'.

Victimhood and the global 'geography of anger'

There are many dimensions to victimhood. Arjun Appadurai, writing about terrorism in the contemporary world, emphasizes that we need to go beyond explanations that locate the perpetrators of the bombings in London in July 2005 within religious minorities. The bombers were not content to reside in the 'isolating world of national minorities'. Instead they chose to identify with networks of global terror. 'Thus they morph from one kind of minority – weak, disempowered, disenfranchised, and angry – to another kind of minority – cellular, globalized, transnational, armed, and dangerous' (Appadurai 2006: 112–13). In the same process their sense of victimhood is transformed as they come to identify with Muslims in Palestine, Iraq, Gujarat and elsewhere:

> Young Muslims (of Indian and Pakistani origin) in Britain could not have failed to make the connections between 9/11 in New York, the war in Iraq and Afghanistan, the ongoing brutalization of their fellow Muslims in Palestine, the pogrom against Muslims in Gujarat in 2002...
>
> (Appadurai 2006: 112)

The result is that

> their self-perception as injured minorities gives way to a different sense of themselves as a vanguard minority who actually speak for a sacred majority – the Muslims of the world ... it is the rogue voice of an injured global majority.
>
> (ibid.: 111)

The account offered by Appadurai is interesting because he incorporates a strong global dimension in his account of minorities, ethnic conflict, and terror. He also shows how minorities marginalized from national structures of governance can connect with global networks and in doing so transform their minority status into something new: a form of global victimhood which also offers a new form of empowerment. The result is not a 'clash of civilizations' but a conflict between what Devji terms 'two kinds of global network – one of terror and the other of security, to employ the US administration's terminology' (Devji 2005: xii). Appadurai formulates this idea in a slightly different way. For him, the upshot is 'a new sort of emotional Cold War between those who identify with the losers in the new game and those who identify with the small group of winners, notably the United States' (Appadurai 2006: 23).

Clearly, victims are not to be simply equated with losers: the status of victimhood is a key stake in the struggle for hearts and minds. We have seen how both the UK and the US have positioned themselves as victims, by being subject to 'asymmetric scrutiny' in the conduct of war in the case of the UK, and in the immediate aftermath of 11 September in the case of the US, a status which did them no harm when attempting to assemble a 'coalition of the willing'. Mestrovic provides a context for understanding the desirability of victimhood status through its centrality to what he terms postemotionalism. This status derives from the licence accorded victims seeking redress, retribution and revenge. What Appadurai demonstrates is how victimhood can 'go global' and create a new form of equivalence between the powerful and the powerless leading to what he terms an 'emotional Cold War'.

Discussion and concluding comments

In this emotional universe the world does not 'make sense' in expected ways, but rather than bemoaning this departure from political rationality perhaps we should address it on its own terms rather than trying to translate it into a conventional language of politics. I will close with a suggestive reading of two contemporary novels which provide very interesting accounts of responses to terrorism, and which engage with themes central to this paper; Liz Jensen's *The Paper Eater* (2001), and J. G. Ballard's *Millennium People* (2004). The novels suggest that the attempt to 'find meaning in meaningless times' is perhaps not the most productive way forward, at least not in terms of the 'politics of emotion' currently on offer. It is suggested that contemporary literature can offer some pointers for future academic research, particularly if we are willing to focus less on fear and trepidation and more on awe and wonder.

Ballard's novel deals centrally with the issue of 'finding meaning in meaningless times' and speaks directly to the issue of the relation between rational understanding and terrorist violence. The novel deals with both the aftermath of a terrorist bombing (the central character's ex-wife is killed by an explosion at Heathrow) and the insurrection of middle-class residents in Chelsea. The latter is caused in part by minor local issues (rising service charges on their accommodation) coupled with a growing sense of the erosion of their living standards and their exploitation (they begin to realize that the system that they have bought into in such a big way has taken them for granted and their skills are undervalued in a job market increasingly dominated by technology and finance, to the extent that they feel they have been transformed into a 'new working class'). They are pushed to the point where they become amenable to manipulation by urban terrorists. Ballard's central theme is that we rely upon motive, reason, explanation in order to 'keep the world sane'. 'Kick those props away and we see that the meaningless act is the only one that has any meaning' (Ballard 2004: 255). As one character says of the deaths caused by the bomb at Heathrow, 'the deaths were pointless and inexplicable, but maybe that *was* the point. A motiveless act stops the universe in its tracks' (ibid.: 255). This theme is reiterated elsewhere in the book. Earlier, one of the central characters states that, 'people who find the world meaningless find meaning in pointless violence' (ibid.: 81). Terrorism is portrayed as being something which cannot be apprehended by rationality; it evades meaning in conventional terms. Another character states that 'a truly pointless act of violence, shooting at random into a crowd, grips our attention for months. The absence of rational motive carries a significance of its own' (ibid.: 194).

We can interpret these insights through the postemotional lens. On Mestrovic's account we have become habituated to synthetic or recycled emotions to such an extent that we no longer know how to be genuinely angry, as opposed to being indignant. Additionally, we are so accustomed to media images of suffering and accounts of tragedy that we have exhausted our fund of appropriate responses. Disaster is commonplace – a flood in Bangladesh today, an earthquake in Pakistan yesterday, starvation in Darfur tomorrow – and such events are emotionally pre-packaged for us by news channels demanding a slice of the prime-time audience. Earthquakes, floods and famine rarely provoke an emotional reaction in us, unless we are led towards particular emotional exits – donating aid to victims of the tsunami or making poverty history by consuming the correct colour of wristband – by media-led appeals to our generous nature and/or humanitarian sensibilities, which in turn are fed by a consumerist logic (Stevenson 2007). Otherwise it is difficult for news of disasters to grab our attention in a way that can compete with the 'drama' of reality TV. For Mestrovic, postemotionalism means that TV is able to generate a greater display of emotions over the result of a talent contest than when transmitting accounts of wars or natural disasters. This helps us understand why in such a society, a seemingly random or meaningless act of violence can carry a new meaning: the power to arrest the gaze of the postemotional TV viewer.

Jensen's novel, which might be described loosely as science fiction, deals directly with the de-politicization of governance and the creation of 'consumer government' where opting for who runs the country is the equivalent of deciding which brand to buy at the supermarket. This is akin to what Philip Bobbitt has called a 'market state' 'in which citizens have become like consumers' (Ash 2006). In Jensen's novel the government skilfully manipulates (dis)information to create the threat of terrorism, in order to deflect attention from the geological and ecological instability of the artificial island (Atlantica) on which the story is set. The terrorists are constructed by the authorities as eco-Luddites and enemies of the people. But the government's strategy doesn't fool everyone. As one character says, 'who in their right mind would turn on the very technology that allows them to live on Atlantica in the first place?... It doesn't make sense. It's meaningless. Motiveless' (Jensen 2001: 132). There exists a clear correspondence here between Jensen's novel and Ballard's: terrorist acts as deliberately meaningless. But Jensen explores the theme of meaninglessness in more depth. One character in the novel offers the following explanation for the fabricated eco-terrorism; that it is designed to deflect attention away from a more fundamental concern. The ecological change brought about by the geological instability of the island 'has been a source of *wonder*, rather than *apprehension*' (Jensen 2001: 132; emphasis in original). Jensen has touched on something very important here. Wonder is a vastly under-researched aspect of the 'politics of emotion', certainly since interest in what the Romantic thinkers of the eighteenth and nineteenth centuries termed 'the sublime' disappeared from the social science agenda (Rumford and Inglis 2005). In its original formulation, the sublime referred to the awe experienced in the face of the vastness of nature, and the realization of human frailty in the face of the power of the natural elements. The sublime is a valuable concept and allows us to understand how wondrous and awe-inspiring events are difficult to comprehend or assimilate into the existing vocabulary of politics. For example, the devastation caused in and around New Orleans by Hurricane Katrina can be seen as awe-inspiring because of the destructive power of nature, on the one hand, and because the response by the

US authorities was not only totally inadequate, but almost unbelievable in the context of the resource mobilization of which the world's most powerful nation-state is capable. The devastation of New Orleans, the tardiness and inadequacy of the response, the breakdown of law and order that ensued, and the fortitude of many who suffered there as a result was truly awe-inspiring.

To return to the quotation from Jensen above, it is useful to view terrorism as 'a source of wonder, rather than apprehension' because the proximity of terror, or, as in the case of her novel, the fabrication of a terrorist threat, can be used to generate a sense of awe or wonder in the population. And on this basis they can be more easily governed. Expressed in other terms, a population is likely to acquiesce in the face of wonder, whereas fear may lead them towards panic and unruliness. As I have argued elsewhere (Rumford 2008) new opportunities for governance often accompany awe-inspiring events, particularly where governments are capable of rendering the unfamiliarity of the wondrous in very familiar and reassuring terms. Attempts to understand the emotional dimension to contemporary politics, for example Bauman's *Liquid Fear* (2006), Appadurai's *Fear of Small Numbers* (2006), Robin's *Fear, The History of a Political Idea* (2004), and Clarke *et al.*'s *Emotion, Politics and Society* (2006) have resulted in an overdue emphasis on fear, anxiety, risk and trepidation. Wonder may yet prove to be a better key for unlocking the 'meaning' of terror and the political responses to it.

References

Abrams, C., Albright, K. and Panofsky, A. (2004), 'Contesting the New York community: from liminality to the "new normal" in the wake of September 11', *City and Community* 3(3): 189–220.

Alexander, J. (2004), 'Towards a theory of cultural trauma', in J. Alexander *et al.* (2004).

Alexander, J., Eyerman, R., Giesen, B., Smelser, N. and Sztompka, P. (2004), *Cultural Trauma and Collective Identity*, Berkeley, CA: University of California Press.

Appadurai, A. (2006), *Fear of Small Numbers: An Essay on the Geography of Anger*, Durham, NC: Duke University Press.

Ash, T. G. (2006), 'A false metaphor has been written out in blood. We need to think again', *Guardian*, 2 November. Available at: www.guardian.co.uk/commentisfree/2006/nov/02/comment.politics1.

Ballard, J. G. (2004), *Millennium People*, London: Harper Perennial.

Bauman, Z. (2006), *Liquid Fear*, Cambridge: Polity Press.

BBC News (2006a), 'US fears home-grown terror threat', 24 June. Available at: http://news.bbc.co.uk/1/hi/world/americas/5112354.stm.

BBC News (2006b), 'Chicago plot suspects denied bail', 5 July. Available at: http://news.bbc.co.uk/1/hi/world/americas/5152652.stm.

BBC News (2006c), 'Terror controls "may get tougher"', 17 October. Available at: http://news.bbc.co.uk/1/hi/uk/6057562.stm.

BBC News (2006d), 'Reid makes Nazi terror comparison', 31 October. Available at: http://news.bbc.co.uk/1/hi/uk/6102508.stm.

Beck, U. (2006), *Cosmopolitan Vision*, Cambridge: Polity Press.

Butler, J. (2004), *Precarious Life: The Powers of Mourning and Violence*, London: Verso.

Clarke, S., Hoggart, P. and Thompson, S. (eds) (2006), *Emotion, Politics and Society*, Houndmills: Palgrave.
Coomarasamy, J. (2006), 'Home front fears in war on terror', *BBC News 24*, 4 June.
Devji, F. (2005), *Landscapes of the Jihad: Militancy, Morality and Modernity*, London: Hurst and Co.
Gillan, A. (2005), 'Europe condemns UK's terror control orders', *Guardian*, 9 June. Available at: www.guardian.co.uk/politics/2005/jun/09/humanrights.terrorism1.
Ignatieff, M. (2001), 'It's war – but it doesn't have to be dirty', *Guardian*, 1 October. Available at: www.guardian.co.uk/world/2001/oct/01/afghanistan.terrorism9.
Jenkins, S. (2006), 'Blair is wildly exaggerating the threat posed by terrorism', *Guardian*, 22 November. Available at: www.guardian.co.uk/commentisfree/story/0,,1953857, 00.html.
Jensen, L. (2001), *The Paper Eater*, London: Bloomsbury.
Mestrovic, S. (1997), *Postemotional Society*, London: Sage.
Reid, J. (2006), Speech to Kings College, London, 20 February.
Robin, C. (2004), *Fear: The History of a Political Idea*, Oxford: Oxford University Press.
Rumford, C. (2008), *Cosmopolitan Spaces: Globalization, Europe, Theory*, London: Routledge.
Rumford, C. and Inglis, D. (2005), 'The Cosmopolitan Sublime: Romanticism, subjectivity, and the infinities of nature'. Paper presented at the Millennium Annual Conference, 'Between Fear and Wonder: International Politics, Representation and "the Sublime"', London School of Economics.
Runciman, D. (2006), *The Politics of Good Intentions: History, Fear and Hypocrisy in the New World Order*, Princeton, NJ: Princeton University Press.
Smelser, N. (2004), 'September 11, 2001 as cultural trauma', in J. Alexander *et al.* (2004).
Stevenson, N. (2007), 'Cosmopolitan Europe: post-colonialism and the politics of imperialism', in C. Rumford (ed.), *Cosmopolitanism and Europe*, Liverpool: Liverpool University Press.
Tempest, M. (2006), 'Britain facing "most sustained threat since WWII" says Reid', *Guardian*, 9 August. Available at: www.guardian.co.uk/politics/2006/aug/09/immigrationpolicy.uksecurity.

10 The ontopolitics of response
Difference, alterity and the face

Madeleine Fagan

Introduction

This chapter is an attempt at beginning to problematize the concept of response in the context of 'responses' to terrorism. Using the work of Emmanuel Levinas, this chapter investigates what response might mean or entail. In it I highlight the relationship between response and responsibility and explore the links between the way in which we conceptualize the other, otherness or difference and the possibilities for thinking about response. The chapter draws on Levinas's approach of distinguishing alterity from difference and uses this to highlight the potential problems with thinking in terms of difference, particularly with respect to the possibility of response and responsibility. I suggest that this thinking in terms of difference is one of the ontopolitical underpinnings of how we often approach response. That is, that difference, rather than alterity (which will be covered in more detail below) acts as one of the fundaments about the necessities and possibilities of human being that is often invoked in the way we think about response.

Using Levinas's work on alterity and the face, the chapter suggests that assumptions about response that are often relied upon are problematic and that by failing to interrogate these assumptions alternative possibilities of response are closed off.

I start from the position, drawn from Levinas, that any response in this context does not only require analysis in terms of politics, but also in terms of ethics and responsibility, that ethics and politics cannot be separated in any straightforward way and as such that any question of the politics of response is always also about the ethics of response (see Fagan, forthcoming 2008). I suggest, following Judith Butler, that some of what are termed 'responses' to the London bombings can be seen as moves which 'de-face' in the Levinasian sense and so can have the effect of negating the possibility of response (Butler 2004: 130). This in turn closes down possibilities of politics and of responsibility.

This chapter is not an attempt to put forward some kind of programme for how to go about thinking in terms of alterity, or to respond 'better'. Rather, following William Connolly, it is an exercise in trying to project our ontopolitical starting points into analyses, to make them problematic rather than natural-ized (Connolly 1992). This is important because it is precisely these starting points which legitimize some forms of response and obscure the possibilities of others. The chapter is concerned mainly with the UK case, in particular the bombings on 7 July 2005, but since the examples are illustrative as opposed to being case studies, I hope that the conclusions drawn are not limited to this context.

The chapter will proceed in three sections. First, a discussion of the role of stabilization, recognition and identification in some approaches to response. Second, an introduction to Levinas's thought on alterity and the face as an alternative starting point for thinking about response. Third, an analysis of the problems this starting point highlights for some examples of so-called 'responses' to terrorism.

Responses to the London bombings

When we talk about responses to terrorism, to the attacks on the World Trade Center of 11 September 2001, the bombings in Madrid on 11 March 2004, or in London on 7 July 2005 it seems clear what we mean by this word 'response'. Response is often taken to mean reaction (Wilkinson 2007), responses are policies designed to prevent the similar events occurring in the future, policies or discussion regarding immigration, identity cards, community integration, passenger screening on aircraft, baggage restrictions, media reactions and discussion, attempts at understanding radicalisation in order to prevent or reverse it and so on.[1] In the literature attempting to respond to the London bombings, the objective often seems to be to acquire better knowledge in order to avoid a repeat of the tragedy (Black 2005: 8; Gove 2006; Rai 2006: 3; Wilkinson 2007). Response is explicitly linked for these authors in avoiding a repeat performance (Black 2005: 47). We need, it is claimed, to understand better what happened, to make sense of it (Rai 2006: 3). Of course, these investigations are hugely important and necessary – we do need to interrogate the causes, establish or contest the facts as presented, discuss strategies to prevent further loss of life. But, if this is the full extent of our attempt to respond it may impose limitations on our thinking which close down other possibilities.

Response is only possible in this discourse if we can first understand, identify and pin down that to which we are attempting to respond. We must first know what we are responding to; response is something which happens 'after the fact' (Black 2005: 49) and yet we must learn the importance of 'proactively preparing ... responsive measures' (Makarenko 2007: 38), so pinning down the event even before it has happened. We might identify the threat as diffuse, protean, as the 'known unknown', and so on, but it remains recognizable as a threat and from a relatively well-identified group. We may not know who the members of this group are but if we did, if we could identify them correctly, then we would know where the threat was coming from. We know what or who it is we are looking for, the only remaining problem is identifying them correctly. As Black argues, the question of response, for example to suspected suicide bombers, is not whether we should kill them, but 'how can we make sure they are suicide bombers before we act?' (Black 2005: 50).

Underpinning these approaches is the idea that we respond to something, a particular clear-cut event the meaning of which is relatively clear, stable, and accessible to us, and in the creation of which we are not implicated. Or we respond to someone, a recognizable individual whose identity is available to us. The task of responding better is, as in Black's statement above, one of recognizing better. We must be able to identify someone to be able to respond correctly – terrorist or Brazilian electrician? The job is to make sure that we identify correctly. The key assumption is that the thing, event or person is separate or separable from us and yet accessible to us, removed so that we can examine it, understand it, acquire knowledge about it and then make an autonomous decision about what we should do in response. This may explain why some of the key moves involved in 'responses' are attempts to produce narratives or reports, to create an official, stable version of what exactly has happened, for example in the *Report of the Official Account of the Bombings in London on July 7th 2005* (2006).

If we are implicated in the creation of the event or identity then it is no longer something outside of ourselves which we can hold at a distance to examine. If we, or our responses, are implicated in the interpretation of the event then the very meaning of the event or identity of the individual becomes unstable, and again, how can we respond if we are not sure what we are responding to or if we cannot clearly separate the response from the thing to which it responds? Responses are approached as an effect of some cause, on a straight timeline, one clearly following the other. The *Official Account* goes as far as producing such a timeline of the events and responses (*Report of the Official Account* 2006: 2–11).

The key moves then in this way of thinking about response are of thinking in terms of separating and making accessible (which, as I will argue below, actually entails a refusal of separation), separating temporally and spatially, thus allowing for the stabilization of meaning and identity and enabling the gathering of information and knowledge to guide our responses.

However, this way of thinking about response is not as clear-cut as it may initially seem. It foregrounds an understanding in terms of 'reacting to', asking the question of what we should do. In doing so, the element of response as 'answering to' is somewhat neglected. Further, the themes of separation and accessibility, of identity and meaning, of a clear temporal separation between event and response rely on particular ideas about subjectivity and relationality which Levinas's work begins to problematize. Levinas's approach to the themes of difference, alterity and the face are key in beginning to rethink approaches to response and as such will be the focus of the following section of this chapter.

Alterity and the face

Levinas is, in part, concerned with articulating a relationship with the other which preserves them as other. The other is completely other for Levinas, absolute alterity, outside of the realms of knowledge that we may try to reduce them to, there is an absolute distance between the self and the other which means they cannot be totalized (Levinas 1969: 35). Approaching the other in terms of knowledge, understanding or recognition, Levinas argues, is violent towards them; 'Thematization and conceptualization ... are not peace with the other but suppression or possession of the other' (ibid.: 46). This is because for Levinas knowledge is something that subsumes the other within the self and brings it into the realm of the self. The other is something more than an object which can be placed in one of my categories and as such allowed a place in my world (Wild 1969: 13). Once the other has been rendered, a part of the self it becomes impossible to enter into a social relation with them. Knowledge is, for Levinas,

> [A] relation with what one equals and includes, with that whose alterity one suspends, with what becomes immanent, because it is to my measure and my scale ... there is in knowledge, in the final account, an impossibility of escaping the self; hence sociality cannot have the same structure as knowledge.
>
> (Levinas 1985: 60)

Knowledge confers some degree of ownership, as the thing known is brought within the self's comprehension, it becomes possessed or possessable (ibid.: 61).

The other for Levinas is not just different in her or his characteristics, a different person, but still a person *like me*, under a genus, categorizable, an example of a type, or ultimately part of a totality. It is this understanding of difference which Levinas refuses in favour of a more radical view of alterity, as distinct from difference in this sense. The other is completely other for Levinas, absolute, rather than a relative alterity or oppositional difference, outside of the realms of knowledge or understanding that we might try to reduce them to. The other is not considered in terms of an *alter ego*, 'another self with different properties and accidents but in all essential respects like me' (Wild 1969: 13). It is precisely this approach that places the self and the other as in common and which negates the alterity of the other: 'The alterity of the other does not depend on any quality that would distinguish him from me, for a distinction of this nature would precisely imply between us that community of genus which already nullifies alterity' (Levinas 1969: 194).

This alterity then is of a different order, it is not dependent on characteristics of the other, the content of their difference, which make them different from me, rather Levinas suggests that it is otherness itself which is the content of the other. It is not differences (of characteristic, of identity) that constitute this absolute alterity, instead Levinas argues that the alterity is what allows for differences in the first place; 'It is not difference that makes alterity; alterity makes difference' (Levinas with Robbins 2001: 106). It is not that we know the other as such and such a type, as an example of a category who is differentiated by particular aspects or characteristics, but that this initial 'such and such a type' or 'example of a category' are removed, that the difference is not in the attributes, the content of the other, or the identity of the other that differentiates, rather that as Levinas asserts, 'Its formal characteristic, to be other, makes up its content' (Levinas 1969: 35). The alterity of the other, for Levinas, does not result from its identity, but constitutes it (ibid.: 251).

This understanding of the other as absolute alterity in Levinas has implications for the way in which he conceives of interpersonal relationships and sociality. Rather than concern for the other arising from some commonality between us Levinas sees it as arising precisely out of the lack of commonality. Rather than community in some sense being the basis for concern for the other Levinas instead argues that community is a result of the concern which arises from the fact of absolute alterity, claiming that 'it is not because the neighbour would be recognized as belonging to the same genus as me that he concerns me. He is precisely *other*. The community with him begins in my obligation to him' (Levinas 2004: 87). Levinas thus reformulates the interpersonal relationship as a relationship with something completely outside the self and the self's powers to bring it into its grid of understanding and possession. Instead he posits a relationship with something completely other as the only relationship worthy of the name (since all others would be a relationship with something already internal to the self, so not a relationship at all). This relation with something completely other and impervious to my powers of comprehension and control is for Levinas enacted in a face-to-face relation of complete separateness (which will be elaborated below). For him, true togetherness is about this separation of the face-to-face rather than about any degree of synthesis (Levinas 1985: 77). We are not together, for Levinas, in the commonality of being individuals within a genus, an analysis where the fact of the elements of sameness among us would come first (ibid.: 78). The way in which we are together is rather, he argues, through first being completely different and strange to one another. Community and togetherness only then emerge, as in a sense secondary, through the obligation that this alterity enjoins. Community does not found obligation, rather obligation founds community. Togetherness is not found in being in common, but only through being utterly uncommon.

Levinas describes this relation with the Other, with something completely other and impervious to my powers of comprehension and control, in terms of the concept of the face and the face-to-face relation. The face, for Levinas, is fundamentally the point at which we are exposed to the otherness of the Other and as such is what determines my relation with the Other.

The face might be best thought in terms of the site at which the other exposes themselves to me, as the way in which I become aware of the other as other and, consequently, as the way in which I am called to responsibility to this other. For Levinas, encountering the other as face is the only encounter in which they are not stripped of their alterity and approached as an object to be brought within the realm of the self.

Importantly, although the term 'face' immediately suggests a human face, in terms of features, a nose, eyes and a mouth, as an image or something recognizable, Levinas's use of this term is somewhat different. Levinas refuses the idea of the face as an image or an object of perception. He suggests that to encounter the 'face' one cannot look at a human face in the usual way. To look, he argues, is knowledge and perception and so negates the possibility of entering into a non-totalizing relation with the Other because it brings the Other into our own sphere of ownership and thus would be tantamount to entering into a relation with oneself (Levinas 1985: 85). It is the idea of the face as recognizable features which creates the Other as an object. For Levinas

> You turn yourself toward the Other as toward an object when you see a nose, eyes, a forehead, a chin, and you can describe them. The best way of encountering the Other is not even to notice the colour of his eyes.
> (Levinas 1985: 85)

If you notice the colour of the Other's eyes, he argues, you are not in a social (that is, non-totalizing) relation with them (ibid.: 85).

For Levinas, while it is possible to be in a social relationship where elements of perception exist, this is not the case if these are the full content of the relationship. While he admits that the relationship with the face can be dominated by perception, he points out that what is specifically the face, what allows for sociality and what is otherness is precisely what cannot be reduced to perception (ibid.: 86), or what overflows perception (Levinas 1969: 297). The reason that understanding the face in terms of images is problematic for Levinas is that he sees images as being immanent to one's own thought, 'as though they came from me' (ibid.: 297). To appear to me the Other would have to in some way make themselves intelligible to me, to signal to me in a way that I could understand and could thus make my own, thus for Levinas the neighbour as Other does not appear (Levinas 2004: 86). What sort of signalling, he asks, 'could he send before me which would not strip him of his exclusive alterity?' (ibid.: 86).

The face for Levinas is an exposure to the Other and in exposure to or relation with the face the Other is, he argues, both commanding and destitute. Encountering the face means some kind of awareness or realization of the mortality, material misery, defencelessness and vulnerability of the Other; 'the face . . . is like a being's exposure unto death; the without defence, the nudity and the misery of the Other' (Levinas with Robbins 2001: 48). The discovery of the Other as defenceless and before death is for Levinas intimately interwoven with the Other's call to me and demands on me and it is this combination, of exposure and command which for Levinas is the face, it is 'this discovery of his death, this hearing of his call' which he terms 'the face of the Other' (ibid.:108). It is the discovery of the death of the Other, their destitution and what Levinas calls nudity, that calls to me, that institutes responsibility to this Other. In an awareness of or exposure to the defencelessness of the Other the self is called to responsibility and subjection to that Other; the nudity of the face is a call to the self (ibid.: 115).

So there are two strands to the exposure of the face; a contact with the nudity and destitution of the Other, their defencelessness, their being before death, but the face also commands, it is in the face that I find myself responsible for the Other and ordered to respect and protect them. The face is the commandment not to kill; 'The face is what one cannot kill, or at least it is that whose *meaning* consists in saying "thou shalt not kill"' (Levinas 1985: 87). So it is through the face-to-face relation that we are responsible for the Other, immediately infinitely obligated by their call.

So the face for Levinas is an exposure to the other person, to their destitution and their command, but as mentioned above, the face does not, for Levinas necessarily refer to a human *face*, in terms of features. What the face does is to expose the uniqueness and alterity of the other, and announce her or his command not to kill (that is, to do everything possible for them, to not take any action which may result, however inadvertently, in the death of the other). It is not an image of the other nor even necessarily another person at all. Levinas's talk of touching and proximity does not necessarily refer to being close to, or being able to see another person. For him, the face, while very human, is not necessarily a human *face* (Levinas 1996: 167). For Levinas, the face is the expressive in the other 'and the whole human body is in this sense more or less face' (Levinas 1985: 97). However, while it may be easy enough to see how Levinas's sense of face can refer to human expression more generally, he goes even further than this. The face, he argues, does not even have to be a person; 'The possibility for the human of signifying in its uniqueness, of my accountability for him, can come from a bare arm sculpted by Rodin' (Levinas with Robbins 2001: 208). This begins to make clearer the distance between the concept of the human face in terms of recognizable features and Levinas's use of the word 'face'. We can encounter the face as features without encountering the Levinasian face, and similarly, we can encounter the face by means other than direct contact with another person.

What emerges then, from Levinas's idea of the face is a relation with the other that is radically different to the way we usually think this relationship. Rather than image or representation Levinas talks of the face in terms of expression (Levinas 1969: 297). The face is precisely not representable (Levinas 2004: 116), it is non-phenomenal, it concerns me, touches me, otherwise or before any image it may present to me (ibid.: 90). The face does not represent or signal the other which we might think of as lying behind it, the other (as in Derrida's reading of Levinas) 'is not signalled by this face, he is this face' (Derrida 1978: 100). It is in this sense that the face, the other, is something which contacts me outside of the world of my understanding, knowledge, comprehension or ownership, outside of the power and mastery of my self, my ego and my identity. My relation to the other is not something that can be subsumed within consciousness or reduced to a theme. The relation with the other is not something over which my consciousness and mastery has control, for that would reduce the other to the same.

This discussion of the face and alterity is important, in this context, in terms of its implications for how we think about response and responsibility. For Levinas responsibility is understood purely as responsibility for the other, not as something which I bring upon myself, rather as 'responsibility preceding a notion of a guilty initiative' (Levinas with Robbins 2001: 52). Responsibility begins with the other and is for the other. It is not something which I can decide on, or could in any way assume ownership of. One of the ways that Levinas approaches responsibility is as the idea of response to the other *as* other, so a response answering before any understanding or consciousness, a response to what he calls an 'unthematisable provocation' (Levinas 2004: 12).

It is the other then who calls me to this responsibility, through the exposure of the face as destitute and commanding. We cannot hear, are not even exposed to, the commanding address of the other if we do not encounter the face, so there is no possibility of being able to respond to it. And we can miss the face, fail to be exposed to it or to hear its address, we can miss the demands, both political and ethical, that it relays to us. This happens when we approach the face as an image or a signifier of something as Levinas cautions. We miss the face when we do violence to the alterity of the other, when we approach them as an instance of a type, an individual within a genus, or when we force them into our own conceptual grid.

Rethinking response

What then, has been the effect of 7 July 2005 and related events, the representations of these events and the various reactions to them, on the idea of face and the possibility of encountering the face? How has this affected the possibilities of *response* in a Levinasian sense? How do the so-called 'responses' to the London bombings condition or curtail these possibilities of responding? The approach to difference as characteristics that Levinas is troubled by can, I think, be found in a number of contexts, but I want to briefly examine two examples here.

First, drawing on Louise Amoore's work on watchful politics in the War on Terror (Amoore 2007) and second, on the 'One London' campaign instigated in the wake of the 7 July London bombings. What these practices show is a refusal of alterity by both the discourse of identifying the other as threat and as outside of the norm, and by the corresponding discourse of a fixed and unitary identity inside.

In the first instance, Amoore comments on the assumptions underlying security practices such as screening of the population through passenger manifests, CCTV footage, or financial transactions in order to profile a norm of behaviour which allows for an algorithmic approach to determining threat by identifying that which is outside the norm (Amoore 2007: 221). Underlying these practices she argues is

> the assumption is that it is possible to 'build a complete picture of a person', to quite literally see who they are before they board a plane or transfer money, by relating them to the norms of a wider population and identifying their degree of deviance.
>
> (ibid.: 221)

While, as Amoore points out, this attempt to recognize and fix identity is problematic in that it necessarily fails because identity is not fixed (ibid.: 220), it is the normative implications of these practices that are of interest in relation to the concept of response. That is, as R.B.J. Walker argues, that there can be no strangers in a world of friend and foe (Walker 1991: 456). In trying to identify individuals as threats or not, as friends or foe, we lose the possibility of encountering them in their strangeness and alterity.

Identifying a degree of deviance is an exercise in reducing alterity to difference, identifying characteristics, fixing a recognizable identity and so on. The attempt at recognition, particularly visually, assumes that the other is laid open to the self to be recognized or not. As Levinas argues, 'Inasmuch as the access to beings concerns vision, it dominates those beings, exercises power over them. A thing is *given*, offers itself to me. In gaining access to it I maintain myself within the same' (Levinas 1969: 194). The other then remains placed in my grid of intelligibility as subsumed within the same, and other only in relation to it.

The face, as discussed above, cannot be encountered if approached as an image or as an identifier or a signifier of something. Images, in this case of particular human faces, lose their affective effect when they are used to signify something. They cease communicating the precariousness of alterity; misery, suffering and vulnerability, and instead become once again subsumed within the totality of the same, comprehensible and thematizable.

The 'One London' campaign performs a similar function of reducing everything to the same, but through a discourse of unity rather than of deviance. The campaign was launched by the Mayor following the 7 July bombings. It was sold as an attempt to underline how Londoners had united since 7 July, their refusal to be divided by acts of terrorism and their pride in being part of a united and diverse city (Mayor's Press Office 2005). However, in adopting and defending an insistence on unity, any idea of alterity is necessarily marginalized.

The campaign celebrates a pairing of 'diversity and unity', which seems in this context to be diversity *as* unity. There is no space in the discourse for radical diversity, it must be contained within a set of common purposes, common understandings of what it means to be a Londoner, that is, ultimately within an insistence on unity and sameness. The campaign slogan, '7 million Londoners, One London' acts to bring difference into the realm of characteristics. It makes others a constitutive part of a whole, an example of a type, that is, all of the things that Levinas's commitment to alterity and otherness explicitly rejects.

What does this refusal of alterity mean for the possibilities of encountering the face and of responding to it? In refusing to accept the otherness of the other we can, as mentioned above, miss the situation of being addressed, the demand from elsewhere, by which our obligations are articulated and pressed upon us (Butler 2004: 130). This is a refusal of the elsewhere, the outside of the same that the command of the face comes from, and in insisting on the lack of an elsewhere we are refusing the face. Yes, refusing its threat, but also refusing the chance for response and responsibility.

Both of these practices then are examples of placing the self and the other in

The ontopolitics of response 187

a totality through thinking in terms of difference, and so subsuming the other into the self, refusing the possibility of alterity from the start. Thinking in terms of difference is, I argue, a contributing factor in a distortion, both spatial and temporal, in how we conceptualize response. Levinas's work suggests that only in facing alterity is response possible and that thinking about response in relation to difference distorts it temporally by acting to predetermine or technologize response.

This happens because difference presupposes a prior conceptualization of the other as being like me, so bringing them within the same and removing any outside which might be responded to. Refusing alterity is precisely the refusal of this elsewhere, something outside of the same that the command of responsibility comes from. Difference implies an original combination of separation and accessibility, because difference must be thought with reference to the same. Placing the same at the centre of our understandings means that there is nothing outside which can be responded to, we cannot encounter the face. In this circumstance we are left only with the possibility of following codes or being guided by knowledge, nothing can interrupt the realm of the same. If our responses are guided by knowledge they are not responding *to* anything, because that which we have (or think we have) knowledge of is already brought within the same. Thinking in terms of difference then is an attempt to avoid exposure to the otherness of the other, or to anything outside of the same, and avoiding exposure or interruption problematizes the possibility of response, so of decisions and responsibility.

This difficulty in response is also a temporal distortion. The approaches to response mentioned above – advertising campaigns, creating narratives, formulating new security policies, and so on – do not follow the clear-cut temporal guidelines of action-reaction that they rely on. This is due in part to the difficulty in simply distinguishing cause and effect, as Maja Zehfuss highlights in her discussion of arguments for war 'produc[ing] what they claim to name' (Zehfuss 2007: 58). The idea of response is distorted by the attempt to separate the event from the response. It seems that first we must understand, experience or stabilize what has happened in order to then be able to respond, as evidenced in the perceived need for narratives of the events of 7 July 2005. However, this begins to unravel if our responses themselves are implicated in deciding the meaning of what or who has happened. As in Zehfuss's argument, calling the events of 11 September 2001 an act of war in this context acts both as a response and as a determination of what it is we might be responding to (ibid.: 58). The two are not clearly separable. Meaning is not given in these (or any) cases, (if it were so easily available to us there would be no need to stabilize it through official narratives) and responding is one way in which we begin to determine it.

However, and linked to this argument, it is also the case that response does not happen when we might think it does. If we allow nothing outside of the same to interrupt us, if our responses are determined by the way we attempt to determine the event or individual, if we allow ourselves, in terms of our identity, or our knowledge, to guide response then the things we call responses have already been decided, at some other time, in some other way. The response then happens at the points at which we enact or try to stabilize our identities, when we decide what counts as knowledge and expertise and place our faith in them, when we decide where the limits of our community or nation might be drawn and what constitutes a threat to them. Ultimately that is, before the event to which we supposedly respond. Thinking in terms of difference is one example of this predetermining of response. It enables some responses and closes off the possibilities of others in part because this way of thinking determines what or who we understand the event or person to be, and the mechanisms we use in order to comprehend them.

While destined to failure as an attempt to protect against threat or unpredictability from this elsewhere, thinking in terms of difference may be much more successful in obscuring anything outside of the same to which we might be able to respond.

Conclusion

Attempts to respond to terrorism are caught up in a series of difficulties and distortions created by the way that the problematic nature of the assumptions they rely upon is glossed over. Although foregrounding these difficulties does not in itself lead to any 'better', or more coherent way of responding it does highlight the fact that these difficulties are partly difficulties within the concept of response itself and as such that there cannot be any easy answers. It is not a question of getting the response right, of understanding better, having more knowledge, recognising or identifying more accurately. Although these things have an important part to play they are not, in themselves, enough. Through accepting these assumptions other possibilities of response are closed off, the range of options seen is already determined and in a sense the debate and questioning starts too late in the day.

This means that some of the ways response has been attempted in fact make response more difficult, if not impossible, by closing off any outside which might be responded to. Are we, through a discourse of unity and invulnerability, cultivating a society where the face cannot be encountered? Is the precariousness, the agony, the suffering that the face communicates lost in our use of the face as an image? Are Londoners (and others) being created as invulnerable and not afraid, united and not singular, and so not precarious, de-faced?

If so, then response itself becomes problematic. And if we cannot respond to the face, if we cannot hear its command, then there is no possibility of realising our responsibility for it, or of taking up this responsibility. We refuse the first step, of being called by the other to our responsibility for them. We are not open to the competing commands of faces, which institutes politics for Levinas. There is no risk, no space for decision and nothing to judge because the answers are already presented to us. Responses cannot be responses in this context, only problem-solving fixes.

Note

1 See for example *Report of the Official Account* (2006), which is, in part, an attempt to understand the mechanism of radicalization.

References

Amoore, L. (2007), 'Vigilant Visualities: The Watchful Politics of the War on Terror' *Security Dialogue*, 38(2): 215–32.
Black, C. (2005), *7–7 The London Bombs: What Went Wrong*, London: Gibson Square.
Butler, J. (2004), *Precarious Life: The Power of Mourning and Violence*, London: Verso.
Connolly, W. (1992), 'The Irony of Interpretation', in D. W. Conway and J. E. Seery (eds), *The Politics of Irony: Essays in Self-Betrayal*, New York: St Martin's Press.
Derrida, J. (1978), *Writing and Difference*, London: Routledge.
Fagan, M. (2008), 'The Inseparability of Ethics and Politics: Rethinking the Third in Emmanuel Levinas', *Contemporary Political Theory* [forthcoming].
Gove, M. (2006), *Celsius 7/7*, London: Weidenfeld and Nicolson.
Rai, M. (2006), *7/7: The London Bombings, Islam and the Iraq War*, London: Pluto Press.
Levinas, E. (1969), *Totality and Infinity: An Essay on Exteriority* [1961], trans. A. Lingis, Pittsburgh: Duquesne University Press.
—— (1985), *Ethics and Infinity: Conversations with Phillipe Nemo*, trans. R. A. Cohen, Pittsburgh, PA: Duquesne University Press.
—— (1996), 'Peace and Proximity' [1984], in: A. T. Peperzak, S. Critchley and R. Bernasconi (eds), *Emmanuel Levinas: Basic Philosophical Writings*, Bloomington, IN: Indiana University Press.
—— (2004). *Otherwise than Being or Beyond Essence* [1981], Pittsburgh, PA: Duquesne University Press.
Levinas, E. with Robbins, J. (2001), *Is it Righteous to Be?: Interviews with Emmanuel Levinas*, Stanford, CA: Stanford University Press.
Mayor's Press Office (2005), *Royal Mail's Stamp of Approval for One London Campaign*, 24 August. Online. Available at: www.london.gov.uk/view_press_release.jsp?releaseid=5545 (accessed 17 November 2007).
Makarenko, T. (2007), 'International Terrorism and the UK: Assessing the Threat', in P. Wilkinson (ed.), *Homeland Security in the UK: Future Preparedness for Terrorist Attack since 9/11*, London: Routledge.
Report of the Official Account of the Bombings in London on July 7th 2005 (2006), London: The Stationery Office.
Walker, R. B. J. (1991), 'State Sovereignty and the Articulation of Political Space/Time', *Millennium* 20(3): 445–61.
Wild, J. (1969), 'Introduction' to *Totality and Infinity: An Essay on Exteriority* [1961], trans. A. Lingis, Pittsburgh, PA: Duquesne University Press.
Wilkinson, P. (2007), 'Introduction', in P. Wilkinson (ed.), *Homeland Security in the UK: Future Preparedness for Terrorist Attack since 9/11*, London: Routledge.
Zehfuss, M. (2007), 'Subjectivity and Vulnerability: On the War with Iraq' *International Politics* 44: 58–71.

11 2 July, 7 July and metaphysics

Costas Douzinas*

Between mythology and nihilism

'Thanks for coming to support the greatest thing in the history of the world' Chris Martin, the lead singer of pop band Coldplay told the crowd at the Live 8 concert in Hyde Park, London, on 2 July 2005. 'We are not looking for charity, we are looking for justice' was how U2 lead singer and event co-organizer Bono expressed the purpose of the series of concerts that had been organized to coincide with the meeting of the G8 leaders in Scotland. In repeated appeals to the leaders of the eight richest nations of the world, Live 8 demanded that African debt should be written off and aid levels substantially increased. Images of starving tormented suffering Africans – mainly children – were projected on to giant screens while Madonna, The Who and Paul McCartney performed. The crowds had a great time participating in the 'biggest thing ever organised' and protesting against African poverty and disease. Justice 'was the simplest and most pervasive theme.... Everyone is, suddenly, globally, politicised' (Ferguson 2005: 2). Human rights and humanitarianism were placed at the centre of concern of the Western world. Tears and sympathy for African suffering and pain dominated the acres of space dedicated to the concert in the British newspapers. As a combination of hedonism and good conscience, Live 8 will not be easily overtaken in size or hyperbole. This was partying as politics; drinking and dancing as moral calling.

Five days later four bombs exploded in central London, killing 52 and injuring hundreds. Blair left the G8 Scotland retreat a few hours after the explosions to come to London to give a press conference and look in control. Soon, these terrible events became known as 7/7 (in a mediatic imitation of the American tendency to simplify, codify and memorize, a rather ineffectual antidote to postmodern historical amnesia) and drove off the front pages the humanitarian partying of 2/7 and London's victory in the race to host the 2012 Olympics which had been announced on 6 July, between the two events.

After the display of care, empathy and humanity of clubbing, fashionable, cosmopolitan London, after the celebrations of global multicultural financially and athletically powerful London, the muffled tears of suffering London. This third event eclipsed the other two in public space, reminding that woes are more mediatic than triumphs. We were told by the Government and commentators that the 'stoic' Londoners suffered and endured in great dignity like our fathers and grandfathers during the Blitz. There was a major difference of course. Half of the London population in 2007 was born overseas. In the university precinct of Bloomsbury that was hit particularly hard, the proportion of non-UK-born people is even higher. The driver of the no. 30 bus that was bombed on Woburn Place was Greek;[1] one of our students at Birkbeck killed in the explosion, Italian. If patience, perseverance and stoicism in the face of adversity characterized the Londoners' response, it had more to do with the multilayered London of the twenty-first century rather than with the stiff upper lip of late Empire cockneydom.

Can philosophy face these events? Do they have a political dimension? Are they related in ways other than their chronological proximity? A first obvious interpretation would approach such a comparison with suspicion if not outright hostility. Yet like many 'obvious' answers, this too may miss the mark and further investigation may be rewarding. It is the argument of this chapter, that the 'philanthropic' expressions of sympathy and the 'misanthropic' displays of hatred are not isolated and eccentric. Carl Schmitt wrote that the metaphysics of a society and epoch is best displayed in its politics.

> The metaphysical image that a definite epoch forges of the world has the same structure what the world immediately understands to be appropriate as a form of its political organization ... metaphysics is the most intensive and the clearest expression of an epoch.
>
> (Schmitt 1985: 46)

Live 8 and the suicide bombings represent two dominant types of metaphysics, which animate important forms of post-politics. Live 8 promotes a politics that abandons the pursuit of the good and sees its vocation as the combat of evil. Politics becomes a moral calling and humanitarianism the ultimate political ideology. The London bombs express a very different form of action: politics in the service of the good, of a truth given only to the elect. In the face of wide indifference or hostility, this politics assumes the form of witnessing to the truth: martyrdom and murder. On the part of the partygoers, politics as philanthropy; on that of the bombers, politics as sacrifice. Moralistic humanism and terror, two types of post-political politics, share their metaphysical structure. We will examine briefly its general characteristics in this section while the following two will look into greater detail the conceptions of self, otherness and community of humanitarian and terrorist politics.

The modernist philosophical tradition from Nietzsche to Heidegger and Derrida has persuasively argued that the metaphysics of our age is 'the metaphysics of the deconstruction of the essence, and of existence qua sense' (Nancy 1997: 92). In the wake of the final stage of secularization, the dominant political and cultural powers announced the end of history. As Jean-Luc Nancy puts it, value or spirit have no place any longer, 'nor is there any history before whose tribunal one could stand. In other words, there is no longer any sense of the world' (ibid.: 92) Jürgen Habermas agrees from a different perspective: 'Lacking a universe of intersubjectively shared meanings, [individuals] merely observe one another and behave towards one another in accordance with imperatives of self-preservation' (Habermas 1998: 125). Theory, following and articulating the effects of global capitalism, has deconstructed well, a little too well, meaning and value.

This absence of meaning is the expression of an absence of world. A world is not just the context or background of sense; world is precisely our sense, our unique arrangement of meaning and value. Politics is partly the formalization of the struggle for meaning, of the attempt to create a local, transient, weak common cosmos out of conflicting and competing worlds. In the age of globalization, however, we are left without a world, senseless (Nancy 2007: 31–57). We encounter this in the abandonment of any idea of good life which characterizes the humanitarian project of combating evil. We encounter it in the excess of meaning of the terror act and in the response to it by the state and the media. The struggle between terror and the war on terror is that between two types of value voids. Following Nancy, we can call them mythology and nihilism.

Mythological is the name for the belief in the plenitude of value and fullness of meaning. It has been the dominant form of the religious world-view. In modernity, it has been transferred to various secular substitutes of totality that have inherited religious values and forms. In Jean-Luc Nancy's terminology, myth designates absolute value and value as absolute, an ultimate ground of community or indispensable *telos* of its politics and law. After the withdrawal of the premodern figures, such as classical *dike* (the order of the world) and God (source of absolute transcendence), the secular values such as humanity, nation, race, ideology or justice have alternately filled the space of withdrawal of value. From Plato's *Republic* to Augustine's *City of God* to Marx's *Communist Manifesto* and the many paeans to nationalism, these ideals have signalled the foundation or origin of a fallen world or the *eschaton* of a utopian or antinomian future. The future unity of humanity for the communist, the future purification of nation for the nationalist or race for the fascist, the coming justice for the socialist express fullness of meaning in its absence, the promise of a lacking world. As origin or destination, as nostalgia or prophecy the presence of the founding value has been absent, a Deus *absconditus* or a future *parousia* which although always still to come opens the space for absent value. This absent meaningfulness, this lacking but discernible value is the essence of modern mythology. No wonder why nostalgia and utopia, are the revolutionary fantasies of modernity. They are the remnants of religious metaphysics, the ideological secularisations of transcendence.

The terrorist act is a desperate evocation of absolute value in its absence. Its main components and references (martyrdom, sacrifice, murder in the name of higher authority, silence or vague allusions to the aims of the act, suggestions of a wounded God or a suffering community) indicate failure and longing for a metaphysics of fullness. For most commentators, suicide bombing is an expression of a premodern, unreformed, even uncivilized religion. And yet, every aspect of the act directs us not to a strong victorious religion but to modernity's exit from religion, which calls for renewed attempts at a lost mediation between the secular and the holy, for new sacralizations which, in their atrocious consequences, evidence the weakness of religion and the dissolution of the community of the faithful. In this sense, religious terrorism joins various modern attempts to halt, reverse or rectify the modernist deconstruction of transcendence.

Opposite the desperation generated by the decline of mythical fullness stands nihilism proper: the meaninglessness of the relativization or absence of value, in other words the nihilism of global capital and its political representations. Nihilism is the name of a globalization in which value and the good have retreated and have been turned into exchange value. Monetary equivalence, endless technological expansion, the glorification of communication and simulation have replaced the fetishistic commitment to religious or secular transcendence. Governments support the capitalist perpetuation of enormous inequalities; at the same time, they proclaim a virtual equality by placing all before the same commodities and promising the same formal rights. The consumer placed opposite the commodity is ostensibly identical to all others as shopping animal. The main aim of 'market democracy' is to facilitate the circulation of capital and 'free' individual choice. The value of globalization is that of individual unfettered desire, unfettered because controlled; insatiable desire is the only value of our valueless age. It is in this sense that globalized capitalism is inherently nihilistic, based on lack, the negativity of desire.

The globalization of exchange value has been followed closely by the universalization of (human) rights and humanitarianism, the main supports of western subjectivity. The legal person endowed with a bunch of formal (but not socio-economic) rights has been declared virtually free and notionally equal with all others in her abstract humanity. In this sense, rights are the best expression of law's value as the relativization of value. This process reached its apogee in the post-1989 triumph of human rights but has a long provenance. We see it in Hegel's argument that rights support a conception of the subject as this or that person, a universal person, with dignity, respect and self-respect but without interiority or content. We find it in Kant, who inaugurates the *nomophilia* of modernity by insisting that law and right take precedence over any conception of the good or virtue and conceives law as a positive morality. We revisit it in Rawls, for whom liberalism supports subjectivity by being strictly indifferent to any substantive conception of content or substance. We encounter it in various theories of legal formalism and proceduralism, according to which the value of law is precisely its valuelessness, its commitment to rules and procedures and its turning away from value (Douzinas 2007: chapters 2 and 4). Rights express and support individual desire, an absolute desire for which everything in the world except itself is relative. They are the sign of the relativization of value in modernity, another name for the absence of value or nihilism. The value promoted by legal rights is the value of desire or desire as ultimate value. The modern community of rights is indispensably nihilistic, both in the sense that it is based on negativity and in the sense that its end is its endless reproduction and expansion. Let us have a closer look at this type of post-political politics first.

Humanitarian politics

Live 8 is part of the sad recognition that, despite the claims of humanism, humanity is split, the 'human' breaks up into distinct parts. One part is the humanity that suffers, the human as victim; the other is the humanity that saves, the human as rescuer. Humanity's goodness depends on its suffering, but without goodness, suffering would not be recognized. The two parts call each other to existence as the two sides of the same coin. You cannot have a rescuer without a victim and there is no victim unless a rescuer recognizes him as such. But there is a second split. Humanity suffers because parts of it are evil, degenerate, cruel and inflict indescribable horrors upon the rest. There can be no redemption without sin, no gift without deprivation, no Band Aid without famine.

Religious traditions and political ideologies attribute suffering to evil. For Christian, particularly Protestant theology, suffering is a permanent existential characteristic, the unavoidable effect of original sin. Suffering and pain are the result of transgression, of lack or deprivation of goodness but also the sinner's opportunity for salvation by imitating Christ's passion. Indeed, the word pain derives from the Latin *poena*, punishment. The human rights movement agrees. It aims to put cruelty first, to stop 'unmerited suffering and gross physical cruelty' (Ignatieff 2001: 173). In the dialectic of good and evil, evil comes first; the good is defined negatively as *steresis kakou*, as the removal, remedy or absence of evil. Human rights and humanitarianism bring the different parts of humanity together, they try to suture a common human essence out of the deeply cut body. Let us examine briefly the three masks of the human, the sacrificial victim, the atrocious evildoer and the moral rescuer.

First, man as victim. The victim is someone whose dignity and worth has been violated. Powerless, helpless and innocent, her basic nature and needs have been denied. But there is more: victims are part of an indistinct mass or horde of despairing, dispirited people. They are faceless and nameless, the massacred Tutsis, the trafficked refugees, the gassed Kurds, the raped Bosnians. Victims are kept in camps, they are incarcerated in prisons, banned into exitless territories *en masse*. Losing humanity, becoming less than human; losing individuality, becoming part of a horde, crowd or mob; losing self-determination, becoming enslaved; these are the results of evil, otherwise known as human rights violations. Indeed here we may have the best example of what Giorgio Agamben calls 'bare or sacred life' (Agamben 1998) or Bernard Ogilvie, the 'one use human' (Ogilvie in Balibar 1999: 43): Biological life abandoned by the juridical and political order of the nation-state, valueless life that can be killed with impunity. The publicity campaigns with the 'imploring eyes' of dying kids and mourning mothers are 'the most telling contemporary cipher of the bare life that humanitarian organisations, in perfect symmetry with state power, need' (Agamben 1998: 133–4). The target of our charity is an amorphous mass of people. It populates our TV screens, newspapers and NGO fund-raising campaigns. The victims are paraded exhausted, tortured, starving but always nameless, a crowd, a mob that inhabits the exotic parts of the world. As a former president of *Médecins sans Frontières* put it, 'he to whom humanitarian actions is addressed is not defined by his skills or potential, but above all, by his deficiencies and disempowerment. It is his fundamental vulnerability and dependency, rather than his agency and ability to surmount difficulty that is foregrounded by humanitarianism' (Brennan 2000).

The victim is only one side of the Other. The reverse side represents the evil aboard in those scary parts the world. This second half, the cause of the fall and the suffering, the Mr Jeckyll or the wolf-man, is absolute evil. Its names are legion: the African dictator, the Slav torturer, the Balkan rapist, the Muslim butcher, the corrupt bureaucrat, the Levantine conman, the monstrous sacrificer. The beast of Baghdad, the butcher of Belgrade, the warlord, the rogue and the bandit are the single cause and inescapable companion of suffering. As Jacques Derrida puts it, 'the beast is not simply an animal but the very incarnation of evil, of the satanic, the diabolical, the demonic – a beast of the Apocalypse' (Derrida 2005: 97). The victims are victimized by their own, and to that extent their suffering is not undeserved. Famine, malnutrition, disease and lack of medicines result from the intrinsic corruption of the evil Other, signs of divine punishment or of appropriate fate in the form of acts of God or *force majeure*. The Other of the West combines the suffering mass and the radical evil-doer, the subhuman and the inhuman rolled into one.

In this moral universe, the claim that there is a single essence to humanity to be discovered in evil, suffering and its relief, for which debt relief stands as a metaphor, is foundational. Whoever is below the standard is not fully up to the status of human. Indeed, every human rights campaign or humanitarian intervention presupposes an element of contempt for the situation and the victims. Human rights are part of an attitude of the postcolonial world in which the 'misery' of Africa is the result of its failings and corruption, its traditional attitudes and lack of modernization, its nepotism and inefficiency; in a word, of its sub-humanity. We can feel great pity for the victims of human rights abuses; but pity is tinged with a little contempt for their fickleness and passivity and huge aversion towards the bestiality of their compatriots and tormentors. We do not like these others, but we love pitying them. They, the savages/victims, make us civilized.

Finally, the rescuer. The human rights campaigner, the western philanthropist and the humanitarian party-goer are there to save the victims. Participation and contributions to the humanitarian movement may be resulting in some 'collateral benefit', to coin a term. There is a kernel of nobility in joining letter-writing campaigns or giving money to 'good causes' to alleviate suffering. Yet the results of massive humanitarian campaigns are rather meagre. In 2006, an audit of G8 promises made to Live 8 a year earlier found that rich countries are failing badly to meet the targets they themselves set (Elliott 2006). Never before have so many people been subjugated, starved or exterminated in absolute figures. The triumph of humanitarianism is drowned in human disaster. The 'best' and the 'worst' come together, prompting and feeding off each other. But if we approach the rescue missions of humanitarianism as part of a wider project on intervention both in the South and in the North, some of the apparent contradictions start disappearing.

Human rights campaigns construct the post-political western subjectivity: they promise the development of a non-traumatized self (and society) supported by our reflection into our suffering mirror-images and by the displacement of the evil in our midst onto their barbaric inhumanity. Using psychoanalytical terms, we can distinguish three types of otherness that support our selfhood and identity, the imaginary, the symbolic and the real. When defined as victim, as the extreme example of universal suffering, the Other is seen as an inferior I, someone who aspires (or should aspire) to reach the same level of civilization or governance we have. Their inferiority turns them into our imaginary Other in reverse, our narcissistic mirror-image and potential double. These unfortunates are the infants of humanity, ourselves in a state of nascency. In their dark skins and incomprehensible languages, in their colourful and 'lazy' lives, in their suffering and perseverance, we see the beautiful people we are. They must be helped to grow up, to develop and become like us. Because the victim is our likeness in reverse, we know his interests and impose them 'for his own good'.

The cures we offer to this imaginary other follows our own desires and recipes. The humanitarian movement is full of these priority cures: liberalization of trade and opening the local markets is more important than guaranteeing minimum standards of living; democracy is more important than survival. Lack of voting rights in one-party states, censorship of the press or lack of judicial guarantees in China or Zimbabwe are the prime examples of beastliness; death from hunger or debilitating disease, high infant mortality or low life-expectancy are not equally important. In the 1980s, the European Community built wine lakes and butter mountains and preferred to stock uselessly and even destroy the produce to avoid flooding the marketplace and driving prices down. Similarly today democracy and good governance, our greatest exports, must be sold at the right price: they must follow our rules and should not be used against our interests.

The second type of otherness is symbolic. We enter the world through our introduction to the symbolic order, as speaking beings subjected to the law (Douzinas 2007: chapter 2). The others, the unfortunate victims of dictators and tsunamis, have not learned as yet to speak (our) language and accept (our) laws, they are non-proper speakers or in-fants. Consumption of western goods and civil and political rights are signs of progress. If the Chinese have Big Macs and Hollywood movies, democracy and freedom will eventually follow. Learning the importance of consumerism and human rights may take some time, as all education and socialization does. But it takes precedence over economic redistribution and cultural recognition. Our legal culture promotes equality and dignity by turning concrete people to abstract persons, bearers of formal rights. According to Zen Bankowski,

> [I]t is as legal persons, the abstract bearers of rights and duties under the law, that we treat concrete people equally. Thus the real human person becomes an abstraction – a point at which is located a bundle of rights and duties. Other concrete facts about them are irrelevant to the law.... You do not help a person but give them their rights.
>
> (Bankowski 2001: 56–7)

This is the West's considered answer: give these unfortunates human rights and second-hand clothes and they will, in time, attain full humanity.

Finally, we have the evil inhuman, the irrational, cruel, brutal, disgusting Other. This is the other of the unconscious. As Slavoj Žižek puts it,

> [T]here is a kind of passive exposure to an overwhelming Otherness, which is the very basis of being human ... [the inhuman] is marked by a terrifying excess which, although it negates what we understand as 'humanity' is inherent to being human.
>
> (Žižek 2005: 34)

We have called this abysmal other that lurks in the psyche and unsettles the ego by various names: God or Satan, barbarian or foreigner, psychoanalysis, death drive or the Real. Individually and socially we are hostages to this irreducible untameable otherness. Becoming human is possible only against this impenetrable inhuman background. Split into two, according to a simple moral calculus, this Other has both a tormenting and a tormented part, both radical evil and radical passivity. He represents our narcissistic self in its infancy (civilization as *potentia*, possibility or risk), civilization in its cradle; but also what is most frightening and horrific in us, the death drive, the evil *persona* that lurks in our midst. We present the Other as radically different, precisely because he is what we both love and hate about ourselves, the childhood and the beast of humanity. The racial connotations of this hierarchy are not far from the surface. As Makau Mutua has argued, 'Savages and victims are generally non-white and non-Western, while the saviours are white. This old truism has found new life in the metaphor of human rights' (Mutua 2001: 207).

The stakes of humanitarian campaigns are high. Positing the victim and/or savage other of humanitarianism we create humanity. The perpetrator/victim is a reminder and revenant from our disavowed past. He is the West's imaginary double, someone who carries our own characteristics and fears albeit in a reversed, impoverished sense. Once the moral universe revolves around the recognition of evil, every project to combine people in the name of the good is itself condemned as evil. All positive conceptions of value not reducible to exchange value and calculation turn into totalitarianism. This is the reason why the price of human rights politics is conservatism. Moralistic relativism both makes impossible and bars positive political visions and possibilities. Humanitarianism and human rights ethics legitimizes what the West already possesses; evil is what we do not possess or enjoy. But as Alain Badiou puts it, while the human is partly inhuman, she is also more than human. There is a 'superhuman or immortal dimension in the human.' The status of victim 'of suffering beast, of emaciated dying individual, reduces man to his animal substructure, to his pure and simple identity as dying ... neither mortality nor cruelty can define the singularity of the human within the world of the living' (quoted in Halward 2003: 257). We become human to the extent that we attest to a nature that, while fully mortal, is not expendable and does not conform to the rules of the game. This is what the metaphysics of humanitarianism precludes as a matter of principle. This is what is leading us not to the end of history but to the end of politics.

Politics of death

How can we understand the metaphysics of the terrorist act, its actors and victims? What conceptions of self, otherness and community, what understanding of agency and value do terrorist attacks on civilians promote? Are suicide bombings a political act or do they bring politics to an end? To examine these questions, we will look in turn at the main characters of the drama: the suicide bomber, the sacrificial victims, finally, the response of (the community) bystanders.

a The suicide bomber

Let us start with the protagonist. In some instances, the bomber targets a specific person and suicide becomes an assassination weapon. Such was the recent murder of Benazir Bhutto in Pakistan. But in most cases, including the London bombs, the suicide bomber uses his own death as a weapon to kill random others who happen to be in the vicinity of his self-explosion. Death of the actor (suicide) and of others (murder) is central to suicide bombing, it gives it meaning and value. Let us follow these two deaths in turn.

Single and communal suicide in order to avoid a life considered worse than death is well known in the western tradition. Achilles joins the battle although he knows that it will inevitably lead to his death. Ajax, Chrysippus, Zeno and Socrates choose suicide instead of dishonour. Jesus enters Jerusalem knowing that he will die there and only momentarily despairs about his pre-destined passion. Christians, following their saviour's example, willingly go to martyrdom. They choose death gladly, many volunteering to be executed for Jesus or choosing to join their tortured or torched fellow Christians. As Groge and Tabor put it,

> in 185 the proconsul of Asia, Arrius Antoninus, was approached by a group of Christians demanding to be executed. The proconsul obliged some of them and then sent the rest away, saying that if they wanted to kill themselves there was plenty of rope available or cliffs they could jump off.
> (Groge and Tabor 1992: 136)

Religious martyrs reject finitude for the infinite and breach the limit that creates humanity, by sacralizing and fetishizing death. The religious suicide's death is literally martyrdom: a witnessing (in Greek, *martyr* means the witness, *martyria* evidence) and confirmation offered to a higher goal and another world. Based on a two-world metaphysics, in which the Hereafter is of infinitely greater importance and value than life on earth, the martyr's suicide becomes the bridge between the two worlds. In this approach, life is worth living because it inexorably leads to its end, this world has value as the ante-chamber to the other.

Suicide bombers do not just commit suicide or murder. They use their own and their victims death as a symbolic and imaginary (both imagistic and fantastical) act. As symbolic, death becomes a tool for the communication of ideas and ideologies. But what does the suicide bombing communicate? The 'freedom or death' cry has repeatedly echoed during national wars and uprisings but also in insurrectional movements leading to (mass) suicides and immolations in the face of inescapable defeat.[2] But a striking difference separates the political violence of the sixties, seventies and eighties from that of recent suicide attacks. Political violence is precisely that, political. Its actors have certain political aims (even though totally impossible or mad), they choose their targets among (real or imagined) members of the enemy and they claim that their action is a means towards the political end. Political violence is organized around a manifesto that guides the terrorist group; each attack is accompanied and completed by communication. The communiqué, which follows immediately after the action, proclaims the ideology of the group, the aims of the action and, significantly and proudly, undertakes responsibility: 'here we are', pronounces an IRA, an ETA or a November 17 group; 'we did it, it is part of our political struggle'. The terrorist actions of the Red Army Faction or the Red Brigades were aimed at identifiable targets from within the 'establishment' and were supposed to raise popular consciousness about the injustices of capitalism and imperialism.

The London bombings were totally different. The goal of the attacks was not stated until much later and little if any responsibility was undertaken. The actors remained unnamed and anonymous, until their identities were discovered by the police. Like the 11 September perpetrators, the London bombers made no immediate demands. The video statements released to Al Jazeera on 2 September, by two of the bombers, made no specific claims about the bombings nor were they a call to action. No obvious or even tacit change of political behaviour or ideological stance was sought or could be expected. At most, the posthumous videos could be seen as recruitment aids for future jihadists but not as clear and present statements of purpose or act. They were mainly confessional, the last will and testament of people about to die.

In this absence of a clear message, the act is all that happens. Deprived of effective or relevant communication, the event is exhausted in its own 'eventness', it becomes what psychoanalysis calls 'acting out'. The symbolism is contained fully in the act itself, death is both its tool and its meaning. The attack has no immediate label, it does not aim at achieving something, it leaves its comprehension and interpretation to its potential victims.[3] As Jean Baudrillard put it apropos of the attacks in New York and Washington, 'Fundamentalism is a symptomatic form of rejection, refusal; its adherents didn't want to accomplish anything concrete, they simply rise up wildly against that which they perceive as a threat to their own identity' (Baudrillard 2004).

The aimlessness of the attack, the lack of a clear message associated with it, the randomness of the victims link these bombings with the 'propaganda by deed' of the Russian anarchists of the nineteenth century. But while the anarchists attacked the representatives of deficient secularization and democratization, recent religious terrorism combines the metaphysics of religion with death and attempts to re-insert transcendence into the political.

Monotheistic religions are founded on the mythology of truth and the One. Their symbolic order is closed and coherent and can easily reveal the nature of empirical reality as fallen, false, incomplete. Fullness of meaning, absolute value without remainder, complete but distorted representation taken for presence, these are the hallmarks of mythological metaphysics. In the face of overwhelming evidence to the opposite, the religious fanatic proclaims the eternal reality of a community without difference, the omnipotence of its sovereign lawmaker and the sinful nature of the unbeliever. Truth floats on the void created by the 'excess' of meaning of absolute belief and total commitment.

But this 'excess' easily passes into the valuelessness of nihilism. The absence of message is both an attack on instrumental politics and on its medium, language with its openness and interpretative potential. Death, the exit from language and the removal of meaning, becomes the meaning of the act. In this sense, whatever else it may be taken to represent, suicide bombing also symbolizes nothingness, the nihil.

The suicide bomber's exploding body is the hinge between (his) martyrdom and (the victims') sacrifice. Martyrdom and sacrifice are evidence of the absolute, of a truth much more important than life. Martyrdom and sacrifice are the politics of religion and the tools of religion as politics. Religions have always claimed to have direct access to the holy. In this sense, theocratic politics places the political on a continuum with the transcendent and understands human agency as an aspect of destiny. Sacrifice may be related to particular religious practices; but in terms of its function, sacrifice has remained throughout western history the privileged mediation between the visible and the invisible worlds. The stake of sacrificial politics is the relation of finite, immanent life to its limit. Communities have negotiated their finitude, people their mortality, either by crossing the limit and establishing a direct link with totality (martyrdom) or through the action of mediating institutions.

In modernity, it is the prerogative of the Sovereign to demand martyrdom from his subjects and to sacrifice his enemies. After God, the Sovereign has administered and channelled the human 'desire to violate the limit, for the limit exposes finitude' (Nancy 2006: 111). Modern sovereignty performs its theologico-political role by maintaining a separation between the holy and the secular through the political function of the sacred. Sacrifice is an offering to a higher cause and gives access to truth. The Sovereign negotiates the link between secular and holy by making sacred (*sacer facere*): war, the death penalty, rituals of sacrifice and consecration are ways through which the absolute is both acknowledged and kept at a distance. The mediation, exemplified by the King's two bodies and his power to take life and offer mercy, introduces the divine into the secular in a symbolic form and places limits on its action, both necessary for the conduct of social life.

The internal link between sovereignty, sacrifice and politics has been a main motif of Georges Battaille, Jacques Derrida and Jean-Luc Nancy. 'Politics *must* be destiny, must have history as its career, sovereignty as its emblem and sacrifice as its access', writes Nancy. We should

> [R]etrace the striking history of political sacrifice, of sacrificial politics, politics of *truth*, that is to say, of the 'theologico-political': from the expressly religious sacrifice to the diverse Reigns of Terror, and to all national militant and partisan sacrifices. The politics of the *Cause* to which sacrifice is due. In this regard, all theologicopolitics, including its 'secularisation', is and can be nothing other than sacrificial. And sacrifice represents the access to truth ... the world which is not a 'Cause' ... does away with sacrifice.
> (Nancy 1997: 89; translation amended)

All politics of cause call for sacrifice. But in the case of suicide bombing, the martyrdom of self is accompanied, indeed realized, through the sacrifice of the other. As Terry Eagleton puts it, 'The martyr bets his life on a future of justice and freedom; the suicide bomber bets your life on it' (Eagleton 2005: 14).

Accepting finitude, doing away with consecration, going to the limit without crossing it would be the post-metaphysical politics after the end of sovereignty. But are we close to the passing of sovereignty and its religious politics? Over the last 20 years we have been repeatedly told that the Sovereign has been dissolved internally through legal procedures and regulatory mechanisms, that he has been tamed externally by the international commitment to human rights and humanitarianism. However the announcement of the imminent death of the Sovereign was premature. Our recent wars which have removed layers of sovereignty from weak states and 'condensed' them in the hegemonic power, the United States and its allies, put paid to the 'end of sovereignty' idea (Douzinas 2007: chapter 11). Globalization, neo-liberalism and the circuits of capitalist governance did not remove the Sovereign power to suspend the law (this was the case with the clear violation of the principles of international law in the declaration of the war against Iraq or in Guatanamo Bay), to kill in the name of higher goals (democracy and human rights in Afghanistan and Iraq) or to subject his enemies to the lawless status of *homines sacri* (Abu Ghraib and rendition prisoners) (Douzinas 2007: chapters 9 and 10). If the Sovereign of old is on the way out, as Antonio Negri and Michael Hardt and the various cosmopolitans might indicate, then we are still in a period of mourning and have not abandoned the need for its mediation with the invisible. Whether real or as a ghost of his previous life, the

Sovereign is still exercising its power fully, displaying its technological marvels and military prowess in the most demonstrative and extreme way.

It is this function of sovereignty that suicide bombing mimics and fakes. If the Sovereign sheds blood, wages war, suspends the law, all intimate expressions of his theologico-political provenance, the suicide bomber acts in the service of the same principle. He is a warrior and claims all the privileges of the status. Mohammad Sidique Khan, the Edgware Road train bomber, avoids all discussion of religion and theology in favour of a call to violence and war in his posthumously released video. The government perpetuates atrocities, 'the bombing, gassing, imprisonment and torture' of his Muslim brothers and sisters, Khan asserts. His obligation and task is to defend the ummah, the community of the faithful. 'We are at war and I am a soldier.... Our words have no impact. Therefore I am going to talk to you in a language you understand. Our words are dead until we give them life with our blood' (Burke 2005). 'Collateral damage', a term popularized in the recent wars particularly in relation to air bombings, in the form of the death of innocents, is acceptable (ibid.).

The bomber as martyr witnesses in his supposed plenitude of belief and faith the senselessness of life and the world. An action aimed at destroying a world without meaning for a higher meaning confirms the meaninglessness of the ideology from which it proceeds. The centrality of death, death's meaningless meaning, takes on its full force, while the content of the grievance, real or imaginary, becomes of secondary importance. Whether religious or not, the suicide bomber, like the Sovereign and his agents, breaches the limit in order to bring the self face to face with the absolute. In doing so, the bomber combines the mythology of absolute value and the nihilism of death glorified. In this aspect at least, the bomber joins those metaphysicians (religious or secular) who have denied or tried to breach or abolish the limit between the worlds of shadows and forms, the empirical and the noumenal or the terrestrial and the divine.

But there is more. Death is for the suicide bomber the most terribly effective weapon but also a rather pathetic attempt at a recognition withheld from mainstream society. The act follows in a distorted way the dialectics of the Hegelian struggle for recognition. According to Hegel, subjectivity is created intersubjectively through the mediation of the object (Douzinas 2000: chapter 10). Identity is the shifting outcome of reciprocal recognitions and misrecognitions by others, whose acknowledgment the self craves. Similarly, when the self desires a thing, it does not do so just for itself but in order to make someone else recognize his right to that thing and therefore his existence and superiority. This is where the infamous master-and-slave stage enters Hegel's philosophy. Since a multiplicity of selves desire to be recognized in their superiority, their action could turn into a catastrophic war of all against all. The universal struggle for recognition had to be contained. Hegel assumes that one of the combatants must be prepared to risk his life and fight to the end. By being prepared to fight to death, he makes the other surrender and accept his superiority. The death seeker becomes the master, the other the slave. The slave has subordinated his desire for recognition to that for survival.

Unlike Hegel's mythical master however the suicide bomber must go all the way. Death is the only weapon he has in order to witness but also to become a witness, to give name and dignity to a life of insignificant everydayness. As the other's acquiescence is not forthcoming there is no stopping point. Risking life is not enough, the terrorist must take life. And in this final act, he acquires the sought-after recognition. The bomber's death is offered as witness to what can never be witnessed. At the same time, death gives retrospective meaning to an anonymous life. The terrorist dies in order to live, finally (s)he becomes known. Reviled by most, celebrated by few, (s)he becomes somebody, a subject, even a celebrity; life acquires meaning and significance at the point of extinction. As Terry Eagleton put it, death gives

> a taste of freedom. The only form of sovereignty left to you is the power to dispose of your own death. Suicide, as Dostoevsky recognized, means the death of God, since you usurp his divine monopoly over life and death.
> (Eagleton 2005: 14)

Angel of death and dedicated follower of sovereignty; denier of the world and of life, servant of truth – the suicide bomber symbolizes with his death globalized modernity's abandonment and desperate mourning for the politics of truth.

b *The victim*

Let us move to the victims. For the terrorist's suicide to succeed as an act of witnessing, it must be accompanied by indifference for the life of the victims. The other becomes disposable means to the suicide's higher end. In this sense, the victims are the opposite of Giorgio Agamben's *hominess sacri*. The *homo sacer* is the prototype of bare life, life stripped of meaning and which cannot be offered in sacrificial rituals and can be taken with impunity. The victims of the bomber on the other hand represent the essence of the sacrificial victim. The terrorist murder is sacrificial, it sheds innocent blood as an offering to a superior principle (or God) in order to push history forward. The victims' contingent death, the destruction of their world, is for the sacrificer a making sacred: the victims bear witness to the other world which they involuntarily enter. But their death proves the force of decision and the necessity of a high calling which gives meaning to the life of the suicide bomber by turning it from a life ordinary and unremarkable to a life of calling and commitment. If, according to Foucault, the Sovereign's power was to take life and let live, the suicide bomber at the point of his death becomes momentarily a pseudo-sovereign by pitting himself against the Sovereign in a warlike posture.

The victims are chosen randomly, not for who they are, what they do or what they represent, but precisely for not being, acting or representing anything special or concrete. They were unfortunate enough to be in the vicinity of the bombers when they detonated and this is what turned them from ordinary people into central characters of this drama. Their participation was chosen by fate and had nothing to do with their being. For the victims, these attacks are like the strike of lightning: in legal terms, they are an 'act of God', an unpredictable and unpreventable expression of *force majeure* from which nobody can be protected. Isn't the well-rehearsed cliché, according to which 'you can never get absolute security', a contemporary expression of older ideas about the inescapability of fate or destiny?

Modernity tried to tame randomness and contingency by abolishing fate. *Moira* and *fata* have been superannuated; unpredictable events and bad turns have been turned into effects of socio-economic or bio-psychological determinations. The modern individual is told that she is, partly at least, in charge of her fate. The contemporary Oedipus may still (desire to) kill his father and marry his mother but a well-trained psychoanalyst should be able to explain and cure. This taming of (known or unknown) necessity lies at the basis of normative modernity and its claims about dignity, autonomy and respect. The 'risk society' of liberal sociologists is precisely the opposite: a society that sees risk in every activity from eating and drinking to countryside pursuits and global warming. But while danger is an external state that threatens and causes fear as a response, ubiquitous risk leads to a type of free-floating, indistinct, all-pervasive anxiety. Danger leads to active responses, such as flight, defensive postures or counter-attack and helps people come together. Ever-present risk on the other hand has an atomizing effect; it cannot be eliminated or fully repelled. Permanent and invasive vigilance, being always prepared for the worst turns quotidian life into a Maginot line. Suicide bombing returns the self to the realm of fate, of unknown uncontrolled and ubiquitous risks.

This is where the suicide bomber, as an extreme form of terrorism, becomes an ally of the power he aims to attack. The unexpected, sudden and brutal attack is perfectly suited for bio-political exploitation. By striking blindly, terrorism turns the whole of society into potential victims, instils an abject fear and justifies surveillance and control of all aspects of self and community. It allows the transformation of the fear of death into a constant uncanny anxiety. The terrorist joins the innumerable and invisible threats of contemporary life, from passive smoking to genetically modified foods and air pollution as a lethal pollutant, lurking in a corner of the urban sprawl. And as this corner could be any corner, the precautionary principle of advanced capitalism entitles, indeed compels, the adoption of an array of measures such as extensive surveillance, increase of the powers of search, arrest and detention without trial, use of torture, identity cards which have little, if any, effect in the 'war on terror'. In this sense, terrorism becomes synonymous with a ubiquitous but not easily detectable deadly virus and the measures to combat it, the political equivalent of the insurance policy.

c *Community*

How do survivors, bystanders, the community relate to the atrocity and the death of the victims? If the bomber dies in the name of an imaginary wounded community what are the effects of the bombing on the community he attacks?

The death of the other is always singular, it cannot be shared, it is always the other's death, never mine. Death has no meaning for the dead nor can the other's death be shared by the survivors. But the death of the other awakens me from the routine numbness of everydayness and makes me relate to my own mortality. My death is my most intimate and most repelled eventuality. The oft-used cliché 'I may die tomorrow' is a mantra we repeat in bad faith as a talismanic – but utterly ineffectual – protection against its occurrence. And it is precisely what we push away, our own death, that comes closest after the event, in those early moments of stunned uncomprehending reaction. The imminence of death, the most incontrovertible aspect of life takes on at these moments an unusual force: the realization that 'I could have been there', that 'I was in the same underground station the other day' or that 'I passed that place' or 'boarded that bus only yesterday', makes me confront my own mortality. Only my death is fully mine, but I will not experience it. And yet, because I will not experience death, it is through the death of the other I come to a reckoning of death.

> If death is indeed the possibility of the impossible ... then, man, or man as Dasein, never has a relation to death as such, but only to perishing to demising, and to the death of the other.... The death of the other thus becomes ... first, always first.
>
> (Derrida 1994: 75)

The death of the other brings community together. Vikki Bell has argued, in a highly nuanced and sophisticated reaction to a Chechen woman suicide bombing in Moscow in 2003, that the bombers aim to aestheticize politics by creating a scene of devastation and a series of images over the meaning of which people struggle (Bell 2005: 241). The act, an immense and incomprehensible physical and imagistic bombardment, operates at the level of sensibility and dislocates its spectators and survivors in a way similar to that of the sublime. Shocked, humiliated, unable to understand, the subject is asked to articulate a response but her questions have no immediate or satisfactory answers. Questions about the 'big' issues ('why here?', 'why (not) me?', 'what is the meaning of this?') make thinking to face its finitude and its quest for transcendence. Such questions cannot receive definite answers, they float ceaselessly augmented by the silence of the suicide. The 'stoicism' of the Londoners may have had more to do with these tormenting unanswered questions we all faced in the aftermath of the bombings than with our impassive nature.

Hegel wrote in the *Phenomenology* that fear of death gives war its metaphysical value, by confronting combatants with the negativity that surrounds life and helping them to rise from mundane life to the contemplation of the universal:

> In order not to let [people] become rooted and set in this isolation, thereby breaking up the whole and letting the community spirit evaporate, government has from time to time to shake them to their core by war. By this means the government upsets their established order, and violates their right

to independence, while the individuals who, absorbed in their way of life, break loose from the whole and strive after the inviolable independence and security of the person, are made to feel by government in the task laid on them their lord and master, death.

(Hegel 1977: 272–3)

The scale of the atrocity and the randomness of death, alerts people to the inescapability of our 'lord and master' and to our strongest common bond which overrides all other affinities and kinships. When my relation to my death emerges as a key and neglected question in the aftermath of the atrocity, similarly our shared common world, our being-with-others exits its thoughtless 'naturalness': it is staged as a common problem and concern which opens the possibility of exploring the condition of the political.

In an obvious sense, all 'thick' communities (of religion, nation, ideology) use death as proof of their truth. For much social theory, a murder lies at the foundation of community and law. Communities form or confirm themselves through rituals repeating and dissimulating the primordial killing. Sacrifice supports community as communion and promotes the commonality of its members, their link with the 'totality' of meaning and truth community brings forth. In taking life and letting live, the Sovereign repeats the violence of foundations and, as argued above, brings the profane in controlled contact with the holy.

But what community does witnessing and contemplating the random killing of others by the terrorist imitators of sovereignty create? What community does suicide bombing confirm? Angharad Closs Stephens has examined in compelling and revealing detail, the mirroring responses by the Government and the Mayor of London to the July bombings (Closs Stephens 2007: 155). The Government insisted on unity and Britishness and emphasized the Blitz narrative of homogeneity and whiteness. Ken Livingstone's 'We are One' slogan stressed the religious, ethnic and cultural multiplicity of the city but repeated in a shrewder way the theme of unity ignoring 'the critique of British nationalism ... and the pernicious effects of nationalist ambitions to secure historical legacies' (Closs Stephens 2007: 155). In their different narratives, the national and local authorities did what the sovereign has always done. They turned the victims into sacrificial martyrs witnessing and bringing about the immanence of community as communion. It may be that the 'essence' of community was posited in different terms (as One London or as a London made up of many Ones) but the meaning was the same: death attests the following of the law; it answers the call of the Sovereign. Death confirms and consecrates the indelible bonds of communal togetherness.

There is no better way for community building than an atrocity and the response to it. This concern with community and its nature was evident in the debates that have dominated the aftermath of the London bombings. The best known questioned the role of religion in contemporary life. Richard Dawkins, Daniel Dennett and Christopher Hitchens, the theological atheists, have united to condemn the influence of religion generally and – directly or indirectly – of

Islam (Dawkins 2007; Dennett 2007; Hitchens 2007). A second debate, sparked by the fact that the bombers were homegrown British Muslims, has focused on questions of identity, citizenship and culture and has questioned the effects of multiculturalism in contemporary Britain (Modood 2005; Rehman 2007).

Finally, questions about necessary and appropriate force in preventing terrorist attacks and its balance with civil liberties and other legal protections have dominated the debate sparked by the killing of Jean Charles de Menezes. New anti-terrorist legislation is being proposed all the time: extension of detention before charge up to 90 days; detention without trial; control orders; deportation to countries that torture; rendition flights. Racial profiling on passengers, increase of stop-and-search of Asian-looking people, many arrests for terrorism with relatively few convictions. The state's response to blind violence has been equally violent. The two violences seek and find each other in killings or bombardments. They belong to the same plane of blind power, cynical rivalry, the arrogance of self-certitude.

And yet, not just the community of laws, institutions and politics, the community of communion and sacrifice begins with events that place us before death. These are just surface manifestations of humanity's acknowledgment of its deathbound trajectory. The inevitability and singularity of the end, our joint but unshareable death – which is unconcerned with the markers of belonging such as nation, race or ideology – leads to the only community worthy of the name: that of being-with-the-other. As Derrida put it in his eulogy of Jean-François Lyotard,

> [O]ne is never *ensemble*, never together, in an *ensemble*, in a group, gathering, whole or set, for the ensemble, the whole, the totality that is named by this word, constituted the first destruction of what the adverb *ensemble* might mean: to be *ensemble*, it is absolutely necessary not to be gathered into any sort of *ensemble*.
>
> (Derrida 2001: 225)

This 'together' that does not create club, party or people is the community Jean-Luc Nancy has called 'inoperable'. It takes place

> [T]hrough others and for others ... if community is revealed in the death of others, it is because death itself is the true community of *I*'s that are not egos.... A community is the presentation to its members of their mortal truth ... the presentation of the finitude and irredeemable excess that makes up finite being: its death, but also its birth, and only the community can present me my birth, and along with it the impossibility of reliving it, as well as the impossibility of my crossing over into my death.
>
> (Nancy 1991: 14–15)

It is in this sense, that a horrific act like the 7 July bombings can (and did) help deconstruct the sense of communion that the official responses tried to impose on Londoners. Because we share mortality, because the random deaths of others brings finitude to thinking, because the death of the other was not sacrificial but meaningless, for all these reasons 7 July was a political event: not according to the mythological politics of Truth or the Good which come from sovereignty or its fake mimics and call for sacrifice; not according to the humanitarian politics for which humanity is fully defined in its negativity. But according to the politics of responding responsibly to the random death of the other and the chance invasion of our place. In this politics, the immanence of the community of belonging is unravelled and another community of beings-in-common-before-death emerges: London is neither One nor Many Ones, neither the totality of religion nor the majesty of sovereignty, but the infinity of encounters of millions of singular worlds.

Notes

* Professor of Law, Director, Birkbeck Institute for the Humanities, Birkbeck College.
1 In a probably unintended symbolism, the bomber exploded in the bus in front of the offices of the General Medical Council and next to Tavistock Square, the headquarters of English medicine and psychoanalysis.
2 Two indicative examples. *Eleftheria i Thanatos* (freedom or death) has been a persistent theme in Greek culture, from the Trojan wars to the fall of Constantinople in 1453 to the Greek war of independence in 1821 which included many instances of mass suicide in the face of certain defeat. See the classic novel of Nikos Kazantzakis, *Capetan Michalis: Freedom or Death*. In a different context, Emmeline Pankhurst finished a lecture to an American audience on the struggle for women's rights in November 1913 with the words: 'We the women of England will put the enemy in the position where they will have to choose between giving us freedom or giving us death.' Emmeline Pankhurst, 'Freedom or Death', *Guardian*, 27 April 2007, www.guardian.co.uk/greatspeeches/story/0,,2059295,00.html.
3 The attacks on the Madrid trains on 11 March 2004 were interpreted by many as a direct intervention in the pending Spanish elections intended to influence voters against the right-wing government which had supported the Iraq war. However the absence of a statement by the bombers meant that people were left to read their own 'message' into the attacks. The devastation was left unexplained and open to many conflicting interpretations.

References

Agamben, G. (1998), *Homo Sacer: Sovereign Power and Bare Life*, trans. D Heller-Roazen, Stanford, CA: Stanford University Press.
Balibar, E. (1999), *Politics and Truth*, Athens: Nissos.
Bankowski, Z. (2001), *Living Lawfully: Love in Law and Law in Love*, London: Kluwer Academic.
Baudrillard, J. (2004), 'This Is the Fourth World War: The *Der Spiegel* Interview with Jean Baudrillard', trans. S. Gandesha, *International Journal of Baudrillard Studies* 1(1), January. Online. Available at: www.ubishops.ca/BaudrillardStudies/spiegel.htm (accessed 21 November 2007).
Bell, V. (2005), 'The Scenography of Suicide: Terror, Politics and the Humiliated Witness', *Economy and Society* 34(2).

Brennan, R. (2000), 'Contradictions of Humanitarianism', *Alphabet City* 7.
Burke, J. (2005), 'Secrets of the Bomber's Death Tape', *Observer*, 4 September. Online. Available at: www.guardian.co.uk/alqaida/story/0,,1562409,00.html (accessed 21 November 2007).
Closs Stephens, A. (2007), '"Seven Million Londoners One London': National and Urban Ideas of Community in the Aftermath of the 7 July 2005 Bombings in London"', *Alternatives* 32(2).
Dawkins, R. (2007) *The God Delusion*, London: Black Swan.
Dennett, D. (2007), *Breaking the Spell: Religion as a Natural Phenomenon*, New York: Penguin.
Derrida, J. (1994), *Aporias: Dying*, trans. T. Dutoit, Stanford, CA: Stanford University Press.
—— (2001), 'Jean-François Lyotard', in P. Brault and M. Nass (eds), *The Work of Mourning*, Chicago: University of Chicago Press
—— (2005) *Rogues*, trans. P. Brault and M. Naas, Stanford, CA: Stanford University Press.
Douzinas, C. (2000), *The End of Human* Rights, Oxford: Hart.
—— (2007), *Human Rights and Empire: The Political Philosophy of Cosmopolitanism*. Abingdon: Routledge-Cavendish.
Eagleton, T. (2005), *Guardian*, 26 January. Available at: www.guardian.co.uk/comment/story/0,,1398445,00.html.
Elliott, L. (2006), 'A year after Live 8, rich countries have failed to keep their promise', *Guardian*, 30 June. Available at: www.guardian.co.uk/business/2006/jun/30/internationalaidanddevelopment.g8.
Ferguson, E. (2005), *Observer*, 3 July. Available at: www.guardian.co.uk/uk/2005/jul/03/g8.famine.
Groge, A. and Tabor, J. (1992), *Noble Death: Suicide and Martyrdom among Christians and Jews in Antiquity*, San Francisco: HarperCollins.
Habermas, J. (1998), *The Inclusion of the Other*, Cambridge: Polity.
Halward, P. (2003), *Badiou: A Subject to Truth*, Minneapolis, MN: University of Minnesota Press.
Hegel, G. (1977), *The Phenomenology of Spirit*, trans. A. V. Miller, Oxford: Oxford University Press.
Hitchens, C. (2007), *God Is Not Great*, London: Atlantic Books.
Ignatieff, M. (2001), *Human Rights as Politics and Idolatry*, Princeton, NJ: Princeton University Press.
Modood, T. (2005), 'Remaking Multiculturalism after 7/7', *Open Democracy*, 29 September.
Mutua, M. (2001), 'Savages, Victims, Saviours', *Harvard International Law Journal*, 42(1).
Nancy, J. (1991), *The Inoperative Community*, Minneapolis, MN: University of Minnesota Press.
—— (1997), *The Sense of the World*, trans. J Librett, Minneapolis, MN: University of Minnesota Press.
—— (2006), 'State, Church, Resistance', in H. de Vries and L. Sullivan (eds), *Political Theologies: Public Religions in a Post-Secular World*, New York: Fordham University Press.
—— (2007), *The Creation of the World or Globalisation*, trans. F. Raffoul and D. Pettigrew, New York: SUNY Press.
Rehman, J. (2007) 'Islam, "War on Terror" and the Future of Muslim Minorities in the

UK: Dilemmas of Multiculturalism in the Aftermath of the London Bombings', *Human Rights Quarterly* 29: 831–78.

Schmitt, C. (1985), *Political Theology: Four Chapters on the Concept of Sovereignty*, trans. G. Schwab, Cambridge, MA: MIT Press.

Žižek, S. (2005), 'Against Human Rights', *New Left Review*, 34, July–August.

Index

9/11, 24–5, 87, 168–9; critique of 9/11, as shorthand 4, 5–7; ethical responses to 148–52

Ackroyd, Peter 44
Afghanistan 92
Agamben, Giorgio 19–20, 26–7, 36, 105, 107–8, 122–3, 125, 126, 194–5, 203
Ahmed, Nafeez 98, 99, 100, 102, 104
al-Qaeda 82, 113, 166, 171
alterity and the face 180–5
Amin, Ash 73
Amnesty International 125
Amoore, Louise 12, 130–41, 185–6
Amorim, Celso 101
Anti-Terrorist Act (ATA), Canada 112, 124, 125–7
Appadurai, Arjun 165, 172–3, 176
Archibugi, Daniele 148–50, 152–3
Arendt, Hannah 8
Ashley, Richard 84
Australia, multiculturalism 120–1
autoimmune crisis 101–4
autoimmune state 88–92

Badiou, Alain 198
Balibar, Etienne 194
Ballard, J.G. 174
Bankowski, Zen 197
'bare life' 19, 194–5, 203
Baudrillard, Jean 199–200
Bauman, Zygmunt 62
BBC 82
BBC News 166, 172
BBC News Online 1–2, 28, 35, 37, 96, 97, 98, 99, 100, 101, 102
Beck, Ulrich 170
Bell, Vikki 205
Benn, Hilary 130

Bennett, Jane 140
Berman, Marshall 66
Bhabha, Homi 72, 73, 119
Bhutto, Benazir 198
Bigo, Didier 46, 106
Biography of London (Ackroyd) 44
Black, Crispin 97, 179–80
Blair, Sir Ian 63, 96–7, 100–1, 102–3, 106, 108
Blair, Tony 1–2, 5, 35, 60, 61, 63, 64–5, 70–1, 72, 81, 82, 83, 84, 85–6, 87, 91, 92, 132, 147, 148, 154, 155, 164–5
Bono 152, 190
Borcila, Rozalinda 139
bordering practices 104–8; electronic bordering 107
Brassett, James 12, 147–61
Breckenridge, Carol A. 73
Brison, Susan J. 21
British Transport Police (BTP) 69–70
Brown, Wendy 8
Bulley, Dan 11, 81–93
Bush, George W. 6–7, 37, 105, 155, 159, 164–5
Butler, Judith 6, 7, 81, 138, 150–1, 160, 166–7, 178, 186

Cabinet Office 32
Campbell, David 7, 82, 97
Canadian Arab Federation 126
Canadian Council of Muslim Women 117–18
Casualty Bureau 29, 32, 34
CBC News 102–3
Centre for Ethics, Toronto University 118
Chakrabarti, Shami 167
Chakrabarty, Dipesh 73
Charter of Rights and Freedoms, Canada 124

Cheah, Pheng 62
Chertoff, Michael 130, 131, 135
Closs Stephens, Angharad 1–13, 60–75, 152, 206
CNN 116
colonialism 48; post-colonialism 72–3
commemoration 23–6
Commission for Racial Equality 52–3
communism 171–2
community 204–8; and the city 70–5; and cosmopolitanism 70–5; London as multicultural community 63–5, 67–70; London as political community 48–51; rejection of 56–7; and time 66–7; in unity 60–2
concentration camps 107–8
Connolly, William 137, 178–9
control orders 166
cosmopolitanism: and community 70–5; cosmopolitan resistance 156–61; subjects of security 51–7; in a time of terror 148–52, 152–5
Council of Europe 167
Crary, Jonathan 133, 134, 138, 139, 140
Crown Prosecution Service 100
CTV News 122
Cuff, Dana 137

Daily Show 116
Daily Telegraph 31, 69, 96, 97
Dawkins, Richard 206–7
Day, Richard 119
De Goede, Marieke 135, 159
democracy: and human rights 89–92, 103; modern self in 50; phallic democracy 122–3
Dennett, Daniel 206–7
Department of Homeland Security 133
Derrida, Jacques 4, 7, 74, 88, 89–90, 91–2, 97, 101, 102, 103, 104, 105, 131, 136, 140, 151–2, 156, 157–8, 185, 195, 205, 207
detention without trial 90–1, 92, 103
Devji, Faisal 164, 173
Dick, Cressida 99
difference: alterity and the face 180–6; cultural difference 46–8; differentiating 'outside' from 'inside' 84; in Olympics narrative 68–9; and 'othering' process 46–7, 71–2, 180–5; racialization of 47–8; securitization of 46–8; threat/value of 68
Dillon, Michael 19–20, 26, 27, 36–7
Disaster Action 34–5

Disaster Victim Identification (DVI) process 32–6, 38
Douzinas, Costas 13, 190–208

Eagleton, Terry 201, 203
Edkins, Jenny 6, 10, 19–38, 93, 156, 158
Edmunds, Michael 115–17
emergency, production of 35–7
ethics: ethical responses to 9/11 148–52; ethical responses to London bombings 37–8; of forgetting 130–2; global ethics 159
Etobicoke mosque 115, 117
European Union Convention on Human Rights 91, 103, 167

Fagan, Madeleine 13, 178–88
failing states 84–8; deconstruction of 88–92; and foreign terror 86–8
Fatayi-Williams, Marie 8, 19, 20, 21, 27–8, 30–1, 32
Fine, Robert 158
foreign policy, Britain 84–8
foreign terror: and autoimmunity 88–92; and British foreign policy 84–8; exteriorising terror 82–4; and Ken Livingstone's speech 70–5; responding/resisting 92–3
forgetting: ethics of 130–2; struggle of memory against 137–41; war on terror 130–41
Foucault, Michel 46, 47, 48, 49, 50, 131
Freedland, Jonathan 63, 81, 100
Friedberg, Anne 134, 136
Front de liberation du Québec (FLQ) 117

G8 1, 147–8, 152–5, 158–60, 190, 195–6
Gaventa, John 160
Geldof, Bob 158
Gil-Robles, Alvaro 167
Gilroy, Paul 48, 52, 63, 72
Gove, Michael 179
Government of Canada 119, 125
GPS satellite technology 107
Graham, Stephen 66
Gregory, Derek 6
Guantanamo Bay 166–7
Guardian 27–8, 30, 63, 67, 100, 130–1, 190, 195–6
Guild, E. 46

Habermas, Jürgen 149, 192

Hage, Ghassan 120–1, 122–3
Hansen, Randall 117
Hardt, Michael 201
Harper, Stephen 112, 113, 116
Hegel, Georg Wilhelm Friedrich 193, 202, 205–6
Held, David 150
Herouxville decree 121
Hitchens, Christopher 206–7
Hogben, Alia 117–18
human rights: and democracy 89–92; humanitarian politics 194–8; responsibilities 85–6; universalization of 193–4; versus fairness 172
Human Rights Act, Canada 125
Hurricane Katrina 175–6
Hussain, Hasib 82
Huysmans, Jef 46

Ignatieff, Michael 172, 194
Immigration and Refugee Act (1978), Canada 126
Independent 64, 101, 105
Independent Police Complaints Commission (IPCC) 96, 97–8, 99–100
Interpol Manual on Disaster Victim Identification 33
IRA 63, 102
Iraq 86–7, 92
Islamic Human Rights Commission 64

Jabri, Vivienne 11, 47
Jensen, Liz 174, 175–6

Keenan, Thomas 141
Khan, Mohammad Sidique 30, 71, 82, 83, 92, 202
Khawaja, Momin 124, 126
King's Cross memorial garden 23–4
Kittler, Friedrich 136
Kratos policy 92, 101–2, 103, 105, 106, 108
Kristeva, Julia 57
Kundera, Milan 137–8
Kymlicka, Will 45

Laclau, Ernesto 19
Let's All Hate Toronto (Nerenberg) 123
Levinas, Emmanuel 178, 180–5, 186
Liberty 167
Lindsay, Germaine 82
Linklater, Andrew 147, 148
'Live 8' concert 1, 158–9, 160, 190–1, 194, 195–6

Livingstone, Ken 61, 62, 68, 70–3, 206
Lobo-Guerrero, Luis 20
London: as British community 63–5; community and the city 70–5; as a global city 44, 51–7; as multicultural community 67–70
London Assembly 1, 3, 28, 29–30, 31, 32, 35, 37–8, 107
London Blitz 63–4, 67–9, 170
London bombings (2005): aftermath 23–7; cosmopolitan response 154–5; as event in global politics 3–5; goals of 199–200; as inevitable event 5–7; missing persons search 27–32; as 'other' at Gleneagles 152–5; overview 1–7; production of emergency 35–7; responses to 179–80; victim identification 32–5, 38
London bombings: an independent inquiry (Ahmed) 104

Macpherson Inquiry 48
McRobbie, Angela 151
MacShane, Denis 85, 87, 93
Madrid bombings (2004) 60
Make Poverty History 147–8, 151–5, 156–7, 158–60
Manthorpe, Rowland 63
Martin, Chris 190
Mass Fatalities Plan 32
Massey, Doreen 6
Massumi, Brian 6–7, 105–6
Mayo, Marj 160
Menezes 2, 60; Jean Charles de 74; and autoimmune crisis 101–4; events of 22/7, 97–9; juridical-political response to death of 99–100; and new border politics 104–8; public response to death of 100–1
Menezes, Maria Otone de 104
Menezes, Patricia de 105
Mestrovic, Stjepan 165, 169–70, 174–5
Metropolitan Police Service: 'if you suspect it' campaign 133; Menezes shooting 96–109
Millennium Development Goals (MDGs) 153
Millennium people (Ballard) 174
missing persons: posters 24–5; search for 27–32
Mitchell, Tom 139
Modood, Tariq 207
Molloy, Patricia 12, 112–27
mourning, politics of 150–1, 160–1
multiculturalism: Canada 118–23; focus on

multiculturalism *continued*
  61–2; London as multicultural community 67–70; under scrutiny 52–3; *see also* cosmopolitanism
Multiculturalism Act (1988), Canada 119
Munk Centre for International Studies 112–13, 116–18, 126
Muslim Council of Britain 100
Mutua, Makau 197

Nancy, Jean-Luc 62, 191–2, 200–1, 207
National Post 116–17
NBC News 96–7, 106, 108
Negri, Antonio 201
Nerenberg, Albert 123
New Scientist 133
New York Times 114–16, 127, 134, 135, 137

Ogilvie, Bernard 194
Olympics (2012) 1, 67–9
'One London' campaign 61, 68, 69–75, 185–6
ontopolitics of response: alterity and the face 180–5; responses to London bombings 179–80; rethinking response 185–8
Orwell, George 63
Osman, Hussein 98, 99

Pamuk, Orhan 56–7
Paper eater (Jensen) 174
Pereira, Alex 104–5
Pettifor, Ann 153–5
Philips, Trevor 52–3
Poggi, Gianfranco 49
political community 48–51; state capacity to constitute 54–5
politics: of dangerousness 166–7; of death 198–208; of mourning 150–1, 160–1; of origins 65–7; of response 8–10
Pollock, Sheldon 73
postemotional society 169–72
poverty: Make Poverty History 147–8, 151–5, 156–7, 158–60; of response 116–18
Precarious life (Butler) 150–1, 166–7
Pugliese, Joseph 98, 99, 106–7

racial profiling 47–8, 98–9, 114–15, 116–23
Rai, Milan 179
Rammell, Bill 85, 91
Razack, Sherene 126
Reid, Dr John 165, 170–2

Report of the 7 July Review Committee 1, 3, 28, 29–30, 31, 32, 35, 37–8, 107
Report of the official account of the bombings in London on July 7th 7, 64, 82–3, 147, 154, 180
resistance: of British community 63–5; moments of 157–61
response: limits of 150–2; rethinking 185–8
RFID (Radio Frequency Identification Technology) 140
Rice, Condoleeza 116
risk 204
Rose, Nicholas 55
Rumford, Chris 12–13, 164–76
Rumsfeld, Donald 141
Runciman, David 164

Said, Edward 140
Sassen, Saskia 53
Scarman Report 48
Schmitt, Carl 191
Scholte, Jan Aart 159
Scotsman 102
Second World War 63–4, 67–9, 170, 171–2
security: and cultural difference 46–8; subjects of 51–7
Shapiro, Michael J.138
shoot-to-kill policy 90, 92, 101–2, 103, 105, 106, 108
Silverman, Kaja 133
Simmel, Georg 74
Sinclair, Iain 133
Smith, Will 153
Socialist Worker 101
sovereign power 20–2, 26–7, 36, 200–2
space: and the city 51–7, 62, 63–75; government of 48–51; shift away from 47–8
Stamp Out Poverty Briefing 157
Stewart, Jon 116
stop-and-search operations 52
Straw, Jack 82, 85, 86–7, 88–9, 90, 91, 93
Supreme Court, Canada 126–7

Tanweer, Shehzad 30, 82
Taylor, Charles 45
terror, exteriorizing 82–4
terror threat responses: governance of 35–7; politics of dangerousness 166–7; postemotional society 169–72; victimhood and global geography of anger 172–3

terrorism versus cosmopolitanism 147–61
Theory and Event 8, 9–10
Thin Cities project 139
Thrift, Nigel 73
time: and community 66–7; and politics 5–7
Tobin Tax 157
Tonkiss, Fran 73–4
Toronto 17: 113–16; exceptional state 124–7; multiculturalism and other myths 118–23; University of Toronto and the poverty of response 116–18
Toronto Star 114–15, 121, 124
Toynbee, Polly 155, 159
Trainor, Meghan 140
Transport for London 61, 69–70
Tulloch, John 5, 21

United Nations (UN) 123, 153
Unlikely utopia: the surprising triumph of Canadian pluralism (Adams) 121–2
urban communities 65–7; space 48–51
US Canada relations 115–16
US One Campaign Film 153

Vaughan-Williams, Nick 1–13, 91, 96–109
victim identification process 22, 30–6, 38
Virilio, Paul 57

Walcott, Rinaldo 118, 119–20
Walker, R.B.J. 4, 84, 150, 186
Walters, William 107
war on terror 5–7; as dangerous concept 130–2; George Bush on 6–7, 159, 164–5; overview 5–7; responding before the event 132–7; responsibility before the event 137–41; Tony Blair on 60, 61, 64–5, 83, 85–6, 87, 91, 92, 164–5
Weber, Samuel 135
White Nation (Hage) 120
Whose hunger? (Edkins) 156
Wickham-Jones, Mark 85
Wilding, Barbara 101–2
Williams, Melissa 118
Willis, Susan 132
Wolin, Sheldon 9

Zehfuss, Maja 187
Žižek, Slavoj 197

eBooks – at www.eBookstore.tandf.co.uk

A library at your fingertips!

eBooks are electronic versions of printed books. You can store them on your PC/laptop or browse them online.

They have advantages for anyone needing rapid access to a wide variety of published, copyright information.

eBooks can help your research by enabling you to bookmark chapters, annotate text and use instant searches to find specific words or phrases. Several eBook files would fit on even a small laptop or PDA.

NEW: Save money by eSubscribing: cheap, online access to any eBook for as long as you need it.

Annual subscription packages

We now offer special low-cost bulk subscriptions to packages of eBooks in certain subject areas. These are available to libraries or to individuals.

For more information please contact webmaster.ebooks@tandf.co.uk

We're continually developing the eBook concept, so keep up to date by visiting the website.

www.eBookstore.tandf.co.uk